Sport Volunteering

Volunteers are central to sport at all levels, from mega-events to grass-roots clubs. *Sport Volunteering* is a definitive guide to the issues associated with managing volunteers in sport.

The book focuses on the psychology of the voluntary experience, the challenges inherent in managing a volunteer workforce for not-for-profit and other groups, and the development of volunteers. It provides a perspective on the roles of volunteers in the development and delivery of sport in a range of contexts – events, clubs, associations and other non-profit groups – and explores important contemporary issues such as sustainability, diversity and the management of risk.

This book is essential reading for anybody studying sport volunteering or managing volunteers in sport, and a valuable resource for students of sport development, sport management, sport business, sport events, sport administration, sport policy, community sport, sport facilities, sport operations, event management or sport coaching.

Russell Hoye is Pro-Vice-Chancellor for Research Development and Director of Sport at La Trobe University, Australia, where he previously served as Director of the Centre for Sport and Social Impact. He is also Adjunct Professor in the School of Human Kinetics at the University of Ottawa, Canada. His research interests are in corporate governance, public policy, volunteer management and the impact of sport on individuals and society. He is Editor of the Sport Management Series for Routledge and is a member of the editorial boards for the *International Journal of Sport Policy and Politics*, *Sport Management Review* and the *Journal of Global Sport Management*.

Graham Cuskelly is Head of the Department of Tourism, Sport and Hotel Management in the AACSB accredited Business School at Griffith University, Australia. His research interests are in volunteers in sport, the development of community sport, and sport organisation and governance. He has been chief investigator on four Australian Research Council grants

and a Canadian Social Sciences and Humanities Research Council grant. His most recent funded research projects include the resilience of community sport organisations impacted by natural disasters, and the economic value of community club-based sport.

Chris Auld is Dean of Macleay College, Australia. He was previously Deputy Vice Chancellor (Academic) at the International College of Management Sydney and was Dean (International) and Head of Department with the Griffith Business School, Griffith University, Australia. His research interests include community sport, the management of sport volunteers, board performance and governance in third sector organisations, and the impacts of major sport events. In 2010 he was elected Senior Fellow and Founding Member of the World Leisure Academy.

Pam Kappelides is a Lecturer in Sport Management at La Trobe University, Australia, and is an expert in the field of volunteer management, community development, youth and children development, disability and minority groups, and the impact of sport participation and development in the community. She has also secured significant research projects and has consulted with many sport organisations and government agencies such as VicHealth, YMCA, Special Olympics, Masters Sport, Tennis Victoria, Football Federation Victoria, Sport and Recreation Victoria, and various local government councils.

Katie Misener is an Associate Professor in the Department of Recreation and Leisure Studies, Faculty of Applied Health Sciences at the University of Waterloo, Canada. Her primary research focuses on the capacity and social impact of non-profit community sport organisations, with a particular focus on how capacity can be enhanced to support sport service delivery and foster social engagement through sport. Her research interests also include the role of sport organisations in community health promotion and creating collaborative value through inter-organisational relationships.

Sport Volunteering

Russell Hoye, Graham Cuskelly,
Chris Auld, Pam Kappelides and
Katie Misener

Routledge
Taylor & Francis Group

LONDON AND NEW YORK

First published 2020
by Routledge
2 Park Square, Milton Park, Abingdon, Oxon OX14 4RN

and by Routledge
52 Vanderbilt Avenue, New York, NY 10017

Routledge is an imprint of the Taylor & Francis Group, an informa business

British Library Cataloguing-in-Publication Data
A catalogue record for this book is available from the British Library

Library of Congress Cataloging-in-Publication Data
A catalog record has been requested for this book

ISBN: 978-0-367-26277-8 (hbk)
ISBN: 978-0-367-26279-2 (pbk)
ISBN: 978-0-429-29232-3 (ebk)

Typeset in Sabon
by Swales & Willis, Exeter, Devon, UK

Contents

Illustrations

Figures

Tables

Preface

The objective of this book is to provide a definitive guide to the myriad issues associated with managing volunteers in sport. The book explores the psychology of the voluntary experience, the challenges inherent in not-for-profit and other groups in managing a sport volunteer workforce, and the development of volunteers in the central roles associated with sport. Our aim was to include numerous examples of accepted practice and research evidence on a number of key themes in order to review how theory and research have informed (or not!) contemporary volunteer management practices.

In 2006, three of the authors (Cuskelly, Auld and Hoye) published a book *Working with Volunteers in Sport: Theory and Practice* that was well received and was the first book to focus on the core issues of sport volunteerism – government impacts on voluntary sport organisations, the experience of volunteers and specific volunteer contexts. The structure of this book has been very deliberately designed to complement that earlier work by both rewriting some of the core content areas covered in the first book as well as providing entirely new material that covers emerging and important ideas on sport volunteering. We start with three chapters that explore the broad concepts of the scale and nature of sport volunteering, the impact that sport volunteers have on society and the way that government policy and actions affect the sport volunteer experience. The next three chapters focus on the psychology of sport volunteering, the enormous potential that supporting volunteers from more diverse population groups has for sport, and a review of contemporary sport volunteer management practices. We then provide four chapters exploring in greater depth four major volunteer contexts germane and unique to sport volunteering: administration, officiating, coaching and sport event volunteering. Our final chapter reviews the current state of sport volunteering research and makes several suggestions for future research efforts.

We are indebted to Routledge's longstanding Commissioning Editor for Sport, Simon Whitmore, for his belief in us to deliver a quality book on a very important topic. We acknowledge and thank our respective partners and families for their support and patience while we committed to writing this book.

Chapter 1

Volunteers and sport

Volunteers are a central feature of community life in most jurisdictions throughout the world. As indicated by McGregor-Lowndes, Crittall, Conroy, and Keast (2017, p. 1), "giving and volunteering are cornerstones of civil society and organisations that inhabit the space between government, the market and family". A United Nations report further suggested that volunteering "as a universal social behaviour is therefore a critical resource for community resilience" (UN Volunteers, 2018, p. viii). Volunteers fulfil a variety of roles that can range from largely informal and typically unrecorded behaviours (such as caring for a neighbour or friend), to highly structured and formal positions (such as international sport administrators). The interaction between the wide array of functions in which volunteers can be involved, as well as the varying layers of intricacy and formality across different roles, means that trying to comprehend the full extent of the motivations, behaviours and contributions of volunteers can be quite complex.

This complexity is reflected in the many approaches utilised to investigate and explain volunteers and their behaviours, as well as to "quantify" the consequences realised by their efforts (both at the individual and organisational/community level). A variety of methods have been adopted (especially since the 1990s) and in sport volunteering these have become more rigorous as the research has matured (Wicker, 2017). It is also the case that the research on volunteering has occurred in different settings and at varying organisational levels. In the sport sector for example, research has been conducted on community sport clubs, provincial/state sporting associations, peak national level sporting associations, as well as sport events of varying levels of scope and complexity.

The literature reveals a number of different theoretical frameworks and constructs that have played some role in volunteer related research. Examples include:

- social exchange theory;
- social capital and citizenship;

- motivation;
- commitment theory;
- role theory including role ambiguity and role conflict;
- psychological contract;
- identity theory;
- net cost theory;
- serious leisure;
- homologous reproduction theory;
- theory of planned behaviour; and
- pro-social behaviour.

In general terms, much of the earlier research concentrated on the motivations of volunteers and how the antecedents of volunteerism influenced volunteer retention: a perennial and central concern for organisations that rely on volunteer labour. There was also an early focus on related management issues such as improving governance, management and volunteer/paid staff relationships. Drawing from the analysis conducted by Wicker (2017), it can be argued that the emphasis was largely utilitarian, attempting to improve volunteer management processes and overall organisational capacity and efficacy, with a somewhat secondary focus on improving the actual volunteer experience.

While such utilitarian foci are still evident in the contemporary literature, especially those related to the antecedents of volunteering and the motivations of volunteers, it is also apparent that the use of theoretical frameworks has become much more sophisticated. This maturation has accompanied the drive to fundamentally understand the volunteer experience, irrespective of potential implications for managerial practice. Wicker (2017, p. 326) argued that research on volunteering and volunteer management in the event and organisational contexts "can be considered one of the most prominent topics within sport management". In addition, as the research has evolved from an initial mainly descriptive focus to predominantly analytical methods, the findings have resulted in more refined insights into the multiplicity of volunteer motivations, behaviours and consequences, something explored in more detail in Chapter 4.

Together with the evolution of volunteer research (or perhaps also as a consequence of the research) has been the expansion of the terms used to describe and categorise volunteers. Similar to the development of the research process, these terms have become increasingly nuanced and insightful as well as more reflective of the nature of the "lived" volunteer experience. Such terms and categories have included (a number of these categories are described and discussed in more detail below):

- formal/informal;
- core/peripheral;

- career volunteers;
- stalwart volunteers;
- corporate volunteers;
- pioneer volunteers;
- policy/service volunteers;
- spontaneous volunteering;
- episodic/continuous or regular volunteering;
- micro-volunteering; and
- digital or virtual volunteering.

The issues outlined briefly here indicate that while volunteers and volunteer-involving organisations have adapted to a variety of changing circumstances, they are also likely to continue to face many challenges in the future. As will be explored in more depth in this and other chapters, communities are being impacted on by a number of volatile and dynamic trends (e.g., technology and communication, family structures, community demographics and changing work practices), many of which have either direct or indirect implications for volunteer behaviour and the management of volunteers. For example, McGregor-Lowndes et al. (2017) argued that internet-based communication and e-commerce are increasingly influencing the manner in which volunteers engage with voluntary organisations.

Such implications, especially those related to the perceptions and utilisation of time, pose significant challenges not only for individual volunteers, but also for those organisations that rely on volunteer labour. The volunteering context is becoming more complex as these trends interact with other issues such as increasing the professionalisation of non-profit and third sector organisations, in addition to government policies that continue to shift more community reliance and accountability onto these same organisations.

> A number of national governments have concluded in recent years that they alone cannot and should not deliver all social and welfare related services and further, that citizen participation is important in the provision of many services. Hence, many governments have gradually scaled back their involvement in the direct delivery of welfare and social services and now rely more on nonprofit organizations and volunteers to deliver many services, maintain community cohesion, and build mutual trust and social solidarity.
>
> (Cuskelly, Hoye, & Auld, 2006, p. 9)

Governments in many jurisdictions therefore have promoted volunteering as one means to address community malaise through policies and programmes with various titles such as "third way" and "social coalition". For example, the UK government "aims to promote volunteering ... as an expression of active citizenship" (Nichols, 2012, p. 155). The interactions and intersections of the trends and issues highlighted here represent powerful forces shaping people's views about the value proposition under-pinning the decision to volunteer and/or the nature of the volunteer commitment they are willing to undertake.

Sport volunteering

While these observations refer to volunteering generally, they are equally applicable to the specific sport volunteering context. Volunteers play crucial governance and programme delivery roles in sport organisations at local, regional, provincial/state, national and international levels, as well as the broader sport-related recreation sector such as in schools and other youth organisations.

Chelladurai and Kerwin (2017, p. 15) argued that "it is inconceivable that sport and recreation could exist without the services of volunteers" and therefore, in many jurisdictions, sport volunteering typically represents one of the most common/frequent categories of volunteer participation. The delivery of programmes and events in the sport sector has historically been structured on the basis of volunteer labour, and this is true of the smallest informally managed community sport club to the largest and most significant global sport events.

Given that sport clubs and associations are typical examples of mutual support organisations, it is also likely that, for many individuals, their first volunteer experience is in a sport setting and therefore sport may act as an important nursery for volunteers (Cuskelly et al., 2006). Eley and Kirk (2002) argued that sport volunteering can encourage pro-social behaviour and citizenship among young people. In countries with a strong volunteering tradition, "a large proportion of sports participation takes place in clubs run by the members themselves" (Nichols, Goel, Nichols, & Jones, 2014, p. 1) and, as argued by Houlihan (2001, p. 1), "as a source of empowerment for citizens and as institutions of civil society in their own right sport and recreation professions have a significant contribution to make". Thus a comprehensive understanding of the factors influencing the decision to become a sport volunteer, the nature of the sport volunteer experience and the management of sport volunteers is crucial for the sustainability of the sport sector.

This chapter will describe the size and nature of the contribution of sport volunteers to the community sport systems that exist in a number of Commonwealth countries (e.g., Canada, the United Kingdom and Australia). In doing so, the chapter will address the following issues:

- defining volunteering;
- the nature and extent of volunteering in different jurisdictions;

- trends impacting on the nature of sport volunteer participation; and
- categorising the various types of volunteer involvement including that in sport.

Defining volunteering

Defining volunteering, while something that superficially looks relatively straightforward, "is actually quite complex" (Cuskelly et al., 2006, p. 4). The term does not necessarily have a commonly shared meaning, despite being a "universal social behaviour" (UN Volunteers, 2018, p. viii), and could be defined by the same person differently depending on the context (including cultural context). For example, caring for those at risk or in need is likely to be perceived as having a strong altruistic component, whereas volunteering for a major sport event may more likely be seen as an exchange-based experience with the expectation of something in return. The nature of the relative cost–benefit ratio or outcomes of volunteering may therefore influence views about what constitutes being a volunteer. Handy et al. (2000) concluded that when the costs to the individual of volunteering are perceived to be higher, the person is more likely to be considered a volunteer.

Furthermore, the mere absence of financial remuneration does not mean that the activity may be viewed consistently as a volunteer experience by different stakeholders. Similarly, the level of formality involved in the process of becoming a volunteer, as well as in the nature of the volunteer activity itself, may also not be a central feature of whether an experience may be perceived as volunteering. As indicated by UN Volunteers (2018, p. 10), volunteerism

> embraces a diverse set of actors and activities ... depending on the context. This diversity means that the concept is understood in different ways in different countries and even within them ... definitions of volunteerism in cross-national comparisons will inevitably remain contested.

Despite these factors, there have long been calls to better define volunteering in order to assist not only with enhanced precision, but also consistency in measurement and research efforts. More than 20 years ago, Cnaan, Handy, and Wadsworth (1996, p. 380) argued that it was critical to "delineate the boundaries of the term volunteer" rather than allow it to remain "a catch-all for a wide range of non-salaried activities" Cnaan et al. (1996, p. 365). This position is consistent with the evolution of volunteer research noted above. Cnaan et al. identified four key dimensions of volunteering, together with a continuum for each dimension, in order to distinguish between what they termed "pure" and more broadly defined volunteers:

- free choice (free will to obligation);
- remuneration (none to a small stipend);
- structure (formal to informal); and
- the beneficiaries (others/strangers to oneself).

While these dimensions still feature prominently in most descriptions of volunteering, given the factors impacting on the voluntary sector, it is interesting to explore the evolution of volunteering definitions in recent years. In Australia for example, Volunteering Australia (VA), defined volunteering as

> an activity which takes place through not for profit organizations or projects and is undertaken: to be of benefit to the community and the volunteer; of the volunteer's own free will and without coercion; for no financial payment; and in designated volunteer positions only.
>
> (Volunteering Australia, 2005)

However, VA later formed the view that this definition did not accurately reflect the full extent of the ways in which volunteers contributed to society and, in 2013, commenced a review aimed at refining its definition in order, amongst a range of purposes, to:

- resonate with all parts of the Australian community;
- be inclusive, aspirational and enabling;
- be enduring, robust and adaptive, acknowledging the dynamic nature of the sector;
- be measurable, allowing the value of the sector to be better understood;
- be usable, pragmatic and able to be widely adopted, allowing entities to work constructively with the definition (Volunteering Australia, 2015, p. 1).

VA consequently adopted a simplified definition: "Volunteering is time willingly given for the common good and without financial gain" (Volunteering Australia, 2015, p. 2). As indicated by VA, the revised definition is consistent with the UN Volunteers (2011, p. 4) position that volunteering "should be for the common good ... directly or indirectly benefit people outside the family or household or ... a cause, even though the person volunteering normally benefits as well".

It is interesting that the VA definition is accompanied by a set of explanatory notes to "provide clarity on what is considered volunteering and what is outside the definition (but is part of the broader civic participation area)" (Volunteering Australia, 2015, p. 1). The supplementary material indicates, for example when clarifying the meaning of "without financial gain", that volunteers can:

- receive reimbursement for out of pocket expenses;
- be rewarded and recognised;
- receive an honorarium, stipend or similar payment.

The explanatory notes further suggest that while these processes and the receipt of such payments may introduce an element of financial or material benefit to the volunteer, this does not either exclude the activity from being considered volunteering or preclude the person from being considered a volunteer. The perceived need for the explanatory notes on the part of VA (the notes also address the concept of the common good and argue that volunteering requires a donation of time and that direct family responsibilities are excluded) reinforces the observation that volunteering is complex and the evolving nature of how society views this dynamic concept.

The scope of volunteering and sport volunteering

In recognition of the efforts and contributions made by volunteers, governments, academics and peak organisations either individually or collaboratively regularly measure and monitor the nature and extent of volunteer work. As pointed out by UN Volunteers (2018, p. 10), variations

> in people's understanding of volunteerism inhibit global agreement on a definition ... and the logistics of data collection limit the reliability of cross-national data. Unlike paid employment, volunteer work is typically performed irregularly, which complicates the measurement of how much volunteering occurs.

However, while methods and definitions may vary between and even within jurisdictions, some comparisons can be made, including that of trends within and across different countries.

It is also the case that improvements made in this area over the last 20 years "have increased the accuracy of global estimates of volunteerism" (UN Volunteers, 2018, p. 10). UN Volunteers further reported that, in 2013, work conducted through the 19th International Conference of Labour Statisticians (ICLS) and the International Labour Organization(ILO) has resulted in the adoption of a new framework for integrating volunteer work into official work statistics.

A variety of data from different sources underscore the sheer scale and scope of the contribution made by volunteers worldwide. UN Volunteers (2018) reported that the combined global formal and informal volunteer workforce is equivalent to 109 million full-time workers and, further, that a workforce of this magnitude equates to the fifth largest in the world, exceeding that of many major global industries.

While typically recorded somewhat differently (e.g., equivalent full-time workforce vs number of volunteers and/or hours contributed), data from different jurisdictions add support to the UN Volunteers figures. For example, Volunteer Canada (2015) reported that in Canada in 2013, 44% of Canadians (12.7 million) each volunteered an average of 154 hours per year, or close to 2 billion hours in total to non-profit and charity organisations. This was equivalent to about 1 million full-time, year-round jobs. However, 82% of Canadians also volunteered informally – almost double the formal rate. The most popular sectors where Canadians volunteered, both in terms of the volunteer rate and percentage of volunteer hours, were social services, sports and recreation, education and research, and religion (a combined total of 88% of all volunteer hours). Sport volunteering accounted for 24% of volunteers and 18% of all volunteer hours. Statistics Canada (2015) reported that volunteers were most often engaged in organizing events (46%) and raising money on behalf of an organization or group (45%).

Similarly, in Australia, McGregor-Lowndes et al. (2017) reported that in the 12 months prior to a survey conducted in 2016, approximately 8.7 million people (43.7% of the adult population) contributed 932 million hours as formal volunteers. This resulted in an annual average of 134 hours each (or 2.5 hours per week per person). Furthermore, 21.9% of respondents participated in informal volunteering, much lower than that reported in Canada.

In contrast to the figures indicated by McGregor-Lowndes et al. (2017), slightly different data were reported by the Australian Bureau of Statistics (ABS). The ABS (2015) General Social Survey (GSS) found that in 2014, 31.3% of the Australian population aged 15 years and over volunteered for at least one organisation. As noted by McGregor-Lowndes and colleagues, the Giving Australia (2016) results show higher levels of volunteering than those reported by the GSS (ABS 2015) though this observation is qualified due to methodological differences between the Giving Australia surveys and the GSS. These differences are, however, reasonably consistent. For example, McGregor-Lowndes et al. (2017) reported that an earlier Giving Australia report, published in 2005, found over the 12 months to January 2005, an estimated 6.3 million people or 41% of the adult population volunteered. One year later in 2006, the ABS found that 5.2 million people (34% of the adult Australian population) participated in voluntary work.

Very similar to the Canadian data, McGregor-Lowndes et al. (2017) indicated that, in Australia, the most commonly recorded areas of volunteer engagement included religion, sport, social services and health. They reported that sports accounted for 20.1% of all volunteers and that this group contributed an annual average of 91 hours each, realising an estimated total of 142.7 million volunteer hours (15.3% of total volunteer hours). Sport volunteering ranged from 18.4% in the 18–24 age group, to 20.7% (35–44 years) and 30.1% for those aged 45–54 years. Sports volunteering attracted more males than females and higher rates of participation were observed as income increased.

Also of note is that, in Australia, 7% of all volunteers contributed their time to recreation organisations, averaging 100 hours each per annum. This resulted in a total of 53.3 million hours of voluntary labour (5.7% of total volunteer hours). While acknowledging that not all recreation volunteering is directly in organised sport, the combination of the two sets of figures provides a strong indication of the full extent and significance of what could be described as "sport-related" volunteering in Australia (i.e., a total of 27% of volunteers and 21% of total volunteer hours).

In the United Kingdom, figures released in 2018 by the National Council for Voluntary Organisations (NCVO) indicate that, in 2016/17, 11.9 million people (22% of the population) formally volunteered at least once a month and 19.8 million (37%) formally volunteered once a year. In terms of informal volunteering, the report estimated that, in 2016/17, 14.5 million (27% of the population) informally volunteered once a month and 27.6 million (52%) informally volunteered once a year.

Consistent with other jurisdictions, the NCVO (2018) reported that, in the UK, females (23%) have slightly higher participation rates in regular formal volunteering than males (22%) as well as in irregular formal volunteering (39% and 35% respectively). This was also the case, albeit more pronounced, in the case of informal volunteering with 55% of women and 49% of men participating once in the last 12 months and 30% of females and 24% of men participating at least once a month. In terms of formal volunteering activities, males were more likely than females to lead groups, give advice and provide transport, whereas women were more involved in organising events, raising money and providing other practical help.

In terms of sport volunteering the NCVO (2018) report indicated that 57% of the people who volunteer formally at least once in the last 12 months did so with a sport organisation (this was the most popular category). The NCVO also reported that, in 2016/17, 63% of men formally volunteered more often in sports clubs than did women (51%). It should also be noted that, as for Australia, the second most popular category of organisations supported by formal volunteers were those related to hobbies/recreation/arts/social clubs (40%). Furthermore, 44% of people who volunteered formally at least once in the last year were involved in organising or assisting to run an activity or event, and 40% had been involved with raising or handling money/taking part in sponsored events. In addition, just over a quarter led a group and/or were involved as a member of a committee (27%) while a further 25% contributed by providing practical help.

The data from these different jurisdictions strongly suggest that, overall, volunteers continue to make substantial contributions to their communities through a wide range of formal and informal roles. While some of the population-level data may vary between jurisdictions, this is very likely due to definitional and measurement issues which may also vary within the same jurisdiction across different survey periods. Sport continues to be either the most popular or amongst the top two to three areas for volunteer engagement across these jurisdictions. These findings underscore the critical importance of volunteers to the long term viability of the sport sector.

Volunteering and sport volunteering trends

A review of data collected in a variety of different settings indicates that participation in volunteering has likely changed over time. For example, in the United Kingdom, the NCVO (2018) reported that in 2016/17, the level of formal volunteering, both regular (once per month) and irregular (once per year), appears to be similar to those recorded in 2015/16, but lower than that recorded in both 2013/14 and 2014/15. The report suggested that formal volunteering levels may have levelled off but any conclusions drawn from these data should be treated with caution due to changes in survey methodology between 2013/14 and 2016/17. Furthermore, while it is suggested that between 2014/15 and 2016/17 the level of informal volunteering appears to have remained relatively stable, this finding should also be viewed with caution because of methodological changes.

On the other hand, the UK Office for National Statistics (2017) reported that while the proportion of people volunteering had increased in recent years, the average time spent volunteering per day has fallen. Between 2000 and 2015, participation rates increased from 39% to 41% for men and from 39% to 42% for women but the average time spent volunteering decreased from 12.3 to 11.3 minutes for men and 16.3 to 15.7 minutes for women.

Volunteer Canada (2015) reported that 600,000 fewer Canadians volunteered in 2013 compared to 2010. In 2013, 12.7 million Canadians (44%) were reported to have volunteered compared to 13.3 million (47%) in 2010. The average number of hours committed by volunteers also declined. In 2013, volunteers contributed an average of 154 hours to their volunteer activities, a result similar to 2010, but down from a high of 168 hours recorded in 2004. Statistics Canada (2015) reported that the proportion of volunteers providing support to sports and recreation organisations has held steady over the last decade. Further, consistent data were recorded for the number of volunteers engaging in organising events and raising money over the same period.

In contrast to the UK and Canadian data, McGregor-Lowndes et al. (2017) reported that, in Australia, the percentage of those volunteering had increased since 2005 from 41% to 43.7%. Average annual total hours had also increased from 132 to 134 hours. This resulted in an increase in the total number of hours from 836 million to 932 million. However, the ABS (2015) indicated that volunteering rates in Australia had declined for the first time in almost 20 years, when compared to the 2006 and 2010 GSS and the 1995 and 2000 Voluntary Work surveys. The ABS reported that in 2010, 6.1 million people (36% of the Australian population aged 18 years and over) participated in voluntary work whereas in 2014, 5.8 million people or 31% of the Australian population aged 15 years and over participated in voluntary work. McGregor-Lowndes et al. (2017) noted however that sampling differences had occurred across these surveys at different periods.

The overall volunteer participation rates suggest that there is a downward trend, although the picture is not absolutely or consistently clear. In the UK, while there appears to have been a decline in volunteering rates between 2013/14 to 2016/17, this may be an artefact of survey sampling changes. Similarly, the stark differences noted in Australia (one data source indicating an increase in volunteering whereas another reveals a decline) may also be due to the different survey methods as well as changes in sampling across survey periods. On the other hand, the downward trend identified in Canada from 2010 to 2013 appears to be less equivocal. What is clear, however, is the consistent downward trend, across jurisdictions, in the time volunteers are now willing to commit. This trend is reflected in a number of measures including minutes per day, overall hours and average number of hours.

With respect to sport volunteering these more recent data appear to be reasonably robust and consistent with that reported earlier by the Australian Productivity Commission (2010). The Productivity Commission reported that, in Australia, sport and recreation volunteering typically accounts for either the largest or amongst the largest category of total volunteering and that this is relatively consistent across different jurisdictions. For example, more than one-quarter of the total volunteers in both Australia (26%) and England (26.5%) and almost one-fifth of Canadian volunteers (18%) were involved as sport volunteers (Productivity Commission, 2010). It is interesting to note that, in Canada, despite the reported overall decline, volunteering for sport organisations was steady.

The nature of volunteering and sport volunteering

As already outlined, there has been a gradual expansion of different terms used to describe and categorise volunteering behaviours. The utilisation of an increasing number of descriptors has been the consequence of a more mature understanding of volunteering, and as noted by Wicker (2017), partly as a result of the gradual evolution of sport volunteer research. In addition, the research has grappled with the rapidity with which sport volunteering behaviour has changed due to the effects of a wide range of global trends. As noted previously, relevant external trends include technology, perceptions of time and time use, employment patterns, community demographics and related social trends, coupled with evolving social attitudes, government policy and shifting family structures.

One of the main implications of the impacts of these trends has been the manner in which people perceive the amount, value and use of time. Consequently, the nature of engagement in volunteering has also evolved, and with this change has come a concomitant need to continually refine how the different manifestations of volunteer behaviour/participation are categorised. For example, terms such as micro and virtual volunteering were not in use as recently as a decade or so ago. A number of different categories of volunteering are defined/described and discussed below. An important consideration when reviewing these categories and their descriptions is that the categories are not necessarily mutually exclusive. Many of the categories intersect and some behaviours may be a subset or variation of another. For example, skills-based micro-volunteers may engage formally with an organisation in a virtual capacity. Similarly, spontaneous volunteers, who may be skills-based, are likely to engage in an episodic manner. The categories, while broadly described, are pertinent to the specific sport volunteering context.

Virtual volunteers are defined as those volunteers who complete tasks, in their entirety or in part, off-site from the organisation using the internet (Volunteer Canada, 2017). Other interchangeable terms include online volunteering, remote volunteering or e-volunteering. Given the ubiquitous nature of the internet, combined with increasingly time-poor lifestyles, it is little wonder that individuals choose to contribute as a volunteer via this means. There may be variable access issues, however, largely related to socioeconomic status and age. For example, 26% of Canadians aged 35 and under looked for volunteer positions over the internet compared to 7% of those over 55 years (Volunteer Canada, 2015). Volunteering Australia (2016) reported that 44% of volunteers had engaged in virtual volunteering in the last 12 months, and a further 19% wished to do so in the future. It remains to be seen however to what extent emerging concerns about data security and privacy may act to inhibit future growth in this area. Virtual volunteering is also suitable for those who may be restricted from participating in traditional volunteering activities due to mobility issues. Volunteer Canada (2015) reports that 64% of Canadians aged 75 and older indicate that the physical inability to participate in volunteer activities is a barrier to volunteering. Virtual volunteering not only overcomes physical barriers but, irrespective of time or distance, allows an individual to make a contribution. Consequently, the nature and timing of involvement is controlled more by the volunteer than by the organisation.

Career Village (2016) reported that unlike traditional forms of volunteering that typically include physical activity and/or face-to-face interactions, virtual volunteering can occur anywhere in which an internet connection exists. The logistical and cost advantages are obvious:

- online interactions are not restricted by location or time;
- volunteering can become highly scalable, able to cope with almost unlimited numbers of volunteers simultaneously; and
- the scalability is efficient and has relatively low entry costs.

However, the rise of virtual volunteering may have implications for those organisations that have traditionally relied on face-to-face reciprocal membership-based delivery (i.e., mutual support organisations). If more members choose to increasingly engage as virtual volunteers, this is likely to impact on the viability of some aspects of service delivery as well as organisational culture and any social capital that may accrue from volunteering.

Micro-volunteering is a variation on traditional volunteering in that the tasks involved only need a few minutes or hours to complete. Moreover, micro-volunteers are not required to make an ongoing or long-term commitment. Bright (2013) argued that non-profit organisations are creating their own micro-volunteering actions or using the term to describe micro-actions that previously were categorised as traditional volunteering. Micro-volunteering could also be described as a subset of virtual volunteering, as many of the tasks can be distributed and completed online.

As well as the obvious appeal to those individuals who, despite busy lifestyles, want to volunteer, this type of volunteer engagement typically requires minimal formality, time and effort to register and participate (Volunteer Canada, 2017). Given the trends impacting on volunteers and volunteer involving organisations, it is not surprising that micro-volunteering is rising in popularity. Statistics Canada (2015) reported that 66% of non-volunteers indicated they had insufficient time to volunteer and 62% that they were unable to make a long-term commitment. UN Volunteers (2011) reported that micro-volunteering was one of the fastest growing trends in global volunteering.

Spontaneous volunteers is a category most frequently associated with natural and other disasters and typically describes those members of the community who come forward to offer their time and skills when a disaster has occurred. It can be considered as an example of episodic volunteering, especially when large numbers of volunteers are needed over a short time period (Hyde, Dunn, Bax, & Chambers, 2016). Volunteering Queensland (2018, p. 3) defined spontaneous volunteers as "individuals or groups who are not skilled or trained to perform specific roles in disasters and are usually not affiliated with a nominated emergency or other community organisation, but are motivated to help". Spontaneous volunteering can include activities such as donating goods, money and/or offering physical help.

In a 2010 report, the Australian Government argued that spontaneous offers of help during and following a disaster are a growing phenomenon. The report indicated that after Hurricane Katrina in 2005, around 8,000 volunteers registered in the first 24 hours and volunteer coordinators continued to receive an average of 3,500 volunteer registrations per day during the relief operations. The American Red Cross alone used 50,000 volunteers to assist with relief activities in New Orleans. Furthermore, following the 2009 Black Saturday bushfires in Victoria (Australia), more than 22,000 potential volunteers offered their help. While the motivations of such individuals are generally altruistic, the sheer number of spontaneous volunteers as well as the volume of goods donated can sometimes "be overwhelming and place administrative burden and challenges on organisations at critical times" (Department of Families, Housing, Community Services, and Indigenous Affairs, 2010, p. 1).

Skills-based volunteering is described as the volunteering of skills that involve using individual or collective expertise to support the work of a non-profit organisation. It normally involves applying or transferring individual or organisational skills (McGregor-Lowndes et al., 2017).

Episodic volunteers is a category typified by less frequent or less regular involvement compared to regular (or continuous) volunteers. While the boundaries can be blurred (Cnaan & Handy, 2005), continuous volunteers demonstrate regular involvement in the same organisation (Holmes & Smith, 2009; Lockstone-Binney, Holmes, Smith, & Baum, 2010), whereas episodic volunteers tend to be involved on a less frequent basis, ranging from every few months to one-off or occasional events and projects (Handy, Brodeur, & Cnaan, 2006; Low, Butt, Ellis, Paine, & Davis-Smith, 2007). Continuous and episodic volunteers may also be differentiated by duration of involvement and the number of hours donated (Hustinx, Haski-Leventhal, & Handy, 2008). Macduff (2004) identified three types of episodic volunteering: temporary episodic volunteers who give a one-time service; occasional episodic volunteers who volunteer for one activity, event or project for the organization, but at regular intervals; and interim volunteers who serve on a regular basis but only for a short period of less than six months. The data suggest that episodic volunteering is becoming more common (Holmes & Smith, 2009; Mykletun & Himanen, 2016). Volunteer Canada (2015) reported that 37% of all volunteering is episodic in nature and that in stark contrast to episodic volunteers who average 36 hours per year, the 7% of Canadians who volunteer on a daily basis contribute on average 526 hours annually. Volunteer organisations typically allocate ad hoc and noncommittal activities to episodic volunteers whereas tasks requiring specialised responsibilities and skills tend to be assigned to regular volunteers. However, research has demonstrated that episodic volunteers were as equally satisfied as regular volunteers with their experience (Hyde et al., 2016).

The growing trend in episodic volunteering is frequently perceived as being problematic for volunteer reliant organisations. Concerns include the potential impacts of volunteers who may hold different volunteering values and attitudes to long-term and regular volunteers. They may be more noncommittal in nature and focussed on their own needs rather than being motivated by altruism and social issues. Other concerns involve the perceived threats to the traditional approaches to volunteer management and the costs required to develop contemporary management practices.

Core/peripheral volunteers. Ringuet-Riot, Cuskelly, Auld, and Zakus (2014) argued that there were two main categories of sport volunteers:

- core volunteers, who were centrally involved in the sport organisation and exhibit relatively high levels of time commitment; and
- peripheral volunteers, who typically displayed a steady or occasional contribution, but at involvement and commitment levels lower than that of core volunteers.

This view was consistent with those developed earlier by Pearce (1993) who first used the term "core" volunteer to describe the involvement and commitment levels of volunteers in non-profit organisations. Cuskelly et al. (2006) argued that core volunteers in sport organisations usually hold a formal management or governance office (e.g., a board or committee member), are seen as leaders, and display higher levels of involvement and commitment. Core volunteers could also be described as stalwart volunteers. On the other hand, peripheral volunteers tend to commit less time and can be classified as steady or occasional contributors whose involvement and commitment levels are lower than those of core volunteers (Pearce, 1993).

The results of research conducted by Ringuet-Riot et al. (2014) found that consistent with the earlier findings of Pearce, core volunteers contribute significantly more hours per week than peripheral volunteers in both primary and secondary roles, thus exhibiting higher overall levels of organisational engagement and commitment. Core volunteer behaviour is also evident in some national data. For example, Volunteer Canada (2015) reported that over half of all volunteer hours are contributed by only 10% of volunteers with the majority of this group, who volunteer daily or weekly, averaging 372 hours or more per year. Moreover, the top 25% of volunteers contribute 77% of all volunteer hours.

Similar to the concerns expressed above about the rise of episodic volunteering, Ringuet-Riot et al. (2014, p. 130) argued that

> given the trend towards volunteers contributing fewer hours, a lower conversion rate of core to peripheral volunteering not only has implications for VSOs [voluntary sport organisations] in terms of capacity derived from hours of volunteer work but also the quality of VSO services as peripheral volunteers are likely to have only a superficial understanding of VSO operations due to less exposure to organisational issues, tasks and workflow.

Stalwart volunteer is a category that could be described as containing loyal, steady and reliable supporters of an organisation. Stalwart volunteer behaviour is a subset of regular/traditional volunteers and could be contrasted to the behaviour of episodic and/or peripheral volunteers. A large amount of anecdotal evidence suggests this stalwart volunteers are a central feature of many community level sport organisations. Furthermore, the existence of stalwart volunteers is clearly evident in the data on volunteer participation in many jurisdictions (see core/peripheral volunteers above).

Pioneer volunteers are typically linked to events and are described by Fairley, Green, O'Brien and Chalip (2014) as volunteers who engage with an event throughout its entire lifecycle. This includes those individuals who volunteer in a continuous way in the lead up to, as well as during, the event. While the research of Fairley et al. (2014) focussed on a mega-event, this type of volunteer involvement could apply to events at any level. Fairley et al. found that pioneer volunteers experienced a strong and sustained identification with their role (still evident 12 years after the event), and sought out continued opportunities to volunteer in the post-event period.

Corporate volunteering is a category associated with volunteer opportunities sponsored by or organised through an employer. Volunteer Canada (2017, p. 13) also uses the term "employer-supported volunteering" and suggests the following definition: "The practice of employers providing the time, space, infrastructure and support for their employees to volunteer in the communities where they live and work".

Volunteer Canada (2017) argued that such programmes are typically one component of a corporate social responsibility strategy. The benefits can include improved reputation in the community, internal branding/

employee satisfaction, team building, skill development, enhanced productivity, improved staff recruitment/retention and increased profits.
McGregor-Lowndes et al. (2017) reported that 46.2% of respondents in
a 2016 survey in Australia who were employed had volunteered in the
previous 12 months. For 9.5% of these, at least some proportion of their
volunteering occurred through a workplace/employee volunteering programme. An average of 46 hours was volunteered annually through workplace volunteering programmes. Micro-volunteering opportunities may
have particular relevance for corporate volunteering initiatives because, as
indicated by Bright (2013), employees can engage at the office and consequently there is no time lost in planning and organising employees to participate in more traditional volunteering activities.

Event volunteers are a specific subset of volunteers and especially sport
volunteers. Sport events are typically dependent on episodic volunteers
(Holmes & Smith, 2009; Lockstone-Binney et al., 2010). The number of
volunteers involved in major sport events is noteworthy. Wicker (2017)
reported that the total number contributing to the Summer Olympic
Games is consistently recorded in the tens of thousands, including, for
example, Barcelona (35,000), Sydney (50,000), Athens (45,000) and
London (70,000). In addition, the International Olympic Committee
(IOC) indicated that there were more than 240,000 applications to volunteer at Rio 2016. Macur (2014) reported 15,000 volunteers worked at the
2014 FIFA World Cup in Rio de Janeiro and cited various news outlets
that had indicated more than 6,000 volunteers were recruited in Moscow
alone for the 2018 World Cup (which was played across 11 different
cities).

International sport events on this scale would not be viable without the
significant level of hours contributed by voluntary labour. However, this
is also the case for the vast majority of sport events at the local, provin-
cial/state and national levels. McGregor-Lowndes et al. (2017) indicated
that the most common type of volunteering task in a 2016 survey in Australia was helping at or setting up events (15.4% of all volunteers) and
that a further 7.4% indicated that their most frequent volunteer activity
was event planning and organisation. Similarly, the most commonly
reported volunteer activities among Canadians are organising events and
fundraising (Volunteer Canada, 2015). Given the nature of reliance on
volunteers for most events and the sheer scale and significance of large
global sport events, it is not surprising that this group of volunteers
attracts considerable research attention.

Conclusion

The evolving nature of volunteer behaviour (as represented by a number of
the categories described above), as well as the broader global and community

trends addressed in this chapter, have crucial implications for sport organisations that rely on voluntary labour. Consistent with the impacts of disruptive technologies and other global trends on traditional business practices, there have also been similar disruptive impacts on the non-profit/third sectors and the people that work and volunteer within those sectors. The challenge for volunteer agencies, researchers as well as relevant government agencies is how to stay abreast of such changes and ensure that planning, management and communication strategies are designed for optimal effect. For example, Nichols (2012, p. 155) posed a number of searching questions about volunteering arising from perceived changes in society:

- Are perceptions of organisations such as sports clubs changing from an expression of mutual enthusiasm and obligation to "service delivery" organisations in which members buy a service?
- Will traditional volunteers be replaced by paid employees or supplemented by young people seeking a marketable experience to help them gain paid work? And/or
- Is the role of volunteering in providing a collective service and social rewards more important in rural areas, or for particular sports?

Furthermore, accessing, recruiting, managing and retaining volunteers is becoming increasingly complex. For example:

- older volunteers may be less likely to access the internet but tend to have more time than other demographic segments in the community;
- older volunteers are concerned primarily with service provision whereas younger volunteers seek to build relationships and desire social experiences through volunteering (Volunteering Queensland, 2012);
- younger volunteers tend to be relatively time poor and are less willing to commit longer term and are also more likely to only contribute small and disaggregated amounts of time;
- volunteers generally expect the experience to be more tailored to their lifestyle and work commitments and want to engage at a time that suits them – not be constrained by when it may best meet organisational requirements (hence the rise of virtual and micro-volunteering); and
- males tend to engage more than females in formal volunteering whereas the reverse is true for informal volunteering.

Overall, volunteers are seeking shorter, less committed types of experiences and also involvement that they are better able to control. Hence, the rise of micro, virtual, peripheral and episodic volunteering. Such developments are usually perceived as problematic by those managing volunteering involving organisations as, in addition to the long-term challenges about volunteer recruitment and retention, are now added growing concerns that such short- term experiences are attracting individuals with different volunteering values and principles (i.e., motivated less by altruistic and social motivations) than regular core, continuous or stalwart volunteers. Consequently, some organisations perceive these developments as undermining the traditional approaches to volunteer programmes and struggle with adapting to and developing new management practices suitable to the new generation of volunteers. Volunteering Australia (2016) reported that while many volunteer involving organisations are aware of the need to adapt to technology to expand the pool of volunteers, they have insufficient skills and/or funding to do so.

These factors mean that sport organisations must be adaptable, flexible and contemporary in all that they do with regard to volunteers. Sport organisations have to be able to straddle both the more traditional, as well as the emerging wants, needs and behaviours of volunteers. As argued by McGregor-Lowndes et al. (2017), volunteer involving organisations must become more person-centred rather than organisation-oriented. If sport organisations are unable to do so, then their long-term sustainability will be threatened. The alternative future delivery model may be more "paid volunteer" roles (especially those related to predictable and repetitive tasks), a concomitant rise in virtual volunteers and a shifting focus to the use of face-to-face volunteers only in frontline service and programme delivery roles. If so, this will have implications for the nature of the culture in sport organisations and the attractiveness of such organisations for both their members and participants as well as volunteers.

References

Australian Bureau of Statistics. (2015). *General social survey: Summary results, 2014*. Retrieved from www.abs.gov.au/ausstats/abs@.nsf/mf/4159.0

Bright, M. (2013). The rise of microvolunteering. *Volunteer Weekly*. Retrieved from www.volunteerweekly.org/the-rise-of-microvolunteering/

Career Village. (2016). *What is virtual volunteering? Service in the 21st century*. Retrieved from https://medium.com/@do.good/why-virtual-volunteering-21st-century-service-22e07813517b

Chelladurai, P., & Kerwin, S. (2017). *Human resource management in sport and recreation* (3rd ed.). Champaign, IL: Human Kinetics.

Cnaan, R. A., & Handy, F. (2005). Towards understanding episodic volunteering. *Vrijwillige Inzet Onderzocht*, 2(1), 29–35.

Cnaan, R. A., Handy, F., & Wadsworth, M. (1996). Defining who is a volunteer: Conceptual and empirical considerations. *Nonprofit and Voluntary Sector Quarterly*, 25 (3), 364–383.

Cuskelly, G., Hoye, R., & Auld, C. (2006). *Working with volunteers in sport: Theory and practice*. London: Routledge.

Department of Families, Housing, Community Services, and Indigenous Affairs. (2010). *Spontaneous volunteer management resource kit.* Canberra: Commonwealth of Australia. Retrieved from www.dss.gov.au/sites/default/files/documents/05_2012/spontaneous.pdf

Eley, D., & Kirk, D. (2002). Developing citizenship through sport: The impact of a sport-based volunteer programme on young sport leaders. *Sport, Education and Society, 7*(2), 151–166.

Fairley, S., Green, B. C., O'Brien, D., & Chalip, L. (2014). Pioneer volunteers: The role identity of continuous volunteers at sport events. *Journal of Sport and Tourism, 19*(3–4), 233–255.

Handy, F., Brodeur, N., & Cnaan, R. A. (2006). Summer on the island: Episodic volunteering. *Voluntary Action, 7*(1), 31–42.

Handy, F., Cnaan, R. A., Brudney, J. L., Ascoli, U., Meijs, L. C., & Ranade, S. (2000). Public perception of who is a volunteer: An examination of the net-cost approach from a cross-cultural perspective. *Voluntas, 11*(1), 45–65.

Holmes, K., & Smith, K. A. (2009). *Managing volunteers in tourism: Attractions destinations and events.* Oxford: Elsevier.

Houlihan, B. (2001). Citizenship, civil society and the sport and recreation professions. *Managing Leisure, 6*(1), 1–14.

Hustinx, L., Haski-Leventhal, D., & Handy, F. (2008). One of a kind? Comparing episodic and regular volunteers at the Philadelphia Ronald McDonald house. *International Journal of Volunteer Administration, XXV*(3), 50–66.

Hyde, M. K., Dunn, J., Bax, C., & Chambers, S. K. (2016). Episodic volunteering and retention: An integrated theoretical approach. *Nonprofit and Voluntary Sector Quarterly, 45*(1), 45–63.

Lockstone-Binney, L., Holmes, K., Smith, K., & Baum, T. (2010). Volunteers and volunteering in leisure: Social science perspectives. *Leisure Studies, 29*(4), 435–455.

Low, N., Butt, S., Ellis Paine, A., & Davis Smith, J. (2007). *Helping out: A national survey of volunteering and charitable giving.* London: Cabinet Office. Retrieved from http://openaccess.city.ac.uk/2547/1/Helping%20Out.pdf

Macduff, N. (2004). The shrinking volunteer: Where have all those long-term service volunteers gone? Paper presented at the Association for Research on Nonprofits and Voluntary Action, Annual Conference. Los Angeles, CA. Retrieved from www.scribd.com/document/49134581/The-Shrinking-Volunteer

Macur, J. (2014). Many sacrifices, but few perks for event's volunteers, *New York Times* (July 10). Retrieved from www.nytimes.com/2014/07/11/sports/worldcup/world-cup-2014-many-sacrifices-few-perks-for-volunteers.html

McGregor-Lowndes, M., Crittall, M., Conroy, D., & Keast, R. (2017). *Individual giving and volunteering: Giving Australia 2016.* Report series commissioned by the Australian Government Department of Social Services. Brisbane, Queensland: The Australian Centre for Philanthropy and Nonprofit Studies, Queensland University of Technology, Centre for Social Impact Swinburne, Swinburne University of Technology and the Centre for Corporate Public Affairs.

Mykletun, R. J., & Himanen, K. (2016). Volunteers at biking race events: Antecedents of commitment and intention to remain volunteering at future events. *Sport, Business and Management: An International Journal, 6*(3), 246–273.

National Council for Voluntary Organisations. (2018). *UK civil society almanac 2018.* Retrieved from https://data.ncvo.org.uk/a/almanac18/

Nichols, G. (2012). Sports volunteering. *International Journal of Sport Policy and Politics, 4*(2), 155–158.

Nichols, G., Goel, R., Nichols, T., & Jones, W. (2014). Volunteers in British mountain rescue: Responding to increasing demand for rescues and a changed relationship with the state. *Voluntary Sector Review, 5*(2), 213–230.

Pearce, J. L. (1993). *Volunteers: The organizational behavior of unpaid workers.* London: Routledge.

Productivity Commission. (2010). *Contribution of the not-for-profit sector.* Australian Government. Retrieved from www.pc.gov.au/inquiries/completed/not-for-profit/report/not-for-profit-report.pdf

Ringuet-Riot, C., Cuskelly, G., Auld, C., & Zakus, D. (2014). Volunteer roles, involvement and commitment in voluntary sport organisations: Evidence of core and peripheral volunteers. *Sport in Society, 17*(1), 116–133.

Statistics Canada. (2015). *Volunteering in Canada, 2004 to 2013.* Catalogue no. 89-652-X2015003. Retrieved from http://volunteeralberta.ab.ca/wp-content/uploads/2015/11/Volunteering-in-Canada-2004-2013.pdf

UK Office for National Statistics. (2017). *Changes in the value and division of unpaid volunteering in the UK: 2000 to 2015.* Retrieved from www.ons.gov.uk/economy/nationalaccounts/satelliteaccounts/articles/changesinthevalueanddivisionofunpaidcareworkintheuk/2015

UN Volunteers. (2011). *State of the world's volunteerism report, 2011: Universal values for global well-being.* United Nations Volunteers (UNV) Programme. Retrieved from www.unv.org/publications/2011-state-world's-volunteerism-report-universal-values-global-well-being

UN Volunteers. (2018). *2018 State of the world's volunteerism report: The thread that binds.* United Nations Volunteers (UNV) Programme. Retrieved from www.volunteering.com.au/uns-state-of-the-worlds-volunteerism-report-2018-the-thread-that-binds/

Volunteer Canada. (2015). *The Canadian volunteer landscape.* Retrieved from https://volunteer.ca/vdemo/IssuesAndPublicPolicy_DOCS/Canadian%20volunteer%20landscape%20EN.pdf

Volunteer Canada. (2017). Canadian code for volunteer involvement. Retrieved from https://volunteer.ca/vdemo/ResearchAndResources_DOCS/Volunteer_Canada_Canadian_Code_for_Volunteer_Involvement_2017.pdf

Volunteering Australia. (2005). *Definitions and principles of volunteering.* Retrieved from https://volunteeringqld.org.au/docs/Publication_Virtual_Volunteering_Best_Practices_and_Future_Potentials.pdf

Volunteering Australia. (2015). *Volunteering Australia project: The review of the definition of volunteering.* Retrieved from www.volunteeringaustralia.org/wp-content/uploads/Definition-of-Volunteering-27-July-20151.pdf

Volunteering Australia. (2016). *State of volunteering in Australia.* Retrieved from www.volunteeringaustralia.org/research/stateofvolunteering/

Volunteering Queensland. (2012). *Virtual volunteering: Best practices and future potentials.* Retrieved from https://volunteeringqld.org.au/docs/Publication_Virtual_Volunteering_Best_Practices_and_Future_Potentials.pdf

Volunteering Queensland. (2018). *Making it happen.* Retrieved from https://volun teeringqld.org.au/services/building-local-capability-to-manage-spontaneous-volunteers

Wicker, P. (2017). Volunteerism and volunteer management in sport. *Sport Management Review*, 20(4), 325–337.

Chapter 2

The impact of volunteers on sport

Volunteerism is the backbone of civil society, having a tremendous impact by providing social services and by influencing the people receiving these services. Volunteers play a pivotal role in supporting non-profit organisations through individual and collective action. In turn, this action has important implications for democracy, social engagement, social capital and the very nature of community well-being: the building blocks of a healthy civil society. Jarvie (2003) suggested that civil society is

> an arena between the spheres of the state, on the one hand, and domestic or interpersonal relations, on the other ... Thus civil societies today have been described as a constellation of forces that provide a series of checks and balances upon the power of the nation state or local state.
>
> (p. 141)

Jarvie further notes that voluntary organisations, such as sport clubs, among others, "actively hold the middle ground between government, the state, and the individual" (p. 142). Given that these organisations fulfil such a central role in the structure of civil society, volunteerism has naturally held a critical place as a foundational component of modern society. For example, in the United States, the first volunteer firehouse was founded in 1736 by Benjamin Franklin (Dreyfus, 2018). The subsequent rise of the social reform movement mobilised individuals around issues such as poverty and women's rights and led to the founding of several institutions such as the American Red Cross, the United Way and the YMCA which would connect the volunteer force to social services and generate pathways for individuals to improve the quality of life for others (Dreyfus, 2018).

The role of volunteers in civil society has shifted significantly over time, yet, according to Rochester, Paine, Howlett, and Zimmeck (2010), four key sets of values remain which have had a significant impact on how we understand voluntary action and its impact:

1. *altruism or beneficence* is based on the moral imperative of compassion which results in greater care for other people;
2. *solidarity* expresses a feeling of identification with a group and engenders responsibility for the well-being of others in the group;
3. *reciprocity* drives the mutual response where helping others may lead in some way to being helped in return when we are in need;
4. *equity and social justice* counter inequity and injustice and challenge actions that are morally and socially wrong and should be addressed or eliminated.

In formal settings, such values may be taken up differently based on the specific mandate of a voluntary organisation. In informal settings, such as helping a neighbour, values may be further shaped by cultural influence and religious beliefs. However, various forms of these principles, held at a collective level in society, have generally shaped our attitudes to voluntary action and form the basis of civil life for generations (Rochester et al., 2010).

Volunteerism is also part of the early roots of modern sport. For example, the practice of volunteering in sport events can be traced back to the very first Olympic Games of the modern era founded by Pierre de Coubertin (Moreno, de Moragas, & Paniagua, 1999). The Games from Athens in 1896 to Berlin in 1936 were

> characterised by the anonymous volunteer work carried out in federations and clubs and in the organisation of the Olympic Games themselves, all in keeping with the social and educational nature of sport in those years. The main volunteer efforts came from groups such as the boy scouts and the army.
>
> (Moreno et al., 1999, p. 3)

The voluntary efforts of the boy scouts in particular consisted of delivering messages, maintaining safety and public order, and carrying out different physical functions, such as carrying flags and replacing obstacles (Moreno et al., 1999). Now, volunteering is central to the sustainability of the Olympics and other sport events and almost every sport programme around the world.

In civic society more broadly and in sport specifically, the volunteer role and its impact has shifted over time. The trend towards privatisation and professionalisation in sport (e.g., Parent, Naraine, & Hoye, 2018) are among a host of changes causing a major ripple effect for volunteers. For example, the sport landscape today "has encouraged governing bodies at different levels to pressure sport organisations into assuming a more professional approach to the delivery and design of the sport product" (Van Hoecke, Schoukens, & De Knop, 2013, p. 89). Many non-profit sport organisations are adopting a market-driven mindset and business-like practices, which impact on the non-profit sport sector's ability to create and maintain a strong civil society. Other trends include shifting family structures and work obligations, increased requirements for highly skilled volunteers in specific areas, a perceived decrease in people's leisure time, and changing attitudes towards volunteerism and commitment outside the family. These trends will be discussed later in the book as they challenge traditional assumptions about the management of volunteers and can make it difficult to attract and retain volunteers. These shifts also pose important questions for the voluntary sport sector such as whether voluntary action can cope with the resulting challenges and whether it should even attempt to do so. However, volunteers and the voluntary organisations they serve are active agents of transformation and not passive subjects. Indeed, the scope of voluntary action in sport is continually evolving and navigating the tension between prescriptive approaches and the free agency of citizen volunteers. This chapter outlines the impact of volunteers on sport and demonstrates that they are essential to sustaining sport systems and, thus, the contemporary management of them is paramount.

The contribution of volunteers to sport development

Sport is generally comprised of a vertically tiered governance system of clubs and community sport organisations, state (or provincial) associations, national governing bodies and international federations. This integrated system of generally volunteer governed organisations works collectively to facilitate delivery of a sport. In Western countries such as Ireland, Canada, Australia, New Zealand, Denmark and Norway, the majority of sport participation occurs at the local or community level within community sport organisations (CSOs), also known as voluntary sport organisations (VSOs) or voluntary sport clubs (VSCs). At this level, sport organisations are most often self-governing and non-profit, although they are sometimes private, profit-seeking businesses. VSOs usually consist of a volunteer committee or board of directors which oversees the direction of the organisation and is largely comprised of parents of youth athletes or members themselves. Often, VSOs are organised and operated entirely by volunteers and depend on the time and money contributed by them to deliver sporting opportunities. While some non-profit sport organisations employ paid staff who execute the daily operations of the organisation, most have no paid staff, further highlighting the reliance of these organisations on voluntary labour, time and resources to sustain their operations. Although community sport organisations are typically autonomous and generally rely on membership fees for their primary revenue, they also sometimes rely on government funding to assist with delivering their objectives. In these cases, they must therefore follow government mandates to qualify for that funding (Misener & Doherty, 2009; Wicker, Breuer, & Hennings, 2012).

Sport development has been conceptualised in various ways, yet the first and perhaps most widely recognised traditional "pyramid" model of sport development was based on the premise that sport participation comprised four hierarchical levels including:

(1) foundation – where individuals acquired the basic motor and perceptual skills to participate in physical activity;
(2) participation – engagement at a social or regular level through a local club system;
(3) performance – where the emphasis was on providing opportunities to improve performance through access to enhanced coaching and competition; and
(4) excellence – where the emphasis was on elite performance.

(As cited by Houlihan & White, 2002)

The pyramid model emphasised the interdependence between hierarchical levels, in particular the need for lower levels to provide resources (i.e., athletic talent) to improve the outputs of successive levels (i.e., more successful elite athletes). This model was revised by Houlihan and White (2002) to allow for more flexibility and transition between all stages to incorporate the idea that individuals could "shape their pattern of participation to meet changes in lifestyle, family and employment circumstances" (p. 42). Indeed, the notion of "progression" and even the notion of "development" through various stages from participation toward excellence or performance has been critiqued as elitist and may ignore important factors that influence one's ability to participate (and progress) in sport such as class, race, gender and other inequalities (Hylton & Totten, 2008). As conceptualisations of sport development change over time, so do the expectations and role of sport volunteers. Depending on the nature of the task and the current philosophy of sport development, volunteers must navigate between predominantly technical vs other supportive functions (e.g., role model, coach support).

Community sport development

Hylton and Totten (2008) are among those who advance an alternative continuum that encompasses the realm of community development rather than solely the development of sport and advocate for a reconceptualisation of community sport development (see Figure 2.1). At one end of Hylton and Totten's (2008) continuum is traditional sport development, also understood as sport *in* the community, where the focus is on sport as an end in itself. Here, the

Sports Development   Participation   Community Development

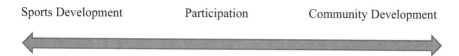

Figure 2.1 The community sports development continuum (adapted from Hylton & Totten, 2008)

primary focus is on interventions designed to allow athletes to progress in skill and sport performance. At the other end of the continuum is the notion of community development where sport is simply a means to human development more broadly. While the term "community" is certainly contested, it implies some notion of collectivity, sense of belonging to a group and/or place, and something shared (Hylton & Totten, 2008). By focusing on sport participation from a community development perspective, attention moves to consideration of a preferred vision of society and what constitutes positive change as well as "the process of change that moves communities and societies closer to that desirable vision" (Sharpe, Mair, & Yuen, 2016, p. 6).

This important repositioning of the nexus between sport and community mirrors the evolution of understandings of recreation and community. Glover and Stewart (2006) argued for a deliberate shift away from the study of community *recreation* to the study of *community* recreation, where the focus ought to start and end with concerns about community rather than the particular aspects of the activity being practised (and managed). Similarly, sport development systems have tended to focus on community *sport* for sport's sake. More often than not, this implies a geographic understanding of community as a municipality or region; and the basis for research is not necessarily community and its connections but one more functional in nature where community is a requirement for the production of sport (cf. Misener, Harman, & Doherty, 2013). Research in this dominant view has tended to concentrate on management systems, governance practices, policy and financial decisions that promote effectiveness and efficiency in sport delivery rather than the social connections, power relations and societal visions that are being developed through sport. This distinction is not trivial but is often ignored in any collective understanding of the sector, its impact and the impact of those who work within it (cf. Glover & Stewart, 2006).

Volunteer roles in (community) sport development

Volunteers make substantial contributions to all aspects of (community) sport development, fulfilling roles in policy development, governance and committee work, facilitating opportunities through fundraising and facility development, and, for the vast majority of volunteers, direct service delivery roles such as coaching, officiating and team management. The vast majority of sport volunteers operate at the community club level in roles which support sport development.

For the sport industry, volunteers frequently fill the role of "aide", serving in numerous capacities and at various levels (Maesen, 1976). They provide economic efficiencies by helping to minimise staff costs and by helping to generate innovative ideas (Cuskelly, 2008; Welty Peachey, 2019). The roles undertaken by volunteers are often to support, organise, manage and run sport and physical activities, programmes or events (Cuskelly, 2004; Ringuet-Riot, Cuskelly, Auld, & Zakus, 2014). Volunteer roles are often diverse and range in nature from formal "positions" to highly informal or undesignated roles and contributions (Ringuet-Riot et al., 2014). Typically, sport volunteers fall under two major groupings, which are identified as strategic or operational (Cuskelly, Hoye, & Auld, 2006; Doherty, 2005; Ringuet-Riot et al., 2014). Strategic volunteer roles can include those who hold positions in managing, governing or administration such as board or committee members of the sport organisations. Operational roles include volunteers acting as officials, coaches and event or general volunteers (Cuskelly et al., 2006; Doherty, 2005; Ringuet-Riot et al., 2014). Furthermore, sport volunteers regularly take on multiple roles and responsibilities and are often sport participants/members themselves (Ringuet-Riot et al., 2014).

Volunteers are also social change agents in and of themselves. New roles are continually being created in community sport in which volunteers are sought and trained to provide important support to organisations undertaking socially innovative programmes to address important social issues such as child welfare, bullying and LGBT advocacy. Volunteers are also engaged as leaders in initiatives to broaden the relevance and impact of sport in the community through socially responsible practices such as humanitarian and environmental work done within the sport club context (Misener & Babiak, 2015).

Volunteers as policy enablers

Voluntary action has a prominent place on the agenda of public policy based on the influence it can have on individual development, social and community cohesion, and addressing pressing social needs (Rochester et al., 2010). Indeed, volunteers themselves can make a powerful contribution to assisting governments in delivering better public programmes and fulfilling policy imperatives, and even one which could assist with the achievement of the UN's Sustainable Development Goals (United Nations, 2015). The expectations of volunteerism and its contribution are no exception in the sport sector, where volunteers are widely cited as critical stakeholders in the achievement of policy objectives (Nichols, Padmore, Taylor, & Barrett, 2012).

Sport policies around the world have long emphasised the critical role of volunteers. While government involvement in sport varies between jurisdictions, most countries have a national sport policy supported by the allocation of public funds and oversight from administrative infrastructure (Houlihan & Malcolm, 2015). Broadly, these policies support strategies such as facilitating opportunities to participate and compete in sport, promoting sport to specific sectors of the community and under-represented groups, providing opportunities to achieve elite excellence, as well as positioning sport as an instrument to achieve other non-sport objectives such as community development, crime reduction, health and diplomatic relations (Houlihan & Malcolm, 2015). While different political ideologies have set the course for the particular resource mix used to support sport policy objectives, governments have historically left much of the provision of sport and physical recreation to unpaid, committed and enthusiastic amateurs. For example, in the UK in the 1970s and 1980s, during rapid expansion of local authority-funded sport provision and large investment into building and staffing sport and leisure centres, the volunteer work force continued to sustain sport development by supplying coaches, administrators and board members "without which most formal competitive sport provision would have disappeared" (Jackson & Bramham, 2008, p. 195). Following the 2010 General Election in the UK, which prioritised deficit reduction through restraint of public expenditure, the "Big Society" ideology emerged, replacing traditional methods of social capital generation with informal opportunities such as volunteering, to allow citizens to contribute to their communities and build social capital (Morgan, 2013). In this realm, sport has been widely recognised as a contributor to voluntary action and the "Big Society" ideal, and policy makers have pinpointed volunteering in sport as a key way to unlock active citizenship and achieve key policy goals (Nicholson, Hoye, & Houlihan, 2011).

For example, the current strategy for Sport England (2016–2021) explicitly considers volunteering as a "dual benefit" for volunteers themselves and those who benefit from their service. The strategy not only considers volunteers an important resource for sport programme and event success, but also seeks to encourage volunteering for "its own sake as well as an enabler for others to engage, it can contribute to every single one of the five values – physical wellbeing, mental wellbeing, individual development, social and community development, and economic development" (Sport England, 2016b, p. 22). The strategy outlines specific measurable indicators related to volunteerism including increasing the number of people volunteering in sport at least twice in the last year and changing the demographics of sport volunteers to be more representative of society.

The Canadian Sport Policy, 2012–2022 also sets the direction for all governments, institutions and organisations to make sure sport has a positive impact on the lives of Canadians and communities through five broad objectives: introduction to sport, recreational sport, competitive sport, high performance sport and sport for development (Canadian Sport Policy, 2012). Sport organisations are responsible for achieving the different policy objectives while delivering sport within their respective environments. Volunteers are widely acknowledged as key stakeholders in the implementation of policy objectives. Both recreational and competitive sport include policy objectives stating that "capable volunteers and salaried workers are recruited and retained in order to achieve system objectives" (p. 10).

Similarly, recent governance reform in Australia (Australian Sports Commission, 2016) underscored the passion and commitment of sport volunteers, particularly in local/community sport, to the continued success of the country's sport development. Indeed, Sport 2030, Australia's national sport plan released in 2018, has a bold vision for sport in the country "to ensure we are the world's most active and healthy nation, known for our integrity and sporting success" (Sport Australia, 2018, p. 1). The plan discusses the complex ecosystem of partners at all levels of sport, with more than 75,000 non-profit organisations at its centre (Sport Australia, 2018). It celebrates the contributions of volunteers and participants at the heart and soul of this system, enriching the lives of not only those who volunteer but also those whose sport and physical activity pursuit is facilitated by those volunteers. "Whether preparing a wicket at the local cricket club, keeping score, coaching or umpiring the kids, running a committee, sport in Australia doesn't happen without its selfless volunteer workforce" (p. 29).

From policy to pressure

Government funding plays a key role in many third sector organisations who face pressure to deliver social services and must navigate the threat of instability and even viability depending on government funding. As government funding continues to dwindle, and the voluntary sport sector faces increased scrutiny, the possibility of reduced resources to support sport is increasingly real. For example, community sport trusts in the UK and elsewhere may be in jeopardy and challenge the provision of sport-related services (Parnell, Spracklen, & Millward, 2017). Much as in other policy domains, the rhetoric within sport policy is rich with good intent, yet the coherence and pragmatism of this rhetoric within challenging economic times can be oddly jarring. If policy makers truly want to design and support systems to increase the sport participation rate, strengthen the experience of people involved in sport, and improve performance at elite levels, there must be a more robust inclusion of volunteers as central to these actions at all levels. As Morgan (2013) suggests, the notion of co-production, where public and non-profit organisations work together in a reciprocal relationship, sharing decision-making and delivery, may offer an important paradigm shift for the future of the sport sector. Further, in order for sport volunteers to contribute to policy objectives, they must be aware of and understand the government's agenda. Research has suggested that sport volunteers may be unaware of or lack understanding of government policy, and greater education and involvement is required if they are expected to serve public policy in light of the pressures they face (Harris, Mori, & Collins, 2009).

The role of volunteers in sport for development and peace

In addition to their important role as the lifeblood of community sport organisations, volunteers also play a critical role within sport for development and peace (SDP) organisations, helping them to use sport to attain social development and peace objectives (e.g., Sherry, Schulenkorf, Seal, Nicholson, & Hoye, 2017; Welty Peachey, Bruening, Lyras, Cohen, & Cunningham, 2015). The SDP field has grown rapidly over the past 20 years and there are now hundreds of organisations and groups across the world engaging in related activities and a wide diversity of activities at local, national and international levels (Giulianotti, Hognestad, & Spaaij, 2016). SDP organisations often employ few staff, and therefore volunteers are necessary for the effective planning and implementation of SDP programming (Welty Peachey et al., 2015). SDP events and programmes rely heavily on these individuals to contribute particular skills and knowledge related to community or youth development, as well as time and energy. Consequently, volunteers are a vital component of any given programme or event (Welty Peachey et al., 2015).

The nature of the volunteer role within SDP is highly specific to the context within which the programme operates. For example, Street Soccer USA is an SDP organisation which uses sport to help youth and adults overcome homelessness. In their study of this organisation, Welty Peachey and colleagues (2011) found that volunteers interacted with the homeless participants in numerous ways from actively being involved or playing in game matches, leading structured goal-setting discussions, or organising/arranging informal social gatherings such as trips to the movies or team barbeques. In a later study, Welty Peachey and colleagues (2015) found that volunteers involved in a multinational SDP event often engaged in informal relationship-building activities, such as talking or playing with participants during the downtime around an event. Further, long-time volunteers with the event would assist other volunteers with problems they encountered, and seasoned volunteers of the event would go out of their way to orient new volunteers and introduce them to other long-time volunteers to help with forming connections and optimising everyone's experience (Welty Peachey et al., 2015). Moreover, the findings indicated that volunteers during this event would spend much of their time leading and organising, as well as collaborating and engaging with participants and volunteers (Welty Peachey et al., 2015). In another context, Sherry and colleagues' (2017) research in the South Pacific Region found that local (in-country) volunteers were key community mobilisers who could liaise with village leaders in order to negotiate resources for the programmes and educate participants about the sport activity. Although this is a small glimpse into the various roles that volunteers play in SDP programmes and events, these findings showcase the importance and impact of volunteers as a key aspect of programme/event success and viability.

SDP initiatives are undoubtedly impacted on *by* volunteers, but they can also have a significant impact *on* the volunteers themselves. Scholars suggest that one of the most prominent impacts of volunteering in SDP programmes and events is the development of social capital, along with heightened levels of prosocial behaviour and active citizenship (e.g., Kay & Bradbury, 2009; Welty Peachey et al., 2015; Welty Peachey, Lyras, Cohen, Bruening, & Cunningham, 2013; Wilson & Musick, 1999). Specifically, the mission and social agendas of these SDP events have the potential for volunteers and participants to establish close connections based around serving others for a development-related purpose (Welty Peachey et al., 2015). For example, volunteers in the Street Soccer USA initiative experienced a positive impact in the areas of "enhanced awareness and understanding, building community and relationships, enhanced passion and motivation to work in the social justice field, and the development of self-satisfaction through a feel good mentality" (Welty Peachey et al., 2011, p. 27). Additionally, the findings from Welty Peachey et al.'s (2015) study indicated that the multinational SDP event facilitated the development of social capital for its volunteers by building relationships between volunteers and participants, encouraging learning among a diverse group of individuals, and enhancing volunteer motivation to work for social change and reciprocity. Ultimately, these initiatives can influence volunteers who gain a sense of mission, utility and social purpose as a result of their direct and intimate interaction with participants (Welty Peachey et al., 2015, 2011).

While these outcomes can be very positive for both volunteers and participants, issues of patronage, power and privilege cannot be ignored when considering the role of volunteers in SDP contexts. As sport has entered the agenda of global policies and international aid, it has been largely financed and administered by agents outside local communities with limited local influence on how projects are financed and implemented

(Coalter, 2013). Critical SDP scholars such as Darnell (2012), Hayhurst and Szto (2016), and Spaaij, Schulenkorf, Jeanes, and Oxford (2018) warn of the exploitations and dependencies created by colonialism, ignorance and power imbalance. Giulianotti et al. (2016) argues that the historical roots of North–South partnerships, which are often reinforced in SDP programmes, must be examined in order to reduce the structures of paternalism which are possible when volunteers are used within a "fly in, fly out" model (p. 137). Rather, shared ownership, co-production and locally developed and led projects are considered essential rather than "voluntourism" which has often occurred within the SDP sector (Burnett, 2015).

Volunteers and community capacity building

Sport volunteers also play a unique role in community capacity building. Chaskin (2001) defined community capacity as

> the interaction of human capital, organisational resources, and social capital existing within a given community that can be leveraged to solve collective problems and improve or maintain the well-being of a given community. It may operate through informal social processes and/or organized effort.
>
> (p. 295)

Community capacity demands an intentional focus on using and developing community assets to promote social change and economic development, ultimately addressing the needs of those most affected in a community by including those most affected in the comprehensive planning and change efforts (Chaskin, 2001). This approach involves significant collaboration among community organisations and citizens as well as those with expertise beyond a given community. While various scholars place emphasis on different components, most agree on at least a few factors, including

> (1) the existence of resources (ranging from the skills of individuals to the strength of organisations to access to financial capital), (2) networks of relationships (sometimes stressed in affective, sometimes in instrumental terms), (3) leadership (often only vaguely defined), and (4) support for some kind of mechanisms for or processes of participation by community members in collective action and problem solving.
>
> (Chaskin, 2001, p. 293)

Thus, community-level action cannot be realised without capable and interested individuals, as they drive the success of each of these factors.

Edwards (2015) found that sport can effectively facilitate community capacity building in order to promote community level health objectives. When conducted in intentional, culturally relevant ways, "sport has demonstrated efficacy in building local skills, knowledge, and resources, increasing social cohesion, facilitating structures and mechanisms for community dialog, leadership development, and encouraging civic participation" (p. 6). Moreover, in settings where community capacity is advocated and used, including neighbourhood strategies, sport and recreation, citizen volunteers are central to community capacity building (Edwards, 2015). Further research is needed to understand the specific mechanisms of how sport can promote community capacity building and develop value systems built on collective action which will ultimately strengthen civil society, democracy and inclusion and not just podium performance.

Conclusion

Given their vital role in supporting the delivery of sport, providing independent governance, contributing to community capacity building, supporting sport for development programmes and supporting the delivery of government policies associated with sport, the question arises as to whether volunteers could ever be replaced? In their study of German sports clubs, Breuer, Wicker, and von Hanau (2012) examine whether there is a viable substitute for voluntary work. They compare sports clubs that experienced a decrease in volunteers over four years with clubs that remained stable (i.e., no change in volunteer rate during the same time period). They found that clubs with a decrease in core volunteers replace those individuals by increasing the number of secondary volunteers. Over the long term, an increase in employment of paid staff is also observed within these clubs, acting as a substitute for voluntary work (Breuer et al., 2012). However, this shift is not necessarily a remedy to be sought as the "work" of volunteers is merely one aspect of their overall influence and contribution. Their energy and passion, word-of-mouth support and other intangible contributions to social capital development and community cohesion cannot necessarily be replaced. The chapters which follow will address some of the considerations and innovative responses which transcend the notion of work outputs and may be used to counter the current trend of volunteer decline in order to revitalise the impact of volunteers in sport.

References

Australian Sports Commission. (2016). *Governance reform in sport*. Retrieved from www.sportaus.gov.au/__data/assets/pdf_file/0007/686212/Governance_Reform_in_Sport_June_2016.pdf

Breuer, C., Wicker, P., & von Hanau, T. (2012). Consequences of the decrease in volunteers among German sports clubs: Is there a substitute for voluntary work? *International Journal of Sport Policy and Politics, 4*(2), 173–186. doi:10.1080/19406940.2012.656681

Burnett, C. (2015). Assessing the sociology of sport: On sport for development and peace. *International Review for the Sociology of Sport, 50*(4), 385–390. doi:10.1177/1012690214539695

Canadian Sport Policy. (2012). Ottawa, ON: Government of Canada. Retrieved from https://sirc.ca/sites/default/files/content/docs/pdf/csp2012_en.pdf

Chaskin, R. J. (2001). Building community capacity: A definitional framework and case studies from a comprehensive community initiative. *Urban Affairs Review, 36*(3), 291–323.

Coalter, F. (2013). *Sport for development: What game are we playing?* London: Routledge.

Cuskelly, G. (2004). Volunteer retention in community sport organisations. *European Sport Management Quarterly, 4*(2), 59–76. doi:10.1080/16184740408737469

Cuskelly, G. (2008). Volunteering in community sport organisations: Implications for social capital. In M. Nicholson, & R. Hoye (Eds.), *Sport and social capital*. Retrieved from https://ebookcentral.proquest.com

Cuskelly, G., Hoye, R., & Auld, C. (2006). *Working with volunteers in sport: Theory and practice*. London: Routledge.

Darnell, S. (2012). *Sport for development and peace: A critical sociology*. London: Bloomsbury Academic.

Doherty, A. (2005). *A profile of community sport volunteers*. Ontario: Parks and Recreation Ontario and Sport Alliance of Ontario. Retrieved from http://wm.p80.ca/Org/Org185/Images/Resource%20Documents/Volunteer%20Resources/Phase1_finalReport.pdf

Dreyfus, S. N. (2018, August 29). *Volunteerism and US civil society*. Retrieved from https://ssir.org/articles/entry/volunteerism_and_us_civil_society

Edwards, M. B. (2015). The role of sport in community capacity building: An examination of sport for development research and practice. *Sport Management Review, 18*, 6–19. doi:10.1016/j.smr.2013.08.008

Giulianotti, R., Hognestad, H., & Spaaij, R. (2016). Sport for development and peace: Power, politics, and patronage. *Journal of Global Sport Management, 1*(3-4), 129–141. doi:10.1080/24704067.2016.1231926

Glover, T., & Stewart, W. (2006). Rethinking leisure and community research: Critical reflections and future agendas. *Leisure/Loisir, 30*(2), 315–327.

Harris, S., Mori, K., & Collins, M. (2009). Great expectations: Voluntary sports clubs and their role in delivering national policy for English sport. *Voluntas, 20*(4), 405–423. doi:10.1007/s11266-009-9095-y

Hayhurst, L. M. C., & Szto, C. (2016). Corporatizating activism through sport-focused social justice? Investigating Nike's corporate responsibility initiatives in sport for development and peace. *Journal of Sport and Social Issues, 40*(6), 522–544. doi:10.1177/0193723516655579

Houlihan, B., & Malcolm, D. (2015). Introduction. In B. Houlihan, & D. Malcolm (Eds.), *Sport and society: A student introduction* (3rd ed., pp. 1–8). London: SAGE.

Houlihan, B., & White, A. (2002). *The politics of sports development*. London: Routledge. Retrieved from www.taylorfrancis.com/books/9781134472611

Hylton, K., & Totten, M. (2008). Community sports development. In K. Hylton, & P. Bramham (Eds.), *Sports development: Policy, process, and practice* (2nd ed., pp. 77–112). London: Routledge.

Jackson, D., & Bramham, P. (2008). Resources for developing sport. In K. Hylton, & P. Bramham (Eds.), *Sports development: Policy, process, and practice* (2nd ed., pp. 185–213). London: Routledge.

Jarvie, G. (2003). Communitarianism, sport and social capital. *International Review for the Sociology of Sport, 38*(2), 139–153.

Kay, T., & Bradbury, S. (2009). Youth sport volunteering: Developing social capital? *Sport Education and Society, 14*, 121–140. Retrieved from www.researchgate.net/publication/248975820

Maesen, W. A. (1976). Evaluation and community volunteer programs: Accountability and impact. *Journal of the Community Development Society, 7*(2), 129–141. doi:10.1080/00103829.1976.10878109

Misener, K., & Babiak, K. (2015, May). A new 'arena': Social responsibility through community sport. Paper presented at the 30th annual conference of the North American Society for Sport Management Conference (NASSM), Ottawa, ON.

Misener, K., & Doherty, A. (2009). A case study of organisational capacity in non-profit community sport. *Journal of Sport Management, 23*, 457–482.

Misener, K., Harman, A., & Doherty, A. (2013). Understanding the local sports council as a mechanism for community sport development. *Managing Leisure, 18* (4), 300–315. doi:10.1080/13606719.2013.809185

Moreno, A., de Moragas, M., & Paniagua, R. (1999). Volunteers, global society and the Olympic movement: The evolution of volunteers at the Olympic Games. *Papers of the Symposium*. Retrieved from http://ceo.uab.cat/en/b/volunteers-olympic-movement-symposium-1999/

Morgan, H. (2013). Sport volunteering, active citizenship and social capital enhancement: What role in the 'Big Society'? *International Journal of Sport Policy and Politics, 5*(3), 381–395. doi:10.1080/19406940.2013.764542

Nichols, G., Padmore, J., Taylor, P., & Barrett, D. (2012). The relationship between types of sports club and English government policy to grow participation. *International Journal of Sport Policy and Politics, 4*(2), 187–200. doi:10.1080/19406940.2012.662693

Nicholson, M., Hoye, R., & Houlihan, B. (2011). Introduction. In M. Nicholson, R. Hoye, & B. Houlihan (Eds.), *Participation in sport: International policy perspectives* (pp. 1–9). London: Routledge.

Parent, M. M., Naraine, M. L., & Hoye, R. (2018). A new era for governance structures and processes in Canadian national sport organisations. *Journal of Sport Management, 32*(6), 555–566.

Parnell, D., Spracklen, K., & Millward, P. (2017). Sport management issues in an era of austerity. *European Sport Management Quarterly, 17*(1), 67–74. doi:10.1080/16184742.2016.1257552

Ringuet-Riot, C., Cuskelly, G., Auld, C., & Zakus, D. H. (2014). Volunteer roles, involvement and commitment in voluntary sport organisations: Evidence of core and peripheral volunteers. *Sport in Society*, *17*(1), 116–133. doi:10.1080/17430437.2013.828902

Rochester, C., Paine, A. E., Howlett, S., & Zimmemeck, M. (2010). *Volunteering and society in the 21st century.* London: Palgrave Macmillan. Retrieved from https://books.google.ca/books?hl=en&id=RVN7CwAAQBAJ&oi=fnd&pg=PP1&dq=role+of+volunteers+in+civil+society&ots=6Funi1I_Gm&sig=epcIQ8-WI07AY1GALNnuvzvR9Xw#v=onepage&q=role%20of%20volunteers%20in%20civil%20society&f=false

Sharpe, E., Mair, H., & Yuen, F. (2016). Community development in leisure: Laying the foundations. In E. Sharpe, H. Mair, & F. Yuen (Eds.), *Community development: Applications for leisure, sport, and tourism* (pp. 3–15). State College, PA: Venture.

Sherry, E., Schulenkorf, N., Seal, E., Nicholson, M., & Hoye, R. (2017). Sport-for-development in the South Pacific region: Macro-, meso-, and micro- perspectives. *Sociology of Sport Journal*, *34*(4). doi:10.1016/j.smr.2016.10.010

Spaaij, R., Schulenkorf, N., Jeanes, R., & Oxford, S. (2018). Participatory research in sport-for-development: Complexities, experiences and (missed) opportunities. *Sport Management Review*, *21*, 25–37. doi:10.1016/j.smr.2017.05.003

Sport Australia. (2018). *Sport 2030: Participation, performance, integrity, industry.* Retrieved from www.sportaus.gov.au/nationalsportplan/home/featured/download/Sport_2030_-_National_Sport_Plan_-_2018.pdf

Sport England. (2016a). *Volunteering in an active nation.* Retrieved from www.sportengland.org/news-and-features/news/2016/december/1/new-volunteering-strategy-published/

Sport England. (2016b). *Sport England: Towards an active nation, strategy 2016–2021.* Retrieved from www.sportengland.org/media/10629/sport-england-towards-an-active-nation.pdf

United Nations. (2015). *Transforming our world: The 2030 agenda for sustainable development.* Retrieved from https://sustainabledevelopment.un.org/content/documents/21252030%20Agenda%20for%20Sustainable%20Development%20web.pdf

Van Hoecke, J., Schoukens, H., & De Knop, P. (2013). Quality and performance management of national sport organisations: Managing and steering the performance of the distribution network. In P. Sotiriadou, & V. De Bosscher (Eds.), *Managing high performance sport* (pp. 87–114). New York, NY: Routledge.

Welty Peachey, J. (2019). SDP and sport management. In H. Collison, S. Darnell, R. Giulianotti, & P. Howe (Eds.), *Routledge handbook of sport for development and peace* (pp. 241–251). London: Routledge.

Welty Peachey, J., Bruening, J., Lyras, A., Cohen, A., & Cunningham, G. B. (2015). Examining social capital development among volunteers of a multinational sport-for-development event. *Journal of Sport Management*, *29*, 27–41. doi:10.1123/JSM.2013-0325

Welty Peachey, J., Cohen, A., Borland, J., & Lyras, A. (2011). Building social capital: Examining the impact of street soccer USA on its volunteers. *International Review for the Sociology of Sport*, *48*(1), 20–37. doi:10.1177/1012690211432068

Welty Peachey, J., Lyras, A., Cohen, A., Bruening, J. E., & Cunningham, G. B. (2013). Exploring the motives and retention factors of sport-for-development volunteers.

Nonprofit and Voluntary Sector Quarterly, *43*(6), 1052–1069. doi:10.1177/0899764013501579

Wicker, P., Breuer, C., & Hennings, B. (2012). Understanding the interactions among revenue categories using elasticity measures – evidence from a longitudinal sample of non-profit sport clubs in Germany. *Sport Management Review*, *15*, 318–329. doi:10.1016/j.smr.2011.12.004

Wilson, J., & Musick, M. (1999). The effects of volunteering on the volunteer. *Law and Contemporary Problems*, *62*, 141–168. Retrieved from www.law.duke.edu/journals/62LCPWilson

Chapter 3

Government impacts on sport volunteers

This chapter explores how government policy and legislation impacts on the ways in which volunteer activities are undertaken in sport, in particular those policies and legislative requirements that have increased the compliance burden for volunteers and voluntary organisations, or directly impacted on volunteering opportunities or programmes in sport. The chapter draws on examples from those jurisdictions most active in supporting or regulating sport volunteers such as Australia, New Zealand, the UK and Canada. The chapter is organised in four parts; the foundations of sport policy and the mechanics of developing sport policy related to volunteers; the nature of the relationship between the government and the non-profit sport sector; an analysis of examples of policies designed to foster volunteer involvement in sport; and finally a review of initiatives that have increased the compliance burden for voluntary sport organizations and their volunteers.

Foundations of sport policy

Contemporary government involvement in sport is broad and extensive (Houlihan, 2005; Hoye, 2013; Kappelides & Hoye, 2014; Strittmatter, Stenling, Fahlen, & Skille, 2018). Governments in Australia, Canada, New Zealand, the UK and many other Western countries have, in consultation with their respective national sport organisations, developed policies designed to foster community involvement in sport and physical activity, regulate the access and use of performance enhancing drugs in sport, and improve the performance of elite athletes and teams. They also seek to deliver economic benefits through supporting infrastructure developments for sport and underwriting major sporting events, and to address issues of equity and access to sport by supporting minority and disadvantaged groups in the community. Policies have also been developed to improve the management and operational performance of organisations involved in delivering sport, and to foster the development of social capital through programmes such as volunteer training and development.

Government intervention in the voluntary sport sector is based on the principle that participation in sport is a merit good, subject to two potential sources of market failure: efficiency and equity (Sandy, Sloane, & Rosentraub, 2004). Efficiency market failure occurs when sport delivery, although efficient for individual participants, may not necessarily be so for society at large if potential additional social benefits are not created due to the actions of individuals. Governments therefore seek to intervene through the provision of publicly funded programmes and facilities to increase sport participation which has the effect of lowering expenditure on public health programmes. Governments may also intervene in sport because of equity related concerns where the market fails to distribute resources and products equitably to all sectors of the community. As outlined in the previous chapter, governments in most Westernised countries with community sport systems can only achieve these policy goals with the assistance of a large and diverse voluntary workforce engaged in many different community sport organisations.

The outcomes sought by governments through various sport policies focussed on elite and/or community level sport are to a large extent focussed on delivering social benefits. Stewart, Nicholson, Smith, and Westerbeek (2004) identified a number of social benefits that result from policies supporting the active participation of communities in sport and physical activity including improvements in community health and productivity, reduced medical costs, reduction in juvenile crime rates, development of character and sense of fair play, and the building of social capital, social cohesion and greater levels of civic engagement. Social benefits claimed to flow from policies that support elite sport include a sense of tribal identification and belonging, civic and national pride, international recognition and prestige along with economic development and tourism (Hoye, Nicholson, & Houlihan, 2010). Governments also seek to address inequities that may exist for individuals and groups accessing resources to participate or otherwise be involved in sport.

Cuskelly, Hoye, and Auld (2006), drawing on the work of Bramham (2001) and Stewart et al. (2004), posited that the extent of government involvement and attempts to intervene in the activities of voluntary sport organisations is dependent on the ideology (conservatism, social reformism or liberalism) of the political party in power at any one time. Stewart et al. (2004, p. 22) argued that sport is "not so much a blind spot as a vacant space" when it comes to conservative governments enacting sport policies. In general, conservative governments on the one hand recognise that sport delivers good outcomes for individuals and society, but on the other hand believe sport is best left to its own devices with little if any government intervention. Stewart et al. (2004, p. 22) argued that conservative governments could be accused of retaining "a romantic belief that sport fulfils its function best when it is done for its own sake, played by amateurs, managed by volunteers, and generally left to look after its own affairs"; clearly a view that fails to acknowledge the increasingly complex sport delivery system dependent on volunteer labour that also underpins the delivery of contemporary sport policy objectives.

Stewart et al. (2004) noted that reformist governments tend to develop programmes for specific interest or minority groups, such as indigenous peoples, women, the disabled and people of non-English speaking backgrounds, and in general focus on community sport rather than elite level sport. Finally, liberals view state-owned enterprises as inefficient and that most economic activity should be driven by the market, with little intervention by the state. Sport is viewed as "an important social institution, but should not be strictly controlled" (Stewart et al., 2004, p. 23). Liberal governments do, however, recognise that sport has its value in nation-building and economic development so it should be supported for those reasons, leading to an emphasis on elite rather than community sport (Stewart et al., 2004). The differences in these three ideologies drives the extent and form that any particular government involvement takes in influencing how sport develops and the activities of sport organisations. This, in turn, creates several challenges for VSOs as "each ideology will produce different sport policy outcomes, strategies and programmes, and the ideology often overrides the claims of interest groups and stakeholders" (Stewart et al., 2004, p. 23).

In pursuing the wide range of outcomes that sport can deliver, governments enact policies that, in a broad sense, either seek to regulate or directly support the activities of organisations involved in the delivery of sport. Governments employ a variety of instruments to achieve policy outcomes: direct funding support for organisations or programmes, enacting legislation or regulations to prohibit or restrict activities of individuals or organisations, acting as an advocate for a cause or idea, or pursuing direct action such as establishing an agency or department to deliver specific programmes directly or via contracts (Baldwin, Cave, & Lodge, 2011; Bridgman & Davis, 2000; Strittmatter et al., 2018). As discussed in the previous chapter, the vast majority of sport organisations are dependent on volunteers, who thus are directly and indirectly affected by government policy initiatives and requirements imposed on VSOs.

Examples of governments providing direct funding support to sport include funding the construction and operation of major stadia and community sporting facilities, providing operational grants to national sport organisations (NSOs) or state or provincial level VSOs, financially supporting the bidding for national and international sporting events, or enacting legislation to control sports betting. Governments enact legislation to control access to free-to-air broadcasting of sporting events in Australia, the distribution of lottery funds for sport in the UK and the creation of national elite sport agencies in most Commonwealth countries.

They also develop generic legislation in areas such as taxation, food safety, privacy or membership rights, human rights and incorporations law which affects VSOs. Governments also act as advocates, directly promoting the benefits of sport participation to individuals through mass media campaigns and supporting the efforts of allied industries and groups that use sport as a vehicle to promote health benefits. Finally, governments are directly involved in delivering services and programmes in sport through national agencies such as Sport Australia (previously the Australian Sports Commission) and Sport England and through elite sport institutes such as the Australian Institute for Sport (AIS) and UK Sport.

Policy developments are driven by the government of the day, the major opposition political parties that develop election policies or platforms that may subsequently become government policy, or the various stakeholder and interest groups involved in sport. Whatever forms that government policy takes or the policy instrument employed, the individuals and organisations affected are part of what is known as a policy community. The policy community for a particular sport policy may comprise organisations as diverse as international sport federations and event organisations, NSOs, state/provincial VSOs, major sport leagues, health and physical education professionals, sponsors, major stadia, elite athletes, media organisations, universities, schools, sport clubs and volunteers. Policy communities provide governments with the opportunity to consult with those who may be directly affected by policy, to access information about the likely impact of any new policy proposals and may help to reduce the potential for conflict over changes to policy.

Interest groups that form part of the policy community comprise four types of structural interest groups: demand groups (sport consumers such as club members or elite athletes), provider groups (service deliverers such as physical education teachers, coaches, club volunteers and VSOs), direct support groups (organisations that provide systemic support such as NSOs, sponsors and schools) and indirect support groups (local government authorities and non-sport funding agencies) (Houlihan, 2005). Volunteers play significant roles in the majority of these interest groups and thus are a core part of sport policy communities. The ability of volunteers and the organisations with which they operate within to influence sport policy depends largely on how governments perceive their legitimacy. Taylor and Warburton (2003) found that third sector organisations interpret their legitimacy as based on how well they represent the views of their constituents and promote values of social justice or equity, whereas governments consider legitimacy in terms of the ability of the organisation to actually deliver policy outcomes. This suggests that third sector organisations, including VSOs, need to demonstrate their capacity to contribute to delivering policy outcomes if they wish to be taken seriously by government and actively engaged in the development of policy. However, this should be carefully managed to ensure organisations can maintain their independence and autonomy.

Fifteen years ago, Stewart et al. (2004, p. 27) highlighted the increasingly complex nature of developing sport policy requiring the interaction of government with a myriad of policy community members and when all the "organizations, activities and facilities are surrounded by a sport culture that has to balance the traditions and history of sport with its commercial imperatives". Sport policy in countries with significant community club based structures such as Australia, Canada, New Zealand and the UK must strike a balance between the economic realities of limited funding being available for sport and the need to deal with issues of gender, race, equity and the particular culture and traditions of different sporting activities. Houlihan (2005, p. 177) noted that there "has been a steady growth in organizational complexity and specialization" for agencies that deal with sport policy. Subsequently, agencies have tended to "develop relatively stable preferences for policy tools, perceptions of problems, and modes of working which constrain their response to new issues" (Houlihan, 2005, p. 177). The increasing complexity of the sport policy environment and the tendency for sport organisations to adopt a relatively narrow perspective for dealing with issues is a source of frustration for governments seeking to enact policy. In addition, Houlihan (2005, p. 177) cites the "recurring complaint from sports ministers that making sport policy normally involves liaison and negotiation with a large number of other departments who have a secondary interest in the area", such as education, health and community development. Contemporary sport policy scholars would argue the complexity of the sport policy environment continues to exist (Nichols, Grix, Ferguson, & Griffiths, 2016; Reid, 2012; Strittmatter et al., 2018).

The claim that developing sport policy in practice is a messy business (Stewart et al., 2004) is still valid today and recently explored in detail by Strittmatter et al. (2018). The multiplicity of outcomes that sport can deliver, the different ideologies that exist within governments, the utility of different policy instruments, the varied source of policy ideas, the wide range of structural interest groups that are involved in delivering policy outcomes, and the inherent complexity of sport issues that cut across areas of government activity such as education, tourism, economic development and health preclude the application of a routine, linear and rational policy process. Sport policy formulation can involve the application of rational planning, political opportunism, the development of suboptimal solutions designed to appease the demands of disparate interest groups, incremental changes and a lot of muddling through (Stewart et al., 2004). There is no single way that governments can best be involved in sport, or "what forms of assistance and regulation will produce the best outcomes" (Stewart et al., 2004, p. 17). Indeed, the recent work by Strittmatter et al. (2018) highlights the ongoing complexity of contemporary sport policy development and implementation. The following sections further explore the nature of the relationship between government and sport and the detail of sport policies that impact on the way in which volunteer activities are undertaken in sport.

Government and sport relationship

The extent and nature of the relationship between sport and government differs by type of organisation involved (NSOs versus small local sports club) and the level of government involved (national versus state/provincial versus local) (Anheier, 2005). The relationship is also dependent on the funding arrangements between government and sport organisations which may encompass grants, fee-for-service contracts, government loans as well as other non-monetary support such as access to facilities, expertise or advice, or general advocacy and organizational support. Relationships also involve mandates where government is required by law to engage with non-profit sport organisations to implement policy and the existence of regulations and accountability mechanisms.

Najam (2000) developed a model of government and non-profit relations based on the extent to which their respective organisational goals and means overlap (see Table 3.1) and proposed that the relationship is either cooperative, complementary, co-optive or confrontational, or indeed some combination of these. If the goals and means are similar then this leads to a cooperative relationship between government and the non-profit sector. In the sport context this would describe the relationship between an elite sport agency or organisation such as the Australian Institute of Sport and NSOs striving to improve the performance of elite athletes and teams. A complementary relationship would evolve if the goals were similar but the means were dissimilar, for example governments promoting higher levels of participation in sport through a mass media campaign supported by NSOs and VSOs offering clinics or other forms of sport participation opportunities in schools. If the goals are dissimilar but the means are similar, this leads to a co-optive

Table 3.1 Government non-profit relations (adapted from Najam, 2000)

		Organizational or policy goals	
		Similar	Dissimilar
Means of achieving policy outcomes or organisational goals	Similar	Cooperation	Co-optation
	Dissimilar	Complementarity	Confrontation

relationship where, for example, government may support the funding of a new multi-purpose sport stadium with matching funds from NSOs or VSOs who wish to use the facility for their own discrete purposes. Finally, if the goals and means are both dissimilar, this sets the scene for a confrontational relationship such as a sports organisation lobbying government for more funding to the sport sector or criticising current sport policies.

The value of Najam's model is that it stresses that all organisations, whether government or non-profit, are "driven not just by the grand schema of sectors and politics, but by the reality and rationality of their institutional interest and priorities" (Najam, 2000, p. 391). As discussed earlier in this chapter, the relationship between government and VSOs is highly variable based on the policy and organisational goals sought by each and the strategies each seeks to employ for their achievement. As governments increasingly look to VSOs for assistance in achieving policy outcomes, VSOs must balance the need to maintain positive relations with government with the needs and interests of volunteers, who provide the dominant means through which VSOs deliver services to their members and the wider community (Wicker, 2017).

In the past two decades, there has been a trend toward governments adopting increasingly interventionist policies that directly impact on how VSOs manage their volunteers. One example of how the relationship between government and non-profit organisations is becoming more formalised and interdependent was the attempt by the British government in the later half of the 1990s to develop a "compact" or agreement between government and the non-profit sector. The agreement sought to foster a closer relationship between government and the non-profit sector in policy development and reviewing the performance of organisations charged with carrying out government policy. Plowden (2003, p. 430) argued that a compact is indicative of "an attempt to change the culture of government/voluntary sector relationships".

Sam and Jackson (2004) highlighted a contradiction of sport policy in New Zealand where the central government sought to coordinate the activities of the sport sector but at the same time empowered organisations within the sector to act more autonomously, seek independent funding and adopt more commercialised management practices. Such contradictions are also apparent in Australia and the UK where central government policy is increasingly focused on funding VSOs for specific policy outcomes but requiring them to become more self-sufficient and independent. The following section explores recent government sport policies in Australia, Canada and the UK in an attempt to identify the elements of current sport policy that directly affect volunteer involvement in sport.

Sport policies and volunteers

Contemporary sport policies developed in Australia, Canada and the UK have followed a similar pattern as each government has attempted to balance supporting a community club-based sporting system while channelling significant funding toward elite sport. Green (2005, p. 161) argued that "the interests of elite sport development have dominated the sport policy-making process in Australia and Canada over the past two to three decades, with a similar scenario emerging in the UK over the past 10 years". The dominance of elite sport has, however, not been the result of sustained lobbying from elite sport interests. Rather it is the result of government "specifying, constructing, and maintaining through resource control and dependency the patterns of values and beliefs supportive of elite achievement" (Green, 2005, p. 161). Nor has community sport been ignored as governments have recognised the need to support other priorities such as "club development, regional development or mass participation" (Green, 2005, p. 161).

In Australia, the impacts of national sport policy on volunteers first came to the fore with Backing Australia's Sporting Ability (BASA), launched in 2001. The approach reflected in the BASA statement required "national sporting organizations to achieve greater rates of active participation and increase registered membership as a condition of funding" (Commonwealth of Australia, 2001, p. 7). The policy also sought to ensure "the adoption of sound business and management practices by national sporting organizations ... (and) ... a higher level of commercial activity on the part of local and national sporting organizations" (Commonwealth of Australia, 2001, p. 8). These outcomes were to be delivered by setting specific performance targets for NSOs in areas of elite sport, participation, fairness, funding, governance, anti-doping and requiring NSOs and their member VSOs to adopt more sophisticated management systems and communication technologies. In essence, these policy settings have remained in Australia with successive national sport policies reliant on volunteers throughout the system to deliver participation programmes, seek accreditation for core volunteer roles such as coaches or officials, and for VSOs to invest in volunteer training and development programmes aimed at recruiting, retaining and ultimately improving the performance of sport volunteers throughout their respective sport delivery systems.

These policy foci and mechanisms used to achieve them in Australia and notably the UK require significant input by volunteers in terms of improving their skills, devoting time in local clubs for achieving national outcomes, such as increased participation levels, and improving the veracity of member registration systems and procedures. At the same time as imposing these requirements on NSOs and their volunteers in return for funding, governments are pushing these same organisations to become more commercialised, adapt better risk management processes and become financially self-sufficient to sustain their operations (cf. Nichols & Taylor, 2010; Nichols, Taylor, Barrett, & Jeanes, 2014; Nichols et al., 2005).

The current Canadian Sport Policy (CSP), endorsed in 2012, has five major policy goals: ensuring Canadians have the fundamental skills, knowledge and attitudes to participate in sport; that they have the opportunity to participate in sport; that they have the opportunity to improve and measure their performance in a safe and ethical environment; that elite athletes achieve world class results; and that sport is used as a tool for social and economic development, and the promotion of positive values (Government of Canada, 2012). The issues being addressed by CSP 2012 are common across other community based sporting systems and include declining participation rates, significant access barriers to minority groups, fostering an effective elite athlete development system, clarifying the values that sport at all levels can deliver to communities and increasing the ability of the sport system to access non-government funding sources. The CSP relies extensively on the efforts of volunteers to deliver outcomes, with a recurring objective being that "capable volunteers and salaried workers are recruited and retained in order to achieve system objectives" (Government of Canada, 2012, p. 10).

The CSP also emphasises the need to enhance interaction between the organisations that make up the Canadian sport system. For example, the CSP aimed to foster stronger relations between VSOs and educational institutions: "linkages and partnerships between and among sport organizations, municipalities/local governments, and educational institutions align and leverage athlete, coach and officials' development and maximize facility utilization" (Government of Canada, 2012, p. 10). The effect of the current policy, and the previous CSP 2002, was to formalise the procedures used by VSOs, increase the reporting requirements of VSOs funded by the government and influence the way VSOs interact with their volunteers.

The implementation of contemporary sport policies of major Commonwealth nations is largely dependent on volunteers continuing to provide the labour for basic service delivery and increasingly the targeted programme and policy support required at all levels of these sport systems. As governments devise more sophisticated policy responses to a wide range of issues within the sport system, such as regulating sports betting and ensuring the integrity of competitions, and look to sport to assist in addressing a range of broader social issues such as childhood obesity and poor community physical activity levels, volunteers and VSOs are being asked to meet an ever growing number of demands. The impacts of these demands are addressed in the following section.

Impacts on voluntary sport organisations

Changes in government sport policy and funding requirements and the subsequent change in the nature of the relationship between government and sport have placed a number of challenges before VSOs. Houlihan and White (2002, p. 213) identified that in the UK

> the steady erosion of the privileged position of sports organizations has enabled local authorities and the Sports Councils to raise their expectations of the contribution that clubs and NGBs [National Governing Bodies] might make to public sports development policy in return for access to public funds, National Lottery income and other public resources.

One of the most significant challenges confronting sport volunteers and VSOs is the erosion of their autonomy and the costs of compliance they must bear if they agree to receive government funding and other support initiatives so that they may access the resources needed to deliver or expand their services. Contemporary sport policies of Australia, Canada and the UK highlight the shift from government simply providing financial grants to sport, to contractual-based partnership arrangements between government and sport with government viewing sport funding as an investment in sport organisations to deliver specified outcomes. Aside from the increased compliance burden of adopting new business practices and more stringent reporting requirements as a result of changes in government sport policy, VSOs and their volunteers have been confronted with many other changes in recent years.

Australian VSOs have been subject to the introduction of child protection legislation requiring changes in operations dealing with adult supervision of children and police checks of volunteer backgrounds, more stringent food safety requirements for VSOs operating food outlets as fund raising activities, and legal requirements for incorporation, volunteer protection legislation and insurance for volunteer directors (Hoye et al., 2010). In Scotland, the introduction of child protection legislation was found to have had a negligible impact on the rates of volunteering in sport clubs, in fact "having to comply with CP procedures is a minor deterrent to volunteers, compared to pressures from lack of time, time at paid work and time with their families" (Nichols & Taylor, 2010, p. 31).

Nichols et al. (2005) and later Nichols and Taylor (2010) cited similar increases in compliance burdens for VSOs in the UK as a result of government funding requirements and policy priorities. While government policies emphasise the use of partnerships, these "are a compromise of objectives, and are influenced by the power relations between partners" (Nichols et al., 2005, p. 40). There is also evidence of resistance on the part of NSOs to implement government policy with the associated increases in administrative and reporting requirements. The increased compliance burden has a direct impact on individual volunteers when "pressures to comply with the conditions of partnerships between NGBs and government cascade down to the volunteers in the sports clubs" (Nichols et al., 2005, p. 40). Further, the partnership arrangements between government and NSOs can be a source of tension if NSOs and their member organisations are viewed by government as service delivery organisations whose funding is tied directly to the delivery of specified outcomes. If government controls the funds, sports have little scope to counteract this control, so volunteers are inevitably asked to perform tasks focussed on achieving government policy targets.

The response of VSOs to these policy requirements is to adopt more professionalised and formalised operating systems, something that may well be at odds with the motivations and expectations of many volunteers. There is evidence to suggest that the adoption of more formalised management practices by VSOs is determined by the motivations of a core set of volunteers, particularly at club level (Nichols et al., 2005). If the core volunteers perceive that adopting such practices as part of the response to government policies and NSO requirements will benefit their club or organisation then they are more likely to do so. Nichols et al. (2016) reviewed the impact of Sport England's Sport Makers programme, the legacy programme from the 2012 London Olympics and Paralympics that aimed to generate new sport volunteers, and found the top-down approach used was counterproductive. They concluded that the county sport partnerships funded under this programme "were not acting in the best interests of increasing volunteers and ultimately sport's participation: they were acting to ensure that targets were met to ensure funding was not reduced or further funding was triggered" (Nichols et al., 2016, p. 71). At the club level, Reid (2012, p. 238) explored the ability of voluntary run sport clubs to support broader government policy objectives and concluded that:

> Voluntary sports clubs are, by their very nature, exclusive and cater for their members and their members' interests rather than wider goals of society, and it is where government policies intersect with these interests that the most progress in increasing sports participation and the health of the nation could be made through voluntary sports clubs.

Government policy has also attempted to influence VSOs to adopt member protection policies that enable players, administrators, coaches, officials and other volunteers to participate in sport free from inappropriate behaviours such as harassment, discrimination or abuse (Sport and Recreation

Victoria, 2005). The rationale for the introduction of member protection policies is that:

> as membership and volunteer numbers decline, organizations need to look at practices and procedures that create safe, welcoming and enjoyable environments. Organizations must comply with legislative requirements (such as anti-discrimination and racial and religious vilification laws), identify the potential for any incidents relating to harassment and abuse of its members and develop strategies to reduce the likelihood or severity of its occurrence.
>
> (Sport and Recreation Victoria, 2005, no page)

Developing member protection policies requires VSOs to adopt formal guidelines and procedures for the recruitment and selection of individuals, particularly those involved with children and adolescents, providing education to members about appropriate standards of behaviour, and appointing volunteers as member protection officers. These officers are the first point of call in a club or sporting organisation for any enquiries, concerns or complaints about harassment and abuse by providing information and moral support to the person with the concern or who is alleging harassment.

A range of other government policy initiatives have added to the complexity of running sport in areas such as anti-doping, conditions under which pregnant women may play sport, insurance, privacy requirements, human rights, incorporation and associated legal requirements, risk management, junior sport policies, and access and equity policies. These are in addition to policies concerning the core business of VSOs in athlete, coach and official development, hosting events, and delivering sport participation and competition opportunities.

Finally, a number of authors have explored the tension of governments seeking more from the network of VSOs while reducing core funding to support their policy objectives, especially in the climate of austerity measures in the UK (Bradford, Hills, & Johnston, 2016; Nichols et al., 2014; Parnell, Millward, Widdop, King, & May, 2018; Walker & Hayton, 2018). Nichols et al. (2014, p. 344) noted that

> sports clubs with junior sections appear to epitomise the ideal of civic activism in a Big Society, but the challenges and opportunities they face illustrate the complex relationship between volunteering and government ... [and that] ... government will need to act with care and sensitivity if it is to promote volunteering in sport.

Their study of volunteering to support youth sport found that "there is a paradox between on the one hand trying to increase volunteering and on the other, increasing pressures on volunteers through cuts in public expenditure and increasing regulatory burdens" (Nichols et al., 2014, p. 345).

Conclusion

This chapter has explored how government policy impacts on the way in which volunteer activities are undertaken in sport, including policies that assist in fostering volunteer involvement in sport and others that have increased the compliance burden for sport volunteers. It has been argued that the multiplicity of outcomes that sport can deliver, the different ideologies that exist within governments, the utility of different policy instruments, the varied source of policy ideas, the wide range of structural interest groups that are involved in delivering policy outcomes and the inherent complexity of sport issues that cut across areas of government activity preclude the application of a routine, linear and rational policy process. The relationship between government and VSOs has evolved towards contractual-based partnership arrangements between government and sport with government viewing sport funding as an investment. The success of government sport policies is largely dependent on the voluntary sector of sport having the capacity and volunteers with motivation to implement such policies. Government sport policy is an important driver of how volunteering takes place in the sport sector and, while it provides many opportunities for sport, it also imposes a number of constraints and challenges on the operations of VSOs and the volunteers on whom they rely.

References

Anheier, H. K. (2005). *Nonprofit organizations: Theory, management, policy.* Oxford: Routledge.

Baldwin, R., Cave, M., & Lodge, M. (2011). *Understanding regulation: Theory, strategy and practice.* New York, NY: Oxford University Press.

Bradford, S., Hills, L., & Johnston, C. (2016). Unintended volunteers: The volunteering pathways of working class young people in community sport. *International Journal of Sport Policy and Politics, 8*(2), 231–244.

Bramham, P. (2001). Sports policy. In K. Hylton, P. Bramham, D. Jackson, & M. Nesti (Eds.), *Sports development: Policy, process and practice* (pp. 7–18). London: Routledge.

Bridgman, P., & Davis, G. (2000). *The Australian policy handbook* (2nd ed.). Crows Nest, NSW, Australia: Allen and Unwin.

Commonwealth of Australia. (2001). *Backing Australia's sporting ability.* Canberra, Australia: Author.

Cuskelly, G., Hoye, R., & Auld, C. (2006). *Working with volunteers in sport: Theory and practice.* London: Routledge.

Government of Canada. (2012). *Canadian sport policy 2012*. Ottawa, Canada: Author.

Green, M. (2005). Integrating macro and meso-level approaches: A comparative analysis of elite sport development in Australia, Canada and the United Kingdom. *European Sport Management Quarterly, 5*(2), 143–166.

Houlihan, B. (2005). Public sector sport policy. *International Review for the Sociology of Sport, 40*(2), 163–185.

Houlihan, B., & White, A. (2002). *The politics of sports development: Development of sport or development through sport*. London: Routledge.

Hoye, R. (2013). Sport governance. In I. Henry, & L. Ming (Eds.), *International handbook of sport policy* (pp. 331–340). London: Routledge.

Hoye, R., Nicholson, M., & Houlihan, B. (2010). *Sport and policy*. Oxford: Elsevier Butterworth-Heinemann.

Kappelides, P., & Hoye, R. (2014). Volunteering and sport. In M. Oppenheimer, & J. Warburton (Eds.), *Volunteering in Australia* (pp. 168–179). Sydney: The Federation Press.

Najam, A. (2000). The Four-C's of third sector–government relations: Cooperation, confrontation, complementarity and co-optation. *Nonprofit Management and Leadership, 10*(4), 375–396.

Nichols, G., Grix, J., Ferguson, G., & Griffiths, M. (2016). How sport governance impacted on Olympic legacy: A study of unintended consequences and the 'Sport Makers' volunteering programme. *Managing Sport and Leisure, 21*(2), 61–74.

Nichols, G., & Taylor, P. (2010). The balance of benefit and burden? The impact of child protection legislation on volunteers in Scottish sport clubs. *European Sport Management Quarterly, 10*(1), 31–47.

Nichols, G., Taylor, P., Barrett, D., & Jeanes, R. (2014). Youth sport volunteers in England: A paradox between reducing the state and promoting a Big Society. *Sport Management Review, 17*, 337–346.

Nichols, G., Taylor, P., James, M., Holmes, K., King, L., & Garrett, R. (2005). Pressures on the UK voluntary sport sector. *Voluntas: International Journal of Voluntary and Nonprofit Organizations, 16*(1), 33–50.

Parnell, D., Millward, P., Widdop, P., King, N., & May, A. (2018). Sport policy and politics in an era of austerity. *International Journal of Sport Policy and Politics, 19* (1), 1–5.

Plowden, W. (2003). The compact: Attempts to regulate relationships between government and the voluntary sector in England. *Nonprofit and Voluntary Sector Quarterly, 32*, 415–438.

Reid, F. (2012). Increasing sports participation in Scotland: Are voluntary sports clubs the answer? *International Journal of Sport Policy and Politics, 4*(2), 221–241.

Sam, M. P., & Jackson, S. J. (2004). Sport policy development in New Zealand. *International Review for the Sociology of Sport, 39*(2), 205–222.

Sandy, R., Sloane, P. J., & Rosentraub, M. S. (2004). *The economics of sport: An international perspective*. New York: Palgrave.

Sport and Recreation Victoria. (2005). *Member protection*. Melbourne: Sport and Recreation Victoria. Online. Retrieved from www.sport.vic.gov.au (Accessed 10 October 2005).

Stewart, B., Nicholson, M., Smith, A., & Westerbeek, H. (2004). *Australian sport: Better by design? The evolution of Australian sport policy*. London: Routledge.

Strittmatter, A., Stenling, C., Fahlen, J., & Skille, E. (2018). Sport policy analysis revisited: The sport policy process as an interlinked chain of legitimating acts. *International Journal of Sport Policy and Politics*, 10(4), 621–635.

Taylor, M., & Warburton, D. (2003). Legitimacy and the role of the UK third sector organizations in the policy process. *Voluntas: International Journal of Voluntary and Nonprofit Organizations*, 14(3), 321–338.

Walker, C. M., & Hayton, J. W. (2018). An analysis of third sector sport organisations in an era of 'super-austerity'. *International Journal of Sport Policy and Politics*, 10(1), 43–61.

Wicker, P. (2017). Volunteerism and volunteer management in sport. *Sport Management Review*, 20(4), 325–337.

Chapter 4

The psychology of sport volunteering

This chapter explores the complexity of the psychology of volunteering in sport, including the key factors of motivation, satisfaction, commitment and increasingly important concepts such as psychological contract and continuity theory in understanding the relationship between sport volunteers and the organisation for which they volunteer. It explores what is currently understood about the psychology of sport volunteers and what future research is required to assist sport organisations develop appropriate volunteer management practices to recruit, support, develop and retain their volunteers.

Much of the early reported literature on sport volunteer psychology focused on sport event volunteers rather than longer term volunteers fulfilling traditional roles as coaches, officials and administrators or other volunteers involved in running sport clubs or programmes over an entire season or annual schedule. This was arguably due to the scale and unique nature of sport events that drove the interests of researchers or agencies seeking to evaluate the experiences of volunteers involved in high profile sport events. In more recent years there has been somewhat of a resurgence of material focussed on more traditional sport volunteering contexts. The distinction between attitudes and behaviours of sport event volunteers versus longer term sport volunteers will therefore be made from time to time throughout this chapter.

Dimensionality of volunteer motives

Much of the early work on volunteer motivation focussed on determining the dimensionality of volunteer motives. The motivation to volunteer in any context can be described as a desire to help others, or for personal and social rewards. In a widely cited work, Stebbins (1996) labelled these motives as altruism and self-interest which, he argued, co-exist within formal organisational settings. Over the last four decades, researchers have developed or argued for models of volunteer motives that comprise a single dimension (Cnaan & Goldberg-Glen, 1991), two dimensions (Smith, 1981), three dimensions (Knoke & Prensky, 1984), four dimensions (Batson, Ahmad, & Tsang, 2002) or more complex models with as many as six unique dimensions (e.g., Clary & Snyder, 1999; Clary, Snyder, & Ridge, 1992; Clary et al., 1998; Finkelstein, Penner, & Brannick, 2005). This lack of agreement on what constitutes volunteer motives was noted by Wang (2004, p. 420) who argued that "despite recent advances in research on volunteer motivations, there is still considerable debate about the underlying structure or dimensionality of volunteer motivations".

This debate has continued, especially in the context of sport event volunteering with at least four scales with different dimensions being developed over the last 20 years. This followed the seminal work by Clary et al. (1998) who utilised functional theory to develop the Volunteer Functions Inventory (VFI). The VFI hypothesised that six functions could be potentially served by volunteering in any context (values, understanding, social, career, protective motives and enhancement). Farrell, Johnston, and Twynam (1998) developed a four dimensional scale, the Special Event Volunteer Motivation Scale (SEVMS) and Monga (2006) developed the five dimensional Motivation to Volunteer (MTV) for Special Events scale. Giannoulakis, Wang, & Gray (2008) developed the three dimensional Olympic Motivation Scale (OVMS), and Bang and Ross (2009) later developed the Volunteer Motivation Scale for International Sporting Events (VMS-ISE) that comprised seven dimensions. This proliferation of scales to measure sport volunteer motives in long term sport volunteering or sport event contexts has been exacerbated by the adoption and adaptation of these scales by a variety of scholars for particular research projects, making it difficult to compare the results of different published research outputs.

As noted earlier, the majority of early research into the motives of sport volunteers has been in the context of large scale sport events (e.g., Allen & Shaw, 2009; Downward & Ralston, 2005; Fairley, Kellett, & Green, 2007; Farrell et al., 1998; Giannoulakis, Wang, & Gray, 2008; Kim, Fredline, & Cuskelly, 2018; Ralston, Downward, & Lumsdon, 2004; Treuren, 2014; Wang, 2004). Relatively fewer studies have focused on the motives of longer term or seasonal volunteers operating at the community level of sport, yet these appear to be increasing in recent times (e.g., Bradford, Hills, & Johnston, 2016; Burgham & Downward, 2005; Cuskelly & O'Brien, 2013; Emrich, Pitsch, Flatau, & Pierdzioch, 2014; Guntert, Strubel, Kals, & Wehner, 2016; Hallmann, 2015; Hallmann & Dickson, 2017; Kim, Zhang, & Connaughton, 2010).

Sport event volunteer motives

One of the earliest reported studies of sport event volunteer motives was conducted by Andrew (1996, p. 24) who concluded that "individuals will be attracted by and expect different material and personal incentives when volunteering for a cause". Andrew (1996) argued that sport event managers needed to understand the variety of motives held by a diverse volunteer labour force and therefore to use a variety of management techniques to sustain these motivations over the duration of an event. In one of the more widely cited works, Farrell et al. (1998, pp. 288–289) identified the importance of sport event organisers understanding volunteer motives so they could "respond effectively to [volunteer] management needs in the areas of recruitment, retention, and daily operations". They also argued that managing volunteer experiences appropriately would assist in the "maintenance of a strong volunteer base in the community for future events" (Farrell et al., 1998, p. 289).

Farrell et al. (1998) was also one of the first reported studies to suggest that sport event volunteer motives differed from those of other types of sport volunteers. They identified four motives of sport event volunteers: purposive, solidary, external traditions and commitments. Purposive motivation is based on a desire to do something useful and contribute to a society or community. Solidary motivation was based on the need for social interaction, group identification and networking. These two categories matched those originally proposed by Caldwell and Andereck (1994) as incentives for volunteering and based on the incentives approach of Knoke and Prensky (1984) who argued that there were three underlying volunteer motives: normative incentives or a desire to help others; affective incentives or social benefits realised from group interaction via volunteering; and utilitarian incentives or material benefits derived from volunteering. The additional factors of external traditions (an emphasis on extrinsic motivations) and commitments (expectations from others for volunteering) were the lowest ranked in terms of importance to event volunteers. In other words, Farrell et al. (1998) argued that the episodic nature of sport events and the different volunteer experiences they provided relative to longer term volunteer settings attracted individuals with different motives.

The uniqueness of volunteering in a sport event context was a focus of Coyne & Coyne (2001) who investigated volunteer motives associated with professional golf events and found that they were initially based on identifiable personal rewards but changed as volunteers remained involved in successive events. They argued that the uniqueness of the sport event and the affinity of volunteers with a particular sport are important reasons volunteers might continue an association with a sport event over a long period of time; essentially that sport event volunteer motives could be considered somewhat "fluid" in that they may change over time as volunteers experience the event and different aspects of their voluntary role.

Ralston et al. (2004, p. 15) investigated the expectations of volunteers prior to the 2002 Manchester Commonwealth Games and reported that sport event volunteering "tends to be sporadic and episodic and is highly dependent on the availability of tangible and intangible incentives and awards to attract and motivate volunteers". Ralston et al. (2004) reported that volunteers were motivated by a feeling of connectedness with something special, an empathy with the spirit or philosophy of the event, a general commitment as local and national citizens, support for an event that leads to the development and image of a local community, region or nation, and volunteers' expectations of the experience itself. Ralston et al. (2004) concluded that three factors were involved in volunteer motives: altruism, involvement and the uniqueness of the event. Understanding these motives is important for designing recruitment and training programmes for sport event volunteers as well as helping to influence volunteer expectations of the particular roles they may play as a volunteer. Similarly, a study by Reeser, Berg, Rhea, and Willick (2005) of the motivations of medical and allied health professional volunteers at the 2002 Salt Lake City Winter Olympic Games yielded similar results to Ralston et al. (2004) with the highest ranked motivating factors being a sense of altruism, wanting to be involved in working with a variety of people including elite athletes and to feel part of a unique event. They concluded that these specialist sport event volunteers were motivated through a complex process described as enlightened self-interest, where volunteer motives were not solely altruistic but based on a sense of reciprocity, with identifiable benefits accruing not just to the event organisers and participants but to the volunteers themselves (Reeser et al., 2005).

Allen and Shaw (2009) used self-determination theory (SDT) to explore intrinsic and extrinsic motives of sport event volunteers, moving beyond mere description of volunteer motives, to explore the processes involved in volunteers' own behavioural regulation. They found that the motivational climate established by the actions of volunteer managers and other volunteers led to their psychological needs for autonomy, competence and relatedness being satisfied and that they felt good about their involvement in the event and therefore appeared more likely to provide the required effort to fulfil their roles. Their study, while exploratory, indicated that deliberative actions by organisations and volunteer managers are associated with volunteer motives, especially during a sport event, and highlight the importance of motives in relation to volunteer effort and future intentions to volunteer.

The reported studies of sport event volunteer motives and their relationship to various attitudes or behaviours have tended to use different measures without significant efforts to test their dimensionality. One of the earliest studies that attempted to do this was undertaken by Wang (2004, p. 421) who claimed that "previous evidence to support the uni-dimensional structure [of volunteer motives] was rather weak" and that the "overwhelming majority of prior studies have suggested that motivation to volunteer is a multidimensional construct". He identified five motives held by sport event volunteers: altruistic value, personal development, community concern, social adjustment and ego enhancement. Wang (2004) outlined each of these values in turn:

(1) the altruistic values dimension is based on people choosing to volunteer because of personal values and beliefs and to derive enjoyment from helping other people and being a person who likes to be involved;
(2) the personal development construct is concerned with motives to volunteer to gain experience, for the challenge and being with people with similar interests;
(3) community concern is focused on volunteering to make a contribution and service to the community;
(4) the social adjustment dimension is based on people volunteering because it is important to significant others who support their volunteer activities; and finally
(5) ego enhancement reflects the notion that people volunteer to feel part of a unique experience or event, because volunteering is fun, and to feel needed or important.

A later study by Fairley et al. (2007) of volunteers travelling to the 2004 Olympic Games identified a similar range of motives.

Giannoulakis et al. (2008) examined the factorial structure of the OVMS through their study of the motives of volunteers at the 2004 Athens Olympics and established three motives: Olympic related, egoistic and purposive. The OVMS was based on the SEVMS developed by Farrell et al. (1998) as discussed earlier. Treuren (2014) further explored the multi-dimensional nature of event volunteer motives through examining volunteers across five different events, including two sport events. He found six different motives existed amongst event volunteers and that most volunteers are motivated by more than one thing. A more recent paper by Kim, Fredline, and Cuskelly (2018) utilised the VMS-ISE originally developed by Bang and Ross (2009) to segment the volunteers associated with three sport events. They found six factors labelled: (1) expression of values; (2) career orientation; (3) love of sport; (4) community involvement; (5) interpersonal contacts; and (6) extrinsic rewards. The unique nature of the events and their respective cohorts of volunteers researched in each of these selected studies over the last 20 years highlights the multi-dimensionality of sport event volunteer motives and that volunteers often hold more than one motive for participating and that motives are likely to change with continuing involvement.

Longer term sport volunteer motives

One of the earlier reported studies of the motives of longer term sport volunteers was carried out by Burgham and Downward (2005) who focused on what they called the "dual decision" that volunteers make: firstly a decision to volunteer at all, and secondly deciding how much time they should commit to a specific sport volunteering activity. They concluded that while individuals may be initially motivated to volunteer, there is, for some, a further trade-off to be made between deciding to volunteer their time to sport or to other activities such as work, family commitments or other leisure activities. Sport organisations therefore need to be cognisant of shaping volunteer roles to maximise their chances of recruiting those individuals with the right mix of motivation, capability and availability.

In a similar approach, Hallmann (2015) used data from a nationwide survey to investigate the determinants of volunteers' decisions to volunteer in organised sport and the factors that influence those people to commit their time to voluntary roles. Being male and slightly less educated were strong predictors of volunteering, as was current membership and engagement with a sport club. These rather unsurprising results do, however, highlight that time and individual resources "seem not to matter regarding the decision to engage as a volunteer [and that] working hours, human capital, age, and migration background do not appear to delimit the potential [volunteer] workforce for sport clubs" (Hallmann, 2015, p. 460).

Cuskelly and O'Brien (2013) used Atchley's (1989, 1999) continuity theory to propose a transition-extension framework that outlined the psychological and social factors that provide the impetus for the transition from playing sport to volunteering in sport. They concluded that individuals transitioning from a playing role to volunteering were doing so in order to "extend both their connection to and involvement in sport, and in most cases within a particular organisational setting" (Cuskelly & O'Brien, 2013, p. 70). Maintaining a sense of identity as a volunteer within sport was also a primary driver of continuing to volunteer as was the desire to maintain continuity of relationships developed through playing sport. This important study highlights the utility of continuity theory in seeking to understand the complex psychology of volunteers involved in sport, particularly in longer term contexts.

An example of some of the emerging research focused on significant cohorts of sport volunteers was the work by Bradford et al. (2016) who explored the pathways of working-class youth as they volunteered in community sport via programmes designed to provide a legacy for the London 2012 Olympic and Paralympic Games. Their study highlighted the important role coaches play in recruiting volunteers amongst young people, the unintended nature of their volunteer experience and the enjoyment they accrued through their voluntary roles in sport. It also highlighted that the young people involved in these programmes developed increased social skills and "heightened employment and educational aspirations that might extend beyond the community sport setting" (Bradford et al., 2016, p. 241).

The previous section reviewed a selected number of attempts to explore the dimensionality of sport event volunteer motives. A modified version of the VFI (Modified Volunteer Functions Inventory for Sports (MVFIS)) was used by Kim et al. (2010) to explore differences between volunteers' motives involved with a range of events and organisations across international, national, local and special-needs youth sport contexts. They found that for all four contexts the values and understanding functions were the highest ranked motives, a result consistent with previous research using the VFI. The absolute scores of the MVFIS also varied across each volunteer cohort, with volunteer motive scores for the international youth sport event being highest, arguably due to people being more motivated to volunteer for a prestigious event, while the scores for the national and local organisations were the lowest. This study again highlighted the multi-dimensionality of sport volunteer motives and the variability of volunteers' motives that exists for different volunteer contexts.

In summary, these published studies on the motivations of sport event and longer term sport volunteers highlight several points. First, the variety of motives held by all sport volunteers indicates that they should not be treated as a homogeneous group but rather as a collection of individuals with different motives for engaging in various forms of volunteering. Second, sport event volunteers tend to be motivated for reasons that differ somewhat from longer term volunteers involved in organised sport. Third, volunteers often have more than one motive for volunteering in sport and efforts to recruit them need to match these motives, something that is discussed later in this chapter. Fourth, volunteer motives are subject to change over time as volunteers engage in their roles and experience various management strategies. Finally, the variety of attempts to develop robust measures of volunteer motives over the last 20 years highlights the current lack of an agreed sport volunteer motivation scale that limits comparability across different sport volunteer settings.

Volunteer satisfaction and commitment

Cuskelly, Hoye, and Auld (2006) noted that volunteer satisfaction, commitment and retention are complex and interrelated phenomena that have attracted an increasing amount of attention from researchers; a trend that has continued since they published their book. In one of the earliest studies of sport event volunteer satisfaction, Elstad (1997) investigated the determinants of volunteer satisfaction amongst volunteers involved in the 1994 Winter Olympic Games in Lillehammer and found that their satisfaction was related to opportunities to expand their personal networks, to be part of the event or to achieve a desired level of job competence.

Farrell et al. (1998) found that sport event volunteer satisfaction was related to the level of communication between volunteers that was facilitated by event organisers and the recognition afforded toward individual volunteers' efforts. Farrell et al. (1998, p. 298) concluded that "volunteer satisfaction with the experience overall is not only a function of fulfilling their expectations, but is also related to their satisfaction with the facilities and the organization of the event". The importance volunteers place on their satisfaction being impacted by how they are treated by event or volunteer organisation managers and supervisors was also supported by Resser, Berg, Rhea and Willick (2005) who concluded that feedback on performance and recognition of volunteer efforts by event managers has a significant effect on the levels of satisfaction felt by volunteers. Giannoulakis, Wang, and Felver (2015) also concluded that sport event volunteer satisfaction was driven by the degree to which their motives were fulfilled. The link between sport volunteer motives and their satisfaction has been well established, but understanding the dynamics of the range of variables that impact on satisfaction is still the subject of contemporary research efforts. The concept of commitment is one of those variables that continues to be a focus.

The concept of organisational commitment amongst sport volunteers has been well researched (e.g. Cuskelly, 1995, 2017; Cuskelly & Boag, 2001; Engelberg, Skinner, & Zakus, 2006; Engelberg, Zakus, Skinner, & Campbell, 2012; Hoye, 2007; Schlesinger, Egli, & Nagel, 2013). These studies have conceptualised organisational commitment as an attitude held by a volunteer toward a sport event or organisation and "reflects the extent to which an individual identifies with and is involved with an organisation" (Cuskelly, 2017, p. 454). Much of the work has focused on the concept of affective commitment (emotional attachment or identification with an organisation), rather than normative commitment (feeling one has to be committed based on socialisation and investments made in an organisation) or continuance commitment (that results from a lack of alternatives or the sacrifice of a high level of sunk costs if one were to leave an organisation) (Cuskelly, 2017). Volunteer levels of commitment have been found to be impacted by their level of understanding of an organisation's goals, opportunities to apply their skills or experience in meaningful volunteer roles, being able to contribute to decision making, and overall job or role satisfaction. In turn, volunteer commitment has been found to be a predictor of volunteer behaviour, performance and future volunteering intentions.

Of all these reported studies, the study by Engelberg et al. (2012) not only explored the dimensionality of commitment amongst sport volunteers but also the targets of their commitment: essentially to what extent does volunteer commitment vary between their role, the immediate team with which they work or to the wider organisation for which they are providing their voluntary efforts? They concluded that volunteers' affective commitment was related to the organisation or the act of volunteering but not necessarily to their immediate team or specific role. Their work highlighted the complexity of the dimensionality of commitment but also the need for greater understanding of the drivers of various forms of volunteer commitment and the implications of commitment for performance and future volunteering intentions. Attention is now turned to two of the more problematic areas of volunteer research: What influences volunteers' decisions to continue volunteering and how can their performance be managed?

Volunteer retention and performance

It is clear that a great deal of published research on sport volunteers has focused on the dimensionality and drivers of volunteer motives, their expectations, antecedents and outcomes of commitment and what factors lead to their satisfaction but less on attempting to explain the behaviour of sport event volunteers, in particular their likelihood of continuing or returning to volunteer again or, indeed, their performance in their voluntary role. Cuskelly (2004) outlined the fact that volunteer retention is recognised as a significant problem for the community sport sector around the globe as it limits the capacity of sport organisations to deliver services to members and other users. However, even in the wider non-profit literature (Gidron, 1985; Mesch, Tschirhart, Perry, & Le, 1998) there are limited studies of volunteer retention. Mesch et al. (1998) identified that motives, meaningful work and satisfaction have been reported to affect volunteer retention. However, the results of various studies using each of these variables are mixed, with arguably only the relationship between volunteer motives and retention being firmly established in the literature. Essentially volunteers are initially motivated to join an organisation but their motives to remain with it might change once they have experienced its culture, management system and interactions with other volunteers or have undertaken other volunteer roles.

This important distinction was the focus of a study by Cuskelly, Auld, Harrington, and Coleman (2004) who investigated the behavioural dependability of volunteers in a number of sport event contexts. They argued that the duration of an event and subsequent expectations placed upon volunteers by event organisers as well as the support they received from family and friends were important determinants of the behavioural dependability of sport event volunteers. Cuskelly et al. (2004, p. 87) concluded that "understanding and influencing the behaviour of major event volunteers is more complicated than ensuring that the motives of volunteers are satisfied by event organizers". The results of Cuskelly et al. (2004) contrast with earlier work reported by Clary et al. (1992), and later Clary and Snyder (1999), who argued that functional theory suggests that volunteers will be satisfied if their volunteer experience matches their motivations and that this will, in turn, lead to volunteers remaining for longer periods. Hoye et al. (2008, p. 46) found that "while volunteer motives are important for understanding the reasons individuals initially choose to volunteer, once engaged in the volunteer experience their motives are not strongly predictive of the likelihood of their continuing to volunteer within the organisation".

Studies of the future intentions of volunteers have increased in recent years and have moved on from the calls made by MacLean and Hamm (2007) and Kim, Chelladurai, and Trail (2007) that there remains much work to be done to investigate the relationship between volunteer motives and retention. More recently reported studies have focused on how future intentions to volunteer in sport may be related to interactions and support (Rundle-Thiele & Auld, 2009), job design (Neufeind, Guntert, & Wehner, 2013), role or job satisfaction (Bang, 2015), role ambiguity (Rogalsky, Doherty, & Paradis, 2016), social interactions amongst volunteers (Lee, Kim, & Koo, 2016) or emotions (Gellweiler, Fletcher, & Wise, 2017).

In a study of volunteer junior football coaches, Rundle-Thiele and Auld (2009) found that aside from factors outside of the control of coaches or their clubs (e.g., illness, relocation) decisions made by volunteers to leave coaching roles are not based on the same factors as decisions to remain. Their study concluded that enjoyment of the role and success in either player development or on-field performance were important factors, but importantly the "nature and level of support from parents, the club, and the league, were identified as the key factors contributing to the decision to stay involved as a volunteer coach" (Rundle-Thiele & Auld, 2009, p. 1). Lee et al. (2016, p. 550) also established that efforts to create a sense of support amongst sport event volunteers "through social media promotes positive team member exchange that further impacts volunteers' future intentions". The work by Gellweiler et al. (2017) points to a need for sport organisations to be more proactive in managing the emotions volunteers associate with the end of their volunteering journey. Their study highlighted the need for further investigation of the processes used to manage volunteer role exit and the implications for future volunteering intentions.

The importance of organisational actions, specifically those that impact on the nature of the sport event volunteer experience on future volunteering intentions, was a focus of a study by Neufeind et al. (2013). They found that

> the design of volunteer jobs varies across event activities and, along with organizational features and appreciation, significantly affects volunteers' satisfaction … [and] … the effects of large sport events on

volunteers' intention to engage traditionally or at an event depend on volunteering history and the type of job they are assigned to.

(Neufeind et al., 2013, p. 548)

Bang (2015, p. 172) found that "as volunteers are younger, their perceived professional respect for leaders and/or members is likely to influence their levels of job satisfaction … [however] … as volunteers are older, their job satisfaction has more influence on their intention to stay". These two studies highlight the importance of job satisfaction, however derived, on the future intentions of sport volunteers.

A study by Rogalsky et al. (2016) explored both the antecedents (role difficulty, supervision, training) and the outcomes (role effort, role performance, role satisfaction) of role ambiguity and their relationship to overall satisfaction and ultimately future sport event volunteering intentions. Role ambiguity, somewhat unsurprisingly, was found (in part) to negatively impact on role performance and role satisfaction as predictors of overall satisfaction and ultimately the future intentions of sport event volunteers, but the study also highlighted the complex interplay of other factors (availability, skills, employment status, etc.) on future volunteering intentions.

The myriad of variables that impact on volunteers' experience and importantly their sense of belonging or connection to an organisation and their subsequent attitude to and behaviour in relation to their voluntary role may be best understood through the lens of the psychological contract. Kappelides, Cuskelly, and Hoye (2018) provide a review of psychological contract (PC) theory and its relevance to volunteering, specifically how it can help understand the set of beliefs a person holds in relation to a voluntary organisation and their perceptions of how that organisation values their contributions. The application of PC theory to sport volunteer research has been very limited to date but it does seem to offer a more holistic framework for exploring the nature of the relationship between volunteers and their organisations and have particular utility for understanding what actions of organisations or volunteer managers might influence this relationship. This influence of psychological contracts on volunteer administrators will be discussed further in Chapter 7.

Conclusion

This chapter on the psychology of sport volunteering has focussed on several core concepts: volunteer motives, satisfaction, commitment, future intentions and performance. The discussion has shown that these concepts are clearly interrelated and that they have important implications for the management of volunteers in sport events and longer or more traditional modes of volunteering. It is worth noting that the majority of volunteers involved in special events (including sport events) conducted on a regular or annual basis in the same locale are repeat volunteers (Treuren & Monga, 2002a, 2002b). As these volunteers are usually sourced from organisations related to the event organisation via the social networks of previous volunteers, or from prior participants, a "combination of targeted recruitment and planned training" may substantially increase the efficacy of volunteer recruitment efforts for repeat sport events (Treuren & Monga, 2002b, p. 226). Similarly, more sophisticated and targeted volunteer recruitment methods are required for other sport volunteers that align to volunteer motives and their expectations of organisational support and personal or professional benefits they may receive in return for their voluntary efforts.

It is clear that there remains much to be discovered about sport volunteers' motivation and commitment, and how volunteer management practices should be designed and implemented to maximise volunteer satisfaction and retention and ultimately their performance. Future research into sport volunteers must continue to move beyond descriptive studies of volunteer motives or satisfaction. The field of sport volunteer research has arguably lacked a consistent and coherent theoretical foundation, has tended to focus on single sport events using convenience sampling and cross-sectional research designs, or has developed measurement tools which are one-off and often event or sport context specific.

Earlier in this chapter the problematic lack of agreement on the dimensionality of sport volunteer motivation and the diverse range of bespoke measurement scales developed by researchers were pointed out. The ability to reliably explain or predict the commitment or future intentions of sport volunteers needs to improve. Cuskelly (2017, p. 457) pointed out that "much of the knowledge base in sport volunteer management is grounded in mainstream management research". He also argued that:

> Volunteer management research in general and sport volunteer management research specifically lacks its own research paradigms, methods and traditions. As a consequence, the field of sport volunteer research has little coherence or agreement about the most important research priorities or directions necessary to advance the body of knowledge independent of the mainstream management literature.
>
> (Cuskelly, 2017, p. 458)

In order to advance the field of sport volunteer research, Cuskelly (2017) posited that a coherent and coordinated international research agenda, an agreed definition and measurement tool for volunteer retention, and a more robust set of measurement tools for variables associated with the psychology of the sport volunteering experience were needed. The application of theoretical frameworks such as continuity theory or the psychological contract seem to afford the opportunity to move beyond simplistic, descriptive studies of attitudes or engagement of sport volunteers to a truly comprehensive understanding of the complexity of the sport volunteer experience. Only then can researchers and managers start to develop more efficacious volunteer management approaches that address individual volunteer needs but also service the requirements of sport organisations in the delivery of sport programmes, participation opportunities and events.

References

Allen, J. B., & Shaw, S. (2009). 'Everyone rolls ups their sleeves and mucks in': Exploring volunteers' motivation and experiences of the motivational climate of a sporting event. *Sport Management Review*, *12*, 79–90.

Andrew, J. (1996). Motivations and expectations of volunteers involved in a large scale sports event: A pilot study. *Australian Leisure*, *7*(1), 21–25.

Atchley, R. C. (1989). A continuity theory of aging. *The Gerontologist*, *29*, 183–190.

Atchley, R. C. (1999). *Continuity and adaptation in aging*. Baltimore, MD: The John Hopkins University Press.

Bang, H. (2015). Volunteer age, job satisfaction, and intention to stay: A case of non-profit sport organizations. *Leadership and Organizational Development Journal*, *36*(2), 161–176.

Bang, H., & Ross, S. D. (2009). Volunteer motivation and satisfaction. *Journal of Venue and Event Management*, *1*(1), 61–77.

Batson, C. D., Ahmad, N., & Tsang, J. (2002). Four motives for community involvement. *Journal of Social Issues*, *58*(2), 429–445.

Bradford, S., Hills, L., & Johnston, C. (2016). Unintended volunteers: The volunteering pathways of working class young people in community sport. *International Journal of Sport Policy and Politics*, *8*(2), 231–244.

Burgham, M., & Downward, P. (2005). Why volunteer, time to volunteer? A case study from swimming. *Managing Leisure*, *10*, 79–93.

Caldwell, L., & Andereck, K. (1994). Motives for initiating and continuing membership in a recreation-related voluntary association. *Leisure Studies*, *16*, 33–44.

Clary, E. G., & Snyder, M. (1999). The motivations to volunteer: Theoretical and practical considerations. *Current Directions in Psychological Science*, *8*(5), 156–159.

Clary, E. G., Snyder, M., & Ridge, R. (1992). Volunteers' motivations: A functional strategy for the recruitment, placement and retention of volunteers. *Nonprofit Management and Leadership*, *2*(4), 333–350.

Clary, E. G., Snyder, M., Ridge, R. D., Copeland, J., Stukas, A. A., Haugen, J., & Miene, P. (1998). Understanding and assessing motivations of volunteers: A functional approach. *Journal of Personality and Social Psychology*, *74*(6), 1516–1530.

Cnaan, R., & Goldberg-Glen, R. S. (1991). Measuring motivation to volunteer in human services. *Journal of Applied Behavioral Science*, *27*(3), 269–284.

Coyne, B. S., & Coyne, E. J. (2001). Getting, keeping and caring for unpaid volunteers for professional golf tournament events: A study of the recruitment/retention of unpaid volunteers for staging large, mass-attended, high-profile Professional

Golf Association (PGA) golf tournaments. *Human Resource Development International*, 4(2), 199–214.

Cuskelly, G. (1995). The influence of committee functioning on the organizational commitment of volunteer administrators in sport. *Journal of Sport Behaviour*, 18, 254–269.

Cuskelly, G. (2004). Volunteer retention in community sport organisations. *European Sport Management Quarterly*, 4, 59–76.

Cuskelly, G. (2017). Volunteer management. In R. Hoye, & M. M. Parent (Eds.), *Handbook of sport management* (pp. 442–462). London: SAGE.

Cuskelly, G., Auld, C., Harrington, M., & Coleman, D. (2004). Predicting the behavioural dependability of sport event volunteers. *Event Management*, 9, 73–89.

Cuskelly, G., & Boag, A. (2001). Organisational commitment as a predictor of committee member turnover amongst volunteer sport administrators: Results of a time-lagged study. *Sport Management Review*, 4, 65–86.

Cuskelly, G., Hoye, R., & Auld, C. (2006). *Working with volunteers in sport: Theory and practice*. London: Routledge.

Cuskelly, G., & O'Brien, W. (2013). Changing roles: Applying continuity theory to understanding the transition from playing to volunteering in community sport. *European Sport Management Quarterly*, 13, 54–75.

Downward, P., & Ralston, R. (2005). Volunteer motivation and expectations prior to the XV Commonwealth Games in Manchester, UK. *Tourism and Hospitality Planning and Development*, 2(1), 17–26.

Elstad, B. (1997). Volunteer perception of learning and satisfaction in a mega-event: The case of the XVII Olympic Winter Games in Lillehammer. *Festival Management and Event Tourism*, 4, 75–83.

Emrich, E., Pitsch, W., Flatau, J., & Pierdzioch, C. (2014). Voluntary engagement in sports clubs: A behavioural model and some empirical evidence. *International Review for the Sociology of Sport*, 49(2), 227–240.

Engelberg, T., Skinner, J., & Zakus, D. H. (2006). Exploring the commitment of volunteers in Little Athletics centres. Volunteering Australia: Inaugural Volunteering Research Symposium. *Australian Journal on Volunteering*, 11(2), 56–66.

Engelberg, T., Zakus, D. H., Skinner, J. L., & Campbell, A. (2012). Defining and measuring dimensionality and targets of commitment of sport volunteers. *Journal of Sport Management*, 26, 192–205.

Fairley, S., Kellett, P., & Green, B. G. (2007). Volunteering abroad: Motives for travel to volunteer at the Athens Olympic Games. *Journal of Sport Management*, 21, 41–57.

Farrell, J. M., Johnston, M. E., & Twynam, G. D. (1998). Volunteer motivation, satisfaction, and management at an elite sporting competition. *Journal of Sport Management*, 12, 288–300.

Finkelstein, M. A., Penner, L. A., & Brannick, M. T. (2005). Motive, role identity, and prosocial personality as predictors of volunteer activity. *Social Behaviour and Personality*, 33(4), 403–418.

Gellweiler, S., Fletcher, T., & Wise, N. (2017). Exploring experiences and emotions sport event volunteers associated with 'role exit'. *International Review for the Sociology of Sport*, 1–17. doi:10.1177/1012690217732533.

Giannoulakis, C., Wang, C. H., & Felver, N. (2015). A modelling approach to sport volunteer satisfaction. *International Journal of Event and Festival Management*, *6*(3), 182–199.

Giannoulakis, C., Wang, C. & Gray, D. (2008). Measuring volunteer motivation in mega-sporting events. *Event Management*, *11*, 191–200.

Gidron, B. (1985). Prediction of retention and turnover among service volunteer workers. *Journal of Social Service Research*, *8*, 1–16.

Guntert, S. F., Strubel, I. T., Kals, E., & Wehner, T. (2016). The quality of volunteers' motives: Integrating the functional approach and self-determination theory. *The Journal of Social Psychology*, *156*(3), 310–327.

Hallmann, K. (2015). Modelling the decision to volunteer in organised sports. *Sport Management Review*, *18*, 448–463.

Hallmann, K. & Dickson, G. (2017). Non-profit sport club members: What makes them volunteer? *Voluntary Sector Review*, *8*(2), 187–204.

Hoye, R. (2007). Commitment, involvement and performance of voluntary sport organization board members. *European Sport Management Quarterly*, *7*(1), 109–121.

Hoye, R., Cuskelly, G., Taylor, T., & Darcy, S. (2008). Volunteer motives and retention in community sport. *Australian Journal on Volunteering*, *13*(2), 40–48.

Kappelides, P., Cuskelly, G., & Hoye, R. (2018). The influence of volunteer recruitment practices and expectations on the development of volunteers' psychological contracts. *Voluntas*, *30*(1), 259–271. doi:10.1007/s11266-018-9986-x.

Kim, M., Chelladurai, P., & Trail, G. T. (2007). A model of volunteer retention in youth sport. *Journal of Sport Management*, *21*, 151–171.

Kim, E., Fredline, L., & Cuskelly, G. (2018). Heterogeneity of sport event volunteer motivations: A segmentation approach. *Tourism Management*, *68*, 375–386.

Kim, M., Zhang, J. J., & Connaughton, D. P. (2010). Comparison of volunteer motivations in different youth sport organizations. *European Sport Management Quarterly*, *10*(3), 343–365.

Knoke, D., & Prensky, D. (1984). What relevance do organization theories have for voluntary associations? *Social Science Quarterly*, *65*(1), 3–20.

Lee, Y., Kim, M., & Koo, J. (2016). The impact of social interaction and team member exchange on sport event volunteer management. *Sport Management Review*, *19*, 550–562.

MacLean, J., & Hamm, S. (2007). Motivation, commitment, and intentions of volunteers at a large Canadian sporting event. *Leisure*, *31*(2), 523–556.

Mesch, D. J., Tschirhart, M., Perry, J. L., & Le, G. (1998). Altruists or egoists? Retention in stipended service. *Nonprofit Management and Leadership*, *9*(1), 3–21.

Monga, M. (2006). Measuring motivation to volunteer for special events. *Event Management*, *10*(1), 47–61.

Neufeind, M., Guntert, S. T., & Wehner, T. (2013). The impact of job design on event volunteers' future engagement: Insights from the European Football Championship 2008. *European Sport Management Quarterly*, *13*(5), 537–556.

Ralston, R., Downward, P., & Lumsdon, L. (2004). The expectations of volunteers prior to the XVII commonwealth games, 2002: A qualitative study. *Event Management*, *9*(1–2), 13–26.

Reeser, J. C., Berg, R. L., Rhea, D., & Willick, S. (2005). Motivation and satisfaction among polyclinic volunteers at the 2002 Winter Olympic and Paralympic Games. *British Journal of Sports Medicine, 39*(4), e20.

Rogalsky, K., Doherty, A., & Paradis, K. F. (2016). Understanding the sport event volunteer experience: An investigation of role ambiguity and its correlates. *Journal of Sport Management, 30*, 453–469.

Rundle-Thiele, S., & Auld, C. (2009). Should I stay or should I go? Retention of junior sport coaches. *Annals of Leisure Research, 12*(1), 1–21.

Schlesinger, T., Egli, B., & Nagel, S. (2013). 'Continue or terminate?' Determinants of long-term volunteering in sports clubs. *European Sport Management Quarterly, 13*(1), 32–53.

Smith, D. H. (1981). Altruism, volunteers and volunteerism. *Journal of Voluntary Action Research, 10*(1), 21–36.

Stebbins, R. A. (1996). Volunteering: A serious leisure perspective. *Nonprofit Voluntary Sector Quarterly, 25*(2), 211–224.

Treuren, G. J. M. (2014). Enthusiasts, conscripts or instrumentalists? The motivational profiles of event volunteers. *Managing Leisure, 19*(1), 51–70.

Treuren, G., & Monga, M. (2002a, July 15–16). Are special event volunteers different from non-SEO volunteers? Demographic characteristics of volunteers in four South Australian special event organizations. In *University of Technology, Sydney, Australian Centre for Event Management, Events and Place Making Conference Proceedings* (pp. 275–304). Sydney: University of Technology.

Treuren, G., & Monga, M. (2002b, July 15–16). Does the observable special event volunteer career in four South Australian special event organizations demonstrate the existence of a recruitment niche? In *University of Technology, Sydney, Australian Centre for Event Management, Events and Place Making Conference Proceedings* (pp. 203–231). Sydney: University of Technology.

Wang, P. Z. (2004). Assessing motivations for sports volunteerism. *Advances in Consumer Research, 31*, 420–425.

Chapter 5

Sport volunteering and diverse populations

Community participation contributes to the development of social support networks, well-being and quality of life (Choma & Ochocka, 2005; Productivity Commission, 2010). Volunteering is an important aspect of community participation and has gained significance over the years in both academia and in practice as an important social activity that provides opportunities for participation and inclusion (Trembath, Balandin, Stancliffe, & Togher, 2010). Volunteers are essential to the operation of sport organisations across national, state, community and grass-roots levels (Donnelly & Harvey, 2011); however, the proportion of the overall population engaging in volunteer roles has been declining (Wicker, 2017). By expanding and providing individuals from diverse backgrounds the opportunity to participate in sport volunteering may increase the overall number of volunteers available for these organisations and provide a meaningful leisure pursuit for individuals (Kappelides & Spoor, 2018).

Individuals with a disability, individuals from a culturally and linguistically diverse (CALD) background, people in retirement or the lesbian, gay, bisexual, transgender, queer and intersex (LGBTQI) community may be an important underutilised resource for not-for-profit and sport organisations that require volunteers for their day to day operations (Baert & Vujić, 2016; Balandin, Llewellyn, Dew, & Ballin, 2006a; Bortree & Waters, 2014). While volunteerism is about helping others, research shows that it also correlates with a host of mental, social, cultural and physical health benefits for volunteers themselves that might be beneficial for a more inclusive volunteer cohort. For example, several studies (Stadelmann-Steffen & Freitag, 2011; Wiepking & Femida, 2016) found social and personal gains were derived from volunteering through such experiences as fun in the actual activities, satisfaction in the volunteer work, doing something with others, helping others, meeting people and building social relationships. In addition, according to Choma and Ochocka (2005), inclusive volunteering positively impacted on individual volunteers through increased self-confidence and more positive feelings about themselves and also assisted organisations in getting necessary jobs completed. Hence, if support from organisations is provided, inclusive volunteering can benefit both the volunteer and the recipient organisation.

This chapter examines the research on the evolving area of inclusive volunteering and explores a range of potential benefits of including volunteers from diverse backgrounds in sport organisations. We will then discuss research on potential barriers to including volunteers from diverse backgrounds as well as future research directions before providing strategies for sport organisations to work with volunteers in this area. This chapter will provide insights to assist sport organisations to alter the conditions and values that shape an individual's choices about volunteering and potentially lead to a more diverse volunteer workforce in community in sport.

Background to inclusive volunteering

Inclusive volunteering is a relatively new area of research and practice. The first researchers to introduce the term "inclusive volunteering" were Miller, Schleien, Rider, and Hall (2002) who studied the involvement of people with an intellectual disability in volunteering. Later, due to its success in engaging with a population that was often excluded from volunteering, that use of the term widened. Inclusive volunteering is currently being used as an umbrella term for involving people at risk of social exclusion, such as CALD communities, older people and the LGBTQI community. For example, Volunteering Australia (2016, p. 30) defined the term of inclusive volunteering as meaning "that anyone can get involved regardless of any barriers they face". Alternatively, Sport England (2016, p. 23) defined inclusive volunteering as "opportunities that allow all individuals to work together to improve their community through voluntary service". Researchers (Kappelides & Spoor, 2018; Miller, Schleien, Brooke, & Merrill, 2010) on inclusive volunteering further emphasise that everyone can be involved; inclusive volunteering is understood as confirming that volunteering is not only for a particular group of people but is open to all without discrimination. Supporters of this view see inclusive volunteering as a tool to address stigmas caused by specific disabilities, disadvantages or limitations (Kappelides & Spoor, 2018; Miller, Simpson, Lieben, & Simpson, 2011). Inclusive volunteering is thus perceived as all individuals working together with the same intent (Spaaij et al., 2018).

Whilst inclusive volunteering is working positively towards increasing volunteering options for all individuals across all sectors, including sport, there are also considerable challenges. In particular, the shift in the nature of paid work, lifestyles, values and new technology has led to a decline in traditional, long-term volunteering (Hustinx & Lammertyn, 2003) and also impacted on the retention of volunteers in the sport sector. Significantly, volunteer strategies in the sport sector still rely heavily on a traditional per-spective of volunteering (Commonwealth of Australia, 2011; McLennan & Birch, 2005) and as such have not fully embraced the opportunities that inclusive volunteers can bring to the sport sector. A study by Kappelides and Spoor (2018) identified that sport organisations can meet ongoing shortfalls in the availability of suitable volunteers, and can become more inclusive by focusing on often marginalised and neglected groups to fulfil their volunteering needs. However, they also identified that volunteering not only requires the willingness of the individuals concerned, but that the environment and the organisations that support the volunteers must also be supportive.

Volunteers with a disability

Research into volunteers with a disability has found that such individuals are interested in volunteering (Balandin et al., 2006b; Bruce, 2006; Kap-pelides & Spoor, 2018; Roker, Player, & Coleman, 1998). Younger indi-viduals with a disability appear to enjoy a range of benefits from volunteering including a greater sense of self-confidence, agency and pur-pose, as well as improved social, practical and work-related skills (Rak & Spencer, 2016; Roker et al., 1998). Similarly, older volunteers with a disability explained how volunteering gives them a sense of purpose (Barlow & Hainsworth, 2001) and that they are able to use their existing skills and life experiences to improve the quality of volunteer services with which they engage (Balandin et al., 2006b).

There is also evidence that sport organisations benefit from utilising volunteers with a disability. In a qualitative study of volunteer managers, all of whom had previous experience working with volunteers with a disability, Kappelides and Spoor (2018) found that the respondents mostly identified benefits to the volunteer experience. This was also found in other non-sport organisations in research conducted by Miller et al. (2010). In both studies paid managers noted that the volunteers often had desirable traits like reliability, a strong work ethic and a willingness to try new tasks. Volunteers with a disability also often had unique skills, inter-ests and an availability that allowed them to fill important roles in the organisations that otherwise might not be met. Similarly, Balandin et al. (2006a) found that volunteer coordinators in a sample of Australian not-for-profit organisations generally had positive attitudes toward volunteers with a disability. The volunteer coordinators recognised the social and self-esteem value of volunteer experiences for this community and that volunteers with a disability could be important role models when working with clients with a disability.

Despite the apparent benefits of including volunteers with a disability, only a small proportion of individuals with a disability actually engage in sport volunteering. Among those with a disability, there is some evidence that they may lack knowledge about what volunteering entails, experience unique constraints and difficulties (e.g., balancing volunteering with other commitments, lack of transport) and may have concerns about social interactions while volunteering (Darcy, Dickson, & Benson, 2014; Dickson, Darcy, & Benson, 2017; Kappelides & Spoor, 2018). Some volunteers with a disability might be more comfortable volunteering in an organisation that provides services and support programmes to individuals with a disability. Furthermore, at the organisation level, the formal processes of volunteer management may also serve as a barrier to including volunteers with a disability. There is growing pressure on sport organisations to take a more professional and formal approach to volunteer management, applying and extending human resource management practices into the volunteer sector, which may act as a constraint to volunteers with a disability if the process becomes over complicated and difficult to understand or follow (Bartram, Cavanagh, & Hoye, 2017; Cuskelly, Taylor, Hoye, & Darcy, 2006; Darcy et al., 2014).

A study of community organisations by Mjelde-Mossey (2006) found that most organisations were concerned that volunteers with a disability would require extra time to be trained and supervised, and most of the organisations believed that they would need external human resource support in the areas of recruitment, training and compliance with legislation in order to include volunteers with a disability. Similarly, Kappelides and Spoor (2018) found that a lack of available paid staff to supervise volunteers with a disability was a barrier to volunteering in sport organisations. Even when event managers and organisations prioritise inclusion of volunteers with a disability, effective human resource management for those volunteers may still be lacking. For example, Darcy et al. (2014) reported that the organising committees for the London 2012 Olympic and Paralympic Games intended to showcase diversity among volunteers, including those with a disability. The organisers used additional outreach activities and extended application periods to improve the recruitment of volunteers with a disability. However, the researchers found that, although many of the volunteers with a disability were satisfied with their overall experience, they also noted significant issues related to recruitment, placement, communication and training relevant to their assigned roles that were inappropriate due to their disability, despite having repeatedly disclosed their disability and accommodation requirements during the selection process. Both the researchers and the volunteers themselves noted that there seemed to be a lack of disability awareness training for sport event managers, staff and volunteers, which probably impeded the volunteers' ability to have meaningful conversations with their supervisors and be provided with appropriate support.

Volunteers from a CALD background

People from CALD backgrounds make an important contribution to volunteering in Australia and other parts of the world. While this remains a largely under-researched area in the sport sector, particularly in emerging migrant communities, there is growing evidence that many thousands of CALD individuals volunteer both within and outside of their respective communities (Volunteering Australia, 2016). CALD communities can be key sources of officials, coaches, administrators and general volunteers, and therefore are critical to the continued growth of sport participation. However, people with CALD backgrounds have traditionally had low levels of involvement in sport and can face many barriers to inclusion. Data from the ABS (2012) reveal that people born in Australia are more likely to participate in sport and physical recreation than those born in other countries (67% and 59% respectively). Similarly, the Canadian Community Health Surveys (Ali, McDermott, & Gravel, 2004; O'Driscoll, Banting, Borkoles, Eime, & Polman, 2014) confirmed lower levels of sport participation by CALD communities compared to those born in Canada. These figures would suggest that people with a CALD background would also be less likely to volunteer with a sport organisation in these communities.

Cultural differences, attitudes (interpersonal and institutional) and a lack of awareness, knowledge and accessibility are all issues that have contributed to the under representation of people from CALD backgrounds in Australian sport (Skene, 2012). Somewhat ironically, sport is seen to be a great "leveller" or an effective way of promoting and supporting inclusivity for CALD populations, but on the other hand, as a social institution, sport is relatively poor at including people from CALD communities in leadership and volunteering roles.

Further, research by the Settlement Council of Australia (SCOA) suggests that sport can and does play a vital role in contributing to positive settlement outcomes, promoting social inclusion and supporting migrant and refugee integration into society. The social interactions that can occur through volunteering in sport organisations and clubs play an important part in shaping and reinforcing patterns of community identification and community belonging. It can also play an important role in the settlement of those newly arrived in countries, including well-documented physical, psychological and social benefits to participants (Spaaij et al., 2014).

As society changes in countries such as Australia, Canada and the UK, sport at all levels needs to adapt and evolve, to reflect the communities they represent, and to provide positive volunteering experiences. Canada was the first country in the world to adopt a multicultural policy (Government of Canada, 2013). The Canadian Government has ensured that multicultural principles are embedded within policy and legislative framework to facilitate the integration and inclusion of CALD communities. This is also the case with sport programmes in Canada. Other countries such as Australia and the UK have also followed suit with policies and frameworks supporting the inclusion of CALD communities (Block & Gibbs, 2017). However, adapting to change can present many challenges for sport organisations if they are unaware of how to involve volunteers from a CALD background (Block & Gibbs, 2017). Below are several practices that can assist sport organisations to better engage with CALD communities, many of which are promoted by the Queensland Government Community Engagement Guides (2016):

- Engage communities early: when planning to include volunteers from CALD backgrounds make sure you involve individuals from your targeted communities early in the process.
- Take the time to build trust and respect: try to understand the situations that individuals from CALD backgrounds are in, particularly if it is early in the settlement process, and engage them accordingly.
- Acknowledge community protocols, beliefs and practices. Identify who the community leaders are. Be clear about expectations and roles for volunteering and how they can be involved.
- Recognise diversity within communities: differences exist between CALD communities. Take time to understand individual communities and offer a range of volunteering options. Find out what "volunteering" means in their CALD community.
- Avoid over-consultation: don't reinvent the wheel. Plan well, liaise and seek advice from others who might also engage the community of interest. Consider partnerships with multicultural organisations and build engagement into existing volunteer programmes and activities.
- Address language issues: consider the need to have written, electronic and verbal information translated and/or made available in plain English. Understand that English may not be a first language for many potential volunteers, so think about the best means of communication.
- Learn about barriers to inclusion: find out more on the barriers to inclusion for people from diverse backgrounds and specific communities; for example, volunteering on religious occasions, alcohol and uniforms.

Older adult volunteers

Increased concern about the possible financial burden of an ageing Western society and ensuring active and healthy ageing have prompted governments and organisations to focus on volunteers who are retired and/or older to support their services and programmes. Volunteering in retirement or later life has been a research area linked to positive ageing theories for some time (Oppenheimer & Warburton, 2014) and a growing interest area in volunteering as a pathway to health and wellbeing in later life. However, these benefits should not be seen as being derived automatically from volunteering, and volunteer opportunities need to be sensitive to the needs and abilities of potential volunteers. Organisations should not assume that older people will necessarily apply to volunteer. Although retired older people may have time to spare, they might not use it to volunteer. Older people give their time to a diverse range of organisations. Much of the research on volunteering in later life has been conducted in Western countries. Examples include the United States (Kaskie, Imhof, Cavanaugh, & Culp, 2008; Morrow-Howell, 2010), Canada (Raymond et al., 2013), the UK (Lie & Baines, 2007), Europe (Haski-Leventhal, 2009) and Australia (Brayley et al., 2014; Paull, 2009; Warburton, Paynter, & Petriwskyj, 2007). As a result of this significant research area the practice of volunteering in later life or during retirement has been a significant contributor to the number of people in this age group that volunteer.

An analysis by Warburton and Jeppsson Grassman (2011) identified that, in the social welfare sectors in Australia and the UK, older volunteers tend to be mostly involved in the delivery of a range of welfare and community services. These may include volunteering in a charity shop, delivering meals on wheels or supporting crisis hotlines. Older people in rural areas tend to volunteer more as opposed to urban areas (Leonard & Johansson, 2008; Warburton & Stirling, 2007). In terms of gender, the ABS (2012) reported that older men are more likely to undertake traditional male-type activities such as volunteering on committees or maintenance work, whilst older women are more likely to be involved in preparing or serving food or befriending activities. Similarly, older men are more likely to volunteer for sports, community/welfare and religious organisations, whereas older women are more likely to volunteer for community/welfare, religious and health organisations (ABS, 2012). These data reinforce the research literature that suggests that both males and females volunteer in later life but have different preferences for their volunteering experiences (Warburton & McLaughlin, 2006).

In relation to sport volunteering for older people the research is sparse. One of the first studies to look at sport and leisure for older adults was by Misener, Doherty, and Hamm-Kerwin (2010) who recognised that fewer older adults were involved in volunteering in comparison to their younger counterparts. However, those who did give their time contributed more hours on average to voluntary sport or leisure organisations. This trend was also consistent outside of North America, as data from Australia and the UK illustrate similar patterns (Gill, 2006). As a result, initiatives have been developed to encourage volunteering among older adults in these countries (Gill, 2006; Price, 2007; VicSport, 2018). Further, in a study by Bang (2015) the findings indicated that the age of volunteers in non-profit sport organisations can be an important factor in increasing organisational success. Therefore, non-profit sport organisations need to put considerable effort into developing strategic approaches to the recruitment and retention of older volunteers, reflecting the needs of volunteers at different life stages. Engelberg, Zakus, Skinner, and Campbell (2012) identified that older volunteers had a stronger commitment to their team than younger volunteers, and that older volunteers were more committed and engaged for longer periods when volunteering in the sport environment. This suggests that it is important to look at volunteer environments to ensure that they are providing appropriate levels of support to facilitate and manage volunteering by older people.

A more recent study by Jenkin, Eime, Westerbeek, O'Sullivan, and van Uffelen (2016) reinforced these findings and suggested there is an opportunity for older adults to contribute to the capacity of sport clubs through volunteering. Overall, the findings indicated that older adults may be motivated to undertake this role for a longer period than younger people due to the increased time they have available. Whilst volunteering by older adults may occur without their active participation in sport, opportunities for them to participate in the sport organisation or club can make them feel valued. Intergenerational opportunities were also identified as a key benefit for sport clubs. The findings of Jenkin et al. suggest that engagement of older adults in sport clubs may influence the participation in sport by their children and grandchildren. The role of older adults in sport clubs may be promoted by providing active participation opportunities to further engage this age group in age-appropriate social play or competitive teams. Engaging older adults is likely to help sport clubs remain sustainable and increase their service capacity.

Volunteers from the LGBTQI community

Despite extensive changes in social attitudes to LGBTQI individuals over the last decade, research shows they still experience significant levels of discrimination and abuse (Symons, Sbaraglia, Hillier, & Mitchell, 2010). There is very little direct research on the sport experience of LGBTQI volunteers. Whilst other disadvantaged groups such as people with disabilities and refugees have been recognised in the diversity research and policy agendas, the existence, experiences and needs of LGBTQI volunteers within sport have largely been ignored. Both implicit discrimination that results from heteronormative attitudes and explicit discrimination that causes LGBTQI sports-people to remain in the closet, become isolated and essentially silenced have created a lack of research on this topic. Sport plays a significant role in many societies such as in Australia, the UK, the USA and Canada; however, it is a place where LGBTQI individuals are largely silent and invisible in terms of what is known of their volunteering experiences.

Research by Symons et al. (2010) was the first comprehensive survey of the LGBTQI sport experience in Australia and provided an insight into the sporting lives, passions, rewards and challenges of LGBTQI sports participants, supporters, volunteers and workers. This study used Griffin's (1998) continuum of social climates (i.e., hostile, conditionally tolerant, and open and inclusive). The continuum described a variety of sports contexts: individual, team, club and league. The research found that LGBTQI volunteers experienced discrimination and exclusion during volunteering in sport. Yet in other volunteering contexts where volunteers are activists or working in grassroots organisations related to the LGBTQI community's rights and specific events, volunteers felt empowered and included (Kuhns & Ramirez-Valles, 2016; Ramirez-Valles, Kuhns, Vázquez, & Benjamin, 2014).

Interestingly, inclusive volunteering opportunities in sports clubs often emerges by chance usually through an individual with a certain standing within the club, such as a committee member or experienced volunteer, who is committed to diversity based on personal values. This was identified in the study by Spaaij et al. (2018) who found that this can be a key tension within diversity work. On the one hand, individual champions are key to the promotion of diversity; without them, it is likely to fall off the agenda. Yet often they are not supported and face unsustainable and insufficient resources to achieve organisational change. The personal commitment of individual volunteers and leadership within sport organisations is a starting point to allow individuals from LGBTQI communities the opportunity to volunteer without discrimination and isolation.

Further, Sport England (2016) has made a commitment in its 2016–2021 strategy to grow the number of volunteers in sport and prioritise diversity including the LGBTQI community. Sport England wants to make the demographics of volunteers in sport more representative of society. The research in this report found that most current volunteers in sport are male, white and from more affluent backgrounds. Sport England has made a commitment that it wants to keep current volunteers, but also attract new and different people that represent the diversity of the UK. The initiative of Sport England (2016) shows commitment to the area of LGBTQI volunteering and hopefully other countries will follow suit. It is important that by creating welcoming and inclusive sports environments, volunteers from the LGBTQI community can be supported to engage in various sport volunteering roles beyond legal compliance and discrimination policies that may exist in sport clubs but are not fully implemented to truly be inclusive of all volunteers.

Strategies towards inclusive volunteering

In understanding the need for inclusive volunteering in sport it is important to remember that individuals may identify with some, or all, of the groups mentioned above. This may mean that individuals wanting to volunteer may face certain barriers, such as language, accessibility, attitudes or even discrimination from others. Inclusion is about taking proactive steps to remove or reduce these barriers that are the result of the way sport products and services are often designed and delivered – not the characteristics of the individual. Every person has the ability and right to volunteer in sport. The strategies below may help to create a welcoming and inclusive environment that can lead to greater involvement by diverse volunteers, administrators, coaches and officials. For example, sporting clubs that are active within a local community, with its own diverse population, may be able to take an inclusive approach by communicating and connecting with the local community to understand their abilities and interests that are relevant to volunteering. This allows the club to take steps to remove or reduce any barriers to volunteering and create opportunities for people to participate. Doing this in partnership with the local community means people have a say in creating volunteer opportunities that work for them. It may also benefit the club by:

- embracing a diverse range of skills, values and characteristics that add vibrancy to the club;
- providing an avenue for new people to volunteer in the club; and
- increasing the number of club members and/or volunteers.

Further, the following strategies may assist in providing inclusive volunteering into a sport organisation:

- avoid segregating or stigmatising any volunteers;
- make the design of the programme appealing to as many volunteers as possible;
- provide adaptability to the volunteer's pace;
- eliminate unnecessary complexity for volunteers;
- accommodate a wide range of literacy and language skills;
- provide effective prompting and feedback during and after volunteering;
- use different modes for presentation of essential information such as rules or procedures.

Future research

It is apparent that future research needs to be conducted in the inclusive volunteering sector of sport. In particular the areas of disability, CALD, older people and LGBTQI communities need additional understanding through research to enhance and support the practice of inclusive volunteering. It would be helpful for future research to explore how organisational leaders and key decision makers in the sport sector, such as committee members and volunteer coordinators, determine what actions may be influencing how they perceive inclusive volunteering and their level of inclusion. This research would have an impact not only on volunteers' perceptions of sport organisations, but would also impact on how paid staff, board members and participants perceive their relationship with the organisation.

There is also a lack of research focussing on current government sport policy in Western countries that includes inclusive volunteering. Current sport policies tend to fail to adequately address the issues outlined in this chapter – the lack of volunteer diversity and inclusion in volunteering. For instance, a research report by the Commonwealth Scientific and Industrial Research Organisation (CSIRO) (2013) in Australia for the Australian Sport Commission reported on megatrends shaping the sport sector, though it has limited analysis of the future involvement of volunteers in sport. If a national sport policy does not address the volunteer sector or indeed inclusive volunteering it may contribute further to declining volunteer numbers. A key challenge is to conduct future research that is committed to catering for all diverse communities in sport volunteering and that can also influence and support national sport policies. This needs to be across both the macro- and micro-levels of sport organisations. If research continues to remain underdeveloped in this area, the understanding and development of the potential of sport to promote volunteer inclusion will be hindered.

Conclusion

This chapter has discussed the opportunity to include a diverse range of communities in sport volunteering, particularly for people with a disability, CALD communities, LGBTQI communities and older people. Sport organisations need to become more aware of how their organisational requirements for voluntary labour can be fulfilled by engaging with communities they may not have previously. Volunteers are clearly essential for the sustainability of the sport sector and there is an opportunity for the sector and the volunteers who currently support this system to more actively engage with diverse population groups to enhance a mutual understanding of how to best manage and support a more inclusive sport volunteer sector. Finally, this chapter may help sport organisations to understand and increase their ability to engage with volunteers from diverse communities by considering these challenges and barriers.

References

ABS (Australian Bureau of Statistics). (2012). *Volunteers in sport, Australia 2010*. Retrieved from www.abs.gov.au/ausstats/abs@.nsf/Products/4440.0.55.001~2010~Chapter~Overview?OpenDocument (Accessed 19 December 2018).

Ali, J. S., McDermott, S., & Gravel, R. G. (2004). Recent research on immigrant health from statistics Canada's population surveys. *Canadian Public Health, 95* (3), 9–13.

Baert, S., & Vujić, S. (2016). Immigrant volunteering: A way out of labour market discrimination? *Economics Letters, 146,* 95–98.

Balandin, S., Llewellyn, G., Dew, A., & Ballin, L. (2006a). 'We couldn't function without volunteers': Volunteering with a disability, the perspective of not-for-profit agencies. *International Journal of Rehabilitation Research, 29*(2), 131–136. doi:10.1097/01.mrr.0000191850.95692.0c

Balandin, S., Llewellyn, G., Dew, A., Ballin, L., & Schneider, J. (2006b). Older disabled workers' perceptions of volunteering. *Disability & Society, 21*(7), 677–692. doi:10.1080/09687590600995139

Bang, H. (2015). Volunteer age, job satisfaction, and intention to stay: A case of nonprofit sport organizations. *Leadership & Organization Development Journal, 36*(2), 161–176.

Barlow, J., & Hainsworth, J. (2001). Volunteerism among older people with arthritis. *Ageing and Society, 21*(2), 203–217. doi:10.1017/S0144686X01008145

Bartram, T., Cavanagh, J., & Hoye, R. (2017). The growing importance of human resource management in the NGO, volunteer, and not-for-profit sectors. *The International Journal of Human Resource Management, 28,* 1901–1911. doi:10.1080/09585192.2017.1315043

Block, K., & Gibbs, L. (2017). Promoting social inclusion through sport for refugee-background youth in Australia: Analysing different participation models. *Social Inclusion, 5*(2), 91–100.

Bortree, D. S., & Waters, R. D. (2014). Race and inclusion in volunteerism: Using communication theory to improve volunteer retention. *Journal of Public Relations Research, 26*(3), 215–234.

Brayley, N., Obst, P., White, K. M., Lewis, I. M., Warburton, J., & Spencer, N. M. (2014). Exploring the validity and predictive power of an extended volunteer functions inventory within the context of episodic skilled volunteering by retirees. *Journal of Community Psychology, 42*(1), 1–18.

Bruce, L. (2006). Count me in: People with a disability keen to volunteer. *Australian Journal on Volunteering, 11*(1), 59–64. Retrieved from http://search.informit.com.au. ez.library.latrobe.edu.au/documentSummary;dn=149212241048831;res=IELFSC

Choma, B. L., & Ochocka, J. (2005). Supported volunteering: A community approach for people with complex needs. *Journal on Developmental Disabilities, 12*(1), 1–18.

Commonwealth of Australia. (2011). National volunteering strategy. Department of the Prime Minister and Cabinet, Canberra Commonwealth of Australia.

Commonwealth Scientific and Industrial Research Organisation. (2013). *The future of Australian sport: Megatrends shaping the sports sector over the coming decades.* Canberra: CSIRO.

Cuskelly, G., Taylor, T., Hoye, R., & Darcy, S. (2006). Volunteer retention: A human resource management approach. *Sport Management Review, 9,* 141–163.

Darcy, S., Dickson, T. J., & Benson, A. M. (2014). London 2012 Olympic and Paralympic Games: Including volunteers with disabilities—A podium performance? *Event Management, 18*(4), 431–446. doi:10.3727/152599514X14143427352157

Dickson, T. J., Darcy, S., & Benson, A. (2017). Volunteers with disabilities at the London 2012 Olympic and Paralympic Games: Who, why, and will they do it again? *Event Management, 21*(3), 301–318.

Donnelly, P., & Harvey, J. (2011). Volunteering and sport. In B. Houlihan & M Green (Eds.), *Routledge Handbook of Sports Development* (pp. 55–71). London: Routledge.

Engelberg, T., Zakus, D. H., Skinner, J. L., & Campbell, A. (2012). Defining and measuring dimensionality and targets of the commitment of sport volunteers. *Journal of Sport Management, 26*(2), 192–205.

Gill, Z. (2006). *Older people and volunteering.* Government of South Australia, Office for Volunteers.

Government of Canada. (2013). Our mandate: Citizenship and immigration. Retrieved from www.cic.gc.ca/english/department/mission.asp

Griffin, G. (1998). Understanding heterosexism: The subtle continuum of homophobia. *Women and Language, 21*(1), 33.

Haski-Leventhal, D. (2009). Altruism and volunteerism: The perceptions of altruism in four disciplines and their impact on the study of volunteerism. *Journal for the Theory of Social Behaviour, 39*(3), 271–299.

Hustinx, L., & Lammertyn, F. (2003). Collective and reflexive styles of volunteering: A sociological modernization perspective. *Voluntas: International Journal of Voluntary and Nonprofit Organizations, 14*(2), 167–187.

Jenkin, C. R., Eime, R. M., Westerbeek, H., O'Sullivan, G., & van Uffelen, J. G. (2016). Are they 'worth their weight in gold'? Sport for older adults: Benefits and barriers of their participation for sporting organisations. *International Journal of Sport Policy and Politics, 8*(4), 663–680.

Kappelides, P., & Spoor, J. (2018). Managing sport volunteers with a disability: Human resource management implications. *Sport Management Review.* doi:10.1016/j.smr.2018.10.004

Kaskie, B., Imhof, S., Cavanaugh, J., & Culp, K. (2008). Civic engagement as a retirement role for aging Americans. *The Gerontologist, 48*(3), 368–377.

Kuhns, L. M., & Ramirez-Valles, J. (2016). Creating identity and community: Latino gay and bisexual men's motives for participation in the AIDS movement. *Journal of Community & Applied Social Psychology, 26*(1), 32–46.

Leonard, R., & Johansson, S. (2008). Policy and practices relating to the active engagement of older people in the community: A comparison of Sweden and Australia. *International Journal of Social Welfare, 17*(1), 37–45.

Lie, M., & Baines, S. (2007). Making sense of organizational change: Voices of older volunteers. *Voluntas: International Journal of Voluntary and Nonprofit Organizations, 18*(3), 225–240.

McLennan, J., & Birch, A. (2005). A potential crisis in wildfire emergency response capability? Australia's volunteer firefighters. *Global Environmental Change Part B: Environmental Hazards, 6*(2), 101–107.

Miller, K. D., Schleien, S. J., Brooke, P., & Merrill, M. (2010). What's in it for me and my agency? A survey on the benefits of engaging volunteers with disabilities. *The International Journal of Volunteer Administration, 27*(2), 65–74.

Miller, K. D., Schleien, S. J., Rider, C., & Hall, C. (2002). Inclusive volunteering: Benefits to participants and community. *Therapeutic Recreation Journal, 36*(3), 247.

Miller, A., Simpson, B., Lieben, J., & Simpson, B. J. (2011). Understanding the role of volunteerism in creating social inclusion. SouthWest Communities Resource Centre. http://swcrc. ca/wp-content/uploads/2013/09/Understanding-the-Role-of-Volunteerism-in-Creating-Social-Inclusion-Final-Report-for-SWCRC-September-2011. Pdf

Misener, K., Doherty, A., & Hamm-Kerwin, S. (2010). Learning from the experiences of older adult volunteers in sport: A serious leisure perspective. *Journal of Leisure Research*, 42(2), 267–289.

Mjelde-Mossey, L. A. (2006). Involving people with disabilities in volunteer roles: Results of a community survey. *Journal of Social Work in Disability & Rehabilitation*, 5(2), 19–30.

Morrow-Howell, N. (2010). Volunteering in later life: Research frontiers. *The Journals of Gerontology: Series B*, 65(4), 461–469.

O'Driscoll, T., Banting, L. K., Borkoles, E., Eime, R., & Polman, R. (2014). A systematic literature review of sport and physical activity participation in culturally and linguistically diverse (CALD) migrant populations. *Journal of Immigrant and Minority Health*, 16(3), 515–530.

Oppenheimer, M., & Warburton, J. (Eds.). (2014). *Volunteering in Australia*. Leichhardt, NSW: Federation Press.

Paull, M. (2009). Sensemaking and the management of older volunteers. *Australian Journal on Volunteering*, 14, 1.

Price, S. (2007). *Volunteering in the third age final report: Findings and conclusions from the VITA programme and looking to the future of older volunteering*. Abingdon, UK: Volunteering in the Third Age.

Productivity Commission. (2010). *Contribution of the not-for-profit sector*, Research Report, Canberra.

Queensland Government Community Engagement Guides. (2016). *A resource for new arts workers in Queensland*. New Farm: QCAN.

Rak, E. C., & Spencer, L. (2016). Community participation of persons with disabilities: Volunteering, donations and involvement in groups and organisations. *Disability and rehabilitation*, 38(17), 1705–1715.

Ramirez-Valles, J., Kuhns, L. M., Vázquez, R., & Benjamin, G. D. (2014). Getting involved: Exploring Latino GBT volunteerism and activism in AIDS and LGBT organizations. *Journal of Gay & Lesbian Social Services*, 26(1), 18–36.

Raymond, É., Sévigny, A., Tourigny, A., Vézina, A., Verreault, R., & Guilbert, A. C. (2013). On the track of evaluated programmes targeting the social participation of seniors: A typology proposal. *Ageing & Society*, 33(2), 267–296.

Roker, D., Player, K., & Coleman, J. (1998). Challenging the image: The involvement of young people with disabilities in volunteering and campaigning. *Disability & Society*, 13(5), 725–741. doi:10.1080/09687599826489

Skene, P. (2012). From barriers to bridges: CALD communities and sport. *Federation of Ethnic Communities' Councils of Australia Mosaic Magazine*, 12(December). Retrieved from www.fecca.org.au/mosaic/archive/mosaic-issue-12-december2018/from-barriers-to-bridges-cald-communities-and-sport

Spaaij, R., Farquharson, K., Magee, J., Jeanes, R., Lusher, D., & Gorman, S. (2014). A fair game for all? How community sports clubs in Australia deal with diversity. *Journal of Sport and Social Issues*, 38(4), 346–365.

Spaaij, R., Magee, J., Farquharson, K., Gorman, S., Jeanes, R., Lusher, D., & Storr, R. (2018). Diversity work in community sport organizations: Commitment, resistance and institutional change. *International Review for the Sociology of Sport*, *53*(3), 278–295.

Sport England. (2016). Towards an active nation. *Sport England*, 1–46.

Stadelmann-Steffen, I., & Freitag, M. (2011). Making civil society work: Models of democracy and their impact on civic engagement. *Nonprofit and Voluntary Sector Quarterly*, *40*, 526–551.

Symons, C., Sbaraglia, M., Hillier, L., & Mitchell, A. (2010). *Come out to play: The sports experiences of lesbian, gay, bisexual and transgender (LGBT) people in Victoria*. Victoria, Australia: Victoria University.

Trembath, D., Balandin, S., Stancliffe, R. J., & Togher, L. (2010). Employment and volunteering for adults with intellectual disability. *Journal of Policy and Practice in Intellectual Disabilities*, *7*(4), 235–238.

VicSport. (2018). *Inclusion and diversity*. Melbourne: Author. Retrieved from. https://vicsport.com.au/inclusion-and-diversity (Accessed 19 December 2018).

Volunteering Australia. (2016). *Research and advocacy*. Melbourne: Author. Retrieved from. www.volunteeringaustralia.org/research-and-advocacy/ (Accessed 19 December 2018).

Warburton, J., & Jeppsson Grassman, E. (2011). Variations in older people's social and productive ageing activities across different social welfare regimes. *International Journal of Social Welfare*, *20*(2), 180–191.

Warburton, J., & McLaughlin, D. (2006). Doing it from your heart: The role of older women as informal volunteers. *Journal of Women & Aging*, *18*(2), 55–72.

Warburton, J., Paynter, J., & Petriwskyj, A. (2007). Volunteering as a productive aging activity: Incentives and barriers to volunteering by Australian seniors. *Journal of Applied Gerontology*, *26*(4), 333–354.

Warburton, J., & Stirling, C. (2007). Factors affecting volunteering among older rural and city dwelling adults in Australia. *Educational Gerontology*, *33*(1), 23–43.

Wicker, P. (2017). Volunteerism and volunteer management in sport. *Sport Management Review*, *20*(4), 325–337.

Wiepking, P., & Femida, H. (2016). *The Palgrave Handbook of Global Philanthropy*. London: Palgrave Macmillan.

Chapter 6

Managing sport volunteers

The recruitment and retention of volunteers within the community sport system is a pivotal issue for all organisations dependent on volunteers for the delivery of services to members, participants and spectators. This chapter reviews the traditional human resource management model of sport volunteer management as well as discussing emerging aspects of how organisations interact and support their volunteers. Volunteers are the quintessential feature of sport systems in many nations. Through roles such as committee or board members, officiating, coaching and managing players and teams, administration and generally helping out, volunteers are integral to the successful management and operation of grassroots community sport organisations to high performance sport and major sport events including the Olympic Games and world championships. Often serving in multiple roles volunteers lead, manage and coordinate service delivery to players, members and spectators as well as to the wider community.

The Australian Sports Commission (ASC) (2018) articulated several key messages about volunteers when they reported that approximately 2.3 million Australians (almost 10% of the population) contribute their time and energy to community sport and recreation clubs. Collectively volunteers contribute significant social and economic value to sport with an estimated labour input value of AUD4 billion annually which may also "provide many psycho-social and self-esteem benefits to the volunteer" (ASC, 2018, no page). The volunteer participation rate quoted for Australia is consistent with sport volunteering in other nations. For example, Sport England (2016) reported than 6.7 million people (14.9% of the population) volunteer in sport and physical activity with an estimated economic value of GBP24 billion or 1.5% of GDP. In Canada, "12% of people aged 15 and over performed volunteer work for sports and recreation organizations" (Vezina & Crompton, 2012, p. 39) for an estimated 30,000 sport clubs across the nation. Such participation rates suggest that the sport sector has a substantial unpaid workforce to manage.

The ASC argued that "the ongoing provision of education and training opportunities, positive recognition, and other forms of support for sport volunteers, has been shown to dramatically improve volunteer recruitment and retention rates, as well as the broader sustainability of Australian sport" (ASC, 2018, no page). Volunteer management practices have an impact on the recruitment and retention of volunteers in sport, a point not lost on the International Labour Organization (2011) which argued that the work of volunteers is most effective when it is properly managed. The capacity of most sport organisations to deliver their programmes and services is largely a function of the size and capability of its volunteer workforce. In effect the volunteer workforce capacity of a sport organisation can be increased in any combination of three approaches: recruiting more volunteers (increasing the size of the workforce), improving volunteer retention rates (decreasing turnover) or increasing volunteer productivity (developing and training volunteers or improving the efficiency of systems and procedures). Recruitment, retention and development processes are core concepts of human resource management (HRM).

The purpose of this chapter is to examine the application of HRM principles to the management of sport volunteers who are increasingly being viewed as a workforce and managed as a resource to facilitate the development and delivery of sport programmes and services. It is no longer a question of whether volunteers *ought* to be managed but *how* can they be managed in a way that does not impinge upon a fundamental condition of volunteering – to freely choose when, where and how to volunteer in sport. The focus of this chapter is the challenging issue of volunteer management. It examines the application of HRM principles and practices to the management of sport volunteers as recommended by government sport agencies and many national governing bodies (NSOs) in sport.

Applying HRM practices to the management of volunteers in sport is based on the presumption that there is a shared understanding of the meaning of HRM. In general management settings, Collings and Wood (2009) argued that HRM is a contested term in which there are rival soft and hard approaches. The soft approach emanates from human relations emphasising human growth and the "role of employees as a valuable asset and a source of competitive advantage through their commitment" (p. 2). In contrast, the hard approach focusses on employees as a resource to be rationally deployed in the attainment of strategic goals. HRM can also be regarded as a simple extension of personnel management or as a collective term to describe "a range of practices associated with managing work and employment relations" (Collings & Wood, 2009, p. 5). The latter notion of a collection of practices perhaps best captures the intended approach of sport club development and volunteer management programmes (VMPs). However, no matter how sophisticated and well intentioned, VMPs cannot be applied without reference to the particular circumstances in different VSOs. Meijs and Karr (2004) opposed the idea that a generic model of volunteer management can be applied across all volunteering contexts. They posit that how volunteers are organised and managed must be adapted to particular situations citing, for example, substantial differences between voluntary organisations that are focussed on service delivery and those which are more membership orientated.

Volunteers and sport club development

Government agencies with responsibility for sport have long recognised the importance of volunteers as the foundation stone of the sport system. Over the past couple of decades government agencies have developed or commissioned programmes or frameworks aimed at the development of sport clubs. Some have taken a standards-based accreditation or benchmarking approach while others have focussed more on a continuous improvement through self-assessment and priority setting approach. Irrespective of the underlying philosophy of such programmes, the recruitment, retention and development of volunteers is a prominent feature.

Clubmark is Sport England's (2018b) sport accreditation scheme for community sport clubs. Its purpose is to support higher standards of welfare, equity, coaching and management as well as ensuring that sport clubs are safer, stronger and more successful. A club improvement tool has been designed by Clubmark for sport clubs to self-assess areas where the club performs well or needs to improve in areas such as managing people (including volunteers), finances and marketing. It includes password protected areas where individual clubs can report, store and monitor their progress. Similarly, Sport New Zealand (2018) and the Australian Sports Commission (2018) offer online tools called Sport Compass and Club Health Check, respectively. Both take a continuous improvement approach to encourage community sport clubs to identify areas where they are performing well and areas in need of improvement. In Canada, a Club Excellence program (Canadian Centre for Ethics in Sport, 2018, no page) was developed with a mission to "increase the capacity of sport clubs and sport organizations to deliver fair, safe and open sport through developmentally appropriate programs for all participants". The programme has operated for about a decade and uses a complex standards-based framework of modules which aim to strengthen sport clubs through improved governance and operational excellence, club partnerships, capacity building and volunteer leadership training. Amongst the common components of these sport club development programmes is a recognition of the importance of effective management of sport volunteers. This has led to the development of VMPs which must be considered within different situational contexts and management approaches. These issues are discussed later in this chapter.

Volunteer management programmes and volunteer standards

Situated within or close to club development programmes are VMPs which aim to help VSOs improve the recruitment, retention and development of volunteers in sports clubs. The practices recommended by the VMPs are largely predicated on an HRM framework. They follow a familiar path which includes planning and the development of job role descriptions, recruitment, induction, training and development, building relationships and motivation, and recognition and retention. For example, under the Club Matters brand, Sport England (2018a) presents a resource kit, online modules, weblinks to other resources within three generic modules for managing volunteers, as well as finding volunteers, keeping volunteers and developing volunteers. The Club Matters resource provides a number of templates (e.g., role descriptions) which are adaptable to local circumstances, though it does not prescribe a particular model for managing volunteers. Rather it aims to guide VSOs to plan more deliberately for the involvement and development of volunteers. Taking a similar approach, The South Australian Government Office for Recreation, Sport and Racing (2018) has developed an online volunteer management tool for sport clubs under the brand V-Star. The management tool comprises a series of modules under the headings "find them", "keep them" and "back them". Reflecting many of the resources provided by Club Matters the V-Star makes extensive use of an online tool for sports clubs to self-assess their areas of need in volunteer management and provides a number of templates as well as a password protected area to develop, store and monitor the club's performance. VMPs are designed to be accessible to a wide variety of VSOs at differing stages of development. Even though the resources provided by VMPs are designed to be adaptable to many different situations they tend to take a programme management approach that prioritises organisational needs over those of volunteers.

Contrasting management approaches

The volunteer management approach advocated by VMPs closely resembles what Meijs and Hoogstad (2001) describe as programme management, which they differentiate from membership management. The programme management approach regards volunteers as a resource. In contrast, membership management focuses on the volunteers themselves taking into account the expectations of existing members and ensuring that volunteer tasks fit these expectations. A comparison between programme management and membership management is summarised in Table 6.1.

Table 6.1 Comparison between programme management and membership management (adapted from Meijs and Hoogstad, 2001)

Criteria	Programme management	Membership management
Structure		
Flexibility of approach	From task to volunteer	From volunteer to task/ assignment
Management	One single manager	Group of "managers"
Executive committee	Arm's length	Close by
Culture		
Organisational culture	Weak	Strong
Volunteer involvement	Low	High
Level of homogeneity among volunteers	Low	High
Relationships between volunteers	People do not know each other	People know each other well or very well
Volunteers' motivation	Goal-orientated	Socially orientated
Process		
Cost of admission	Low social costs	High social costs
Expectations	Explicit	Implicit
Recognition	On basis of performance	On basis of number of years as member
Hours spent/invested	Low	High

Membership management organisations may develop high levels of satisfaction with the volunteer experience because participation tends to be broad and multi-faceted and the organization "shapes itself to the needs and desires of its membership" (Meijs and Karr, 2004, p. 178). However, membership management organisations tend to have problems coping with diversity and such organisations risk stagnation because they are unable to adapt in a timely manner to changes in either their internal or external environments. In contrast, programme management organisations are focused on clearly specified tasks (e.g., delivering a particular service at a scheduled time) in which the priority of volunteer involvement is to carry out such tasks without fear of committing unlimited amounts of time. Volunteers' needs and interests tend to be secondary and they themselves may not identify strongly with these organisations. Because involvement is limited, volunteer entry and exit are easily facilitated. Programme management organisations are more adaptable to their environments but are less personable, risk high rates of volunteer turnover and rely on recruiting new volunteers to ensure continuity of services.

The programme management and membership management approaches vary both in terms of degree of formalisation in volunteer management practices and their suitability for organisations across the spectrum of VSOs. Over-emphasising managerialist approaches to managing sport volunteers exaggerates the risk of subordinating the needs, motives and interests of volunteers to increasing levels of formalisation and standardisation. The dominance of organisational concerns has the potential to disempower sport volunteers and can overlook volunteer involvement which encompasses variability in the duration, frequency and intensity of individual volunteers. In sports clubs there are often marked differences between volunteers in terms of the number of years they have served (duration), how often they volunteer (frequency) and the depth or strength of their involvement (intensity).

Volunteer standards

The programme management approach is reflected in the volunteer standards approach which is increasingly being used to demonstrate best practice in volunteer involvement and management. The Investing in Volunteers (IiV) (2018) programme is the UK quality standard for all organisations who involve volunteers and includes nine indicators: policies, resources, diversity, roles, safety, recruitment, induction, support and recognition for volunteers. The idea germinated in the mid-1990s when concerns were raised about the standard of management and care for volunteers. Reflecting an HRM approach the standard is based on volunteer management planning, recruitment, selection, support and retention. At about the same time as the volunteer standards programme was being developed in the UK, Volunteering Australia, a volunteer advocacy body, formally documented and adopted a set of national standards for involving volunteers in non-profit organisations in 1998. The standards were revised in 2001 and again in 2015 and are now referred to as The National Standards for Volunteer Involvement. Amongst the eight standards are criteria and evidence for leadership and management, recruitment and selection, support and development, workplace safety and wellbeing, volunteer recognition, quality management and continuous improvement. Importantly, the Volunteering Australia standards recognise the benefits of a two-way relationship in "providing an opportunity for organisations to achieve their goals by involving volunteers in their activities, and for volunteers to make meaningful use of their time and skills, contributing to social and community outcomes" (Volunteering Australia, 2015, p. 3).

Perspectives on volunteers and volunteering

Because volunteering involves a two-way relationship between an organisation and its goals and volunteers making meaningful use of their skills and time it is useful to briefly explore different perspectives on volunteering. Rochester (2006) proposed a model which is useful for capturing the diversity of activity which is described by the ubiquitous terms "volunteer" and "volunteering" (see Figure 6.1). The unpaid work perspective suggests that volunteers are helpers that need to be managed using a workplace or HRM approach normally applied to paid staff. From a serious leisure perspective, the focus is on intrinsic rather than extrinsic motivations for volunteering. Serious leisure is the pursuit of a volunteer activity sufficiently substantial and interesting for the participants to find a career within (Stebbins, 2004). The activism perspective suggests a quite different approach where volunteering is regarded as a force for social change. Rochester's model affords an opportunity to move beyond the managerial approach to volunteering in which volunteers in sport are simply managed as an unpaid human resource.

These perspectives enable a more complete understanding of some of the complexities of the act of volunteering as well as managing and working with sport volunteers. For example, one volunteer might feel obligated to volunteer, because their children are involved, but would prefer to volunteer informally and not take on a designated role with a position description such as a team manager. Another volunteer may freely choose to take on the role of coach, but because formal qualifications are required, might expect that the club will reimburse her expenses or provide a stipend. Yet another volunteer might be involved as a social activist

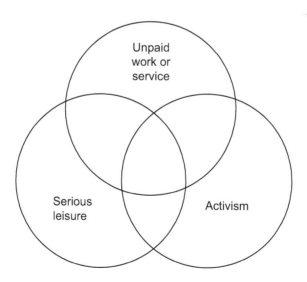

Figure 6.1 Three perspective model on volunteering (adapted from Rochester, 2006)

and sees sport as a vehicle for reaching out to disadvantaged or at-risk youth.

Managing sport volunteers needs to be considered within the context of an increasingly complex and competitive landscape. The ASC (2014, p. 1) reported that in "many instances sporting organisations are competing against other sporting organisations for the same volunteer workforce as well as the myriad of other opportunities for people to volunteer their time in all facets of civil society". Further, it was argued that "increasing cultural diversity and changing generational preferences mean that traditional volunteer recruitment and management practices need to be rethought" ASC (2014, p. 1). Using a market segmentation approach the ASC (2014) developed a needs-based model to better understand sport volunteers and to suggest more effective and relevant approaches to recruit and retain different segments of sport volunteers. In total, ten segments were identified: five that were currently volunteering and the remainder that were not currently volunteering. The five segments of current volunteers were labelled happy helpers, community committed, opportunists, altruists and overcommitted. The happy helpers segment, accounting for 33% of sport club volunteers, preferred support roles, included club sport as one of several volunteer activities and were there to help family and friends. Sport New Zealand (2006) identified nine volunteer segments based on motivation and four underlying core values: generosity, love of sport, social connection and appreciation.

According to Sport New Zealand, generosity may be conditional on the basis that volunteers seek opportunities that:

- have boundaries around their roles and responsibilities;
- reflect a desire to achieve results;
- use their time productively;
- do not waste time; and
- offer an environment that minimises risk.

Love of sport is expressed through supporting people that a volunteer is attached to (e.g., children, partner or friends). Consistent with the transition-extension hypothesis discussed later in this chapter, Sport New Zealand (2006, p. 13) found that "involvement as a player is often a gateway to volunteering and provides fertile ground for recruitment". Social connection describes the bonds formed with others through volunteering in which opportunities to both work and socialise together are important for building links with like-minded people. Finally, appreciation is not necessarily only direct recognition but the expectation or desire sport volunteers have to feel good about giving up their time. Segmentation research is useful to the extent that it recognises and provides evidence that volunteers have a diverse range of values, attitudes and motives. However, adapting volunteer management practices to different sub-groups of volunteers runs the risk of sports clubs losing sight of what they are trying to achieve in the delivery of programmes and services to their members and other stakeholders. An effective volunteer management framework needs to find an appropriate balance between the needs of volunteers and the needs of the organisation in order to effectively and efficiently deliver its services.

Human resource management and sport volunteers

From a strategic perspective volunteers represent the human capital necessary for the achievement of long-term organisational goals. However, it has long been recognised that there is an underlying tension in applying HRM practices to the management of sport volunteers. This tension is captured in an LIRC (2003, p. 80) report for Sport England when commenting on the merits of formal and informal management cultures relative to volunteer motives:

> In particular the importance of shared enthusiasm and social benefits from volunteering militates against a managerialist approach to volunteers, whilst motivations concerned with helping a club improve and succeed, and "giving something back" are more compatible with formal approaches to volunteer management.

Frisby and Kikulis (1996) argued that traditional HRM has the advantage of a planned approach which links the abilities of individuals to organisational needs, but is limited by an emphasis on controlling behaviour and ignoring many of the dynamics that are more evident in interpretive and critical HRM paradigms. The traditional paradigm views HRM processes "as objective realities that can be observed, measured and controlled by management" (Frisby & Kikulis, 1996, p. 109). Traditional HRM ignores matters such as the formation and impacts of groups and coalitions within organisations, organisational cultures and sub-cultures, as well as the broader social and political environments and the influences exerted on individual volunteer behaviour.

While mindful of its limitations the traditional HRM paradigm is considered here because it is dominant amongst VMPs and has been developed and advocated by government agencies, sport NSOs and volunteer advocacy bodies such as Volunteering Australia and Investment in Volunteering in the United Kingdom. Because VMPs have logical and clearly defined processes such an approach is most likely to be adopted by VSOs seeking to improve volunteer management practices. A national survey of Norwegian sports clubs concluded that "55 percent of the organizations emphasize human resources in some variant as the most important obstacle for a better-run organization" (Seippel, 2004, p. 225). It is therefore important to consider the processes and impacts of HRM on VSOs and volunteers. Traditional HRM processes are more prescriptive than adaptive and based on the assumption that the motives, needs and interests of volunteers can be matched with the strategic and operational requirements of VSOs. Further, the performance, commitment, satisfaction and ultimately the retention of volunteers are the logical outcomes of HRM practices. This approach is closely aligned with programme management, discussed earlier, and focuses on recruitment, selection, orientation and training. Traditional HRM is a cyclical process in which human resources are recruited, developed and either retained or replaced by VSOs. Significant components of these processes are outlined and examined within the context of VSOs in the following sections.

Recruiting volunteers

Taking a management perspective, Østerlund (2013) argued that recruiting a sufficient number of volunteers is the main challenge for VSOs and "the way voluntary sport organizations are managed exerts significant influence on the level of difficulty in recruiting volunteers" (p. 144). In a study of 5,000 sport clubs in Denmark, Østerlund found evidence of modest effects of management styles on volunteer recruitment. In most VMPs, the process of recruiting volunteers begins with an examination of current and future demand for volunteers to service existing and planned programmes and events. The task of planning for volunteer recruitment suggests a level of formality in the recruitment process. Given that the main challenge for VSOs is to recruit sufficient volunteers, it is likely that a mix of formal and informal approaches are used in practice. Responsibility for recruiting a replacement volunteer sometimes falls to a volunteer who has decided to leave and because of normative pressures feels obligated to find their own replacement so the organisation can continue to function normally. Whether volunteers are recruited through formal or informal processes they "should be given a realistic overview of what the role entails before they are asked to commit their time and energy to a position" (Taylor, Doherty, & McGraw, 2007, p. 70). A position description with major responsibilities and expected time commitment will help potential volunteers decide if a particular position will suit their availability, skills and experience. Volunteering Victoria (2018) provide a detailed template for a volunteer position description template which includes a position title, supervisor, time commitment, description of the position, responsibilities or list of tasks, qualifications and experience needed, outcomes or goals of the position, a training and support plan, reporting, and benefits the volunteer will gain from the role.

Volunteer recruitment is not only a reflection of the needs of a VSO at a particular point in time but should also consider the volunteer's perspective and their decision to become a volunteer. Hallmann (2015) used a heterodox economic perspective to model the decision to volunteer in organised sports by examining the determinants of volunteering and the time committed to volunteering using demographic, economic, sociological and psychological variables. It was found that human capital, female gender and the motive to shape society negatively influenced the decision to volunteer, whereas the number of voluntary engagements had a positive effect. Time commitment to volunteering was positively influenced by male gender, having children, meeting people, club membership, shaping society and the number of voluntary engagements. Hallmann (2015) concluded that volunteers are heterogeneous and recommended that a sport club does "not need to limit its search to a particular group of people, except for their members, which had the highest effect on the decision to volunteer" (p. 459).

From an HRM perspective, mainstream recruitment practices usually assume that potential volunteers do not have an existing relationship with an organisation. However, as indicated by Hallmann (2015) a rich source of new volunteers is often within the VSO itself. Involvement as a player was discussed earlier as a gateway to volunteering. Schlesinger, Egli and Nagel (2013) found that volunteering in a sport club is influenced by having children belonging to the club, competition experiences and longer club membership. This is not inconsistent with the transition-extension hypothesis advanced by Cuskelly (2004) and introduced in Chapter 4. Based on continuity theory (Atchley, 1989, 1999), the transition-extension hypothesis argued that a decision to volunteer often represents a changed involvement rather than the development of a new relationship with a VSO. Continuity theory posits that individuals are "both predisposed and motivated toward inner psychological continuity as well as outward continuity of social behavior and circumstances" (Atchley, 1989, p. 183). Volunteer recruitment practices therefore need to be varied according to whether volunteers are being recruited from within or outside a VSO. Those being recruited from within an organisation are likely to be extending their participation, perhaps making the transition from another role less difficult than it might be for volunteers recruited from outside the organisation. Those recruited from outside a VSO experience a different and perhaps more difficult transition process as they get to know their roles and key volunteers for the first time.

Screening and selection of volunteers follows the planning and recruitment processes. Screening and selection processes are becoming increasingly important but also more complex as VSOs are required to comply with child protection, member protection, privacy of personal information and other legislation depending upon the jurisdiction in which a club operates. Theoretically, recruitment is designed to attract a pool of appropriately qualified and motivated applicants to a vacant position from which the most appropriate candidate is selected. In practice, many VSOs operate under circumstances where they have a shortage of volunteers. Nichols (2005) reported that almost three-quarters (74%) of sports clubs reported there are not enough people willing to volunteer. VSOs that have more applicants than an available position requires can be in a position to select rather than appoint. Under such circumstances it is important to select the best possible candidate for the position. HRM selection practices in mainstream organisations can include a wide array of techniques which vary in terms of costs, reliability and validity. Selection techniques can include standard and behaviourally based interviews, a work sample, aptitude or cognitive ability tests, personality inventories and assessment centres. Selecting sport volunteers normally includes an interview and depending upon the level of responsibility associated with the position (e.g., controlling valuable assets and cash) reference checks. Interviews might vary from an informal chat about a position to a formal process with a selection committee and a set of predetermined interview questions. The selection process concludes when a volunteer is offered and accepts a position. Other potential volunteers who are not selected might be encouraged to help out with other tasks or roles.

VSOs have little control over the selection process for a number of key positions particularly on committees or boards. VSOs which are incorporated under relevant legislation are bound by democratic convention and their constitution to conduct regular elections for significant leadership and decision-making positions such as president or chair, secretary and treasurer, often annually or biennially. Even if an incumbent committee or board member has fulfilled the responsibilities of their position other members normally have a right to nominate and run for election. The assumption of managerial control which underpins HRM practices is secondary to the democratic principles upon which most VSOs are founded and widely accepted selection practices cannot always be applied. However, in some circumstances an individual can be deemed to be ineligible to hold a volunteer position. Child safety legislation often requires mandatory background checks for volunteers who may come into contact or are working with children.

Developing volunteers

Induction or orientation, training and performance management are important processes in the development of sport volunteers and are a common component of VMPs. A significant event in the HRM process is the transition that occurs when an individual takes up a volunteer role for the first time.

Whether a current or former player, parent or partner of a player, general member or previously having no involvement with a VSO, volunteering, particularly for the first time, deepens or extends and sometimes enriches an individual's level of engagement. However, it cannot be assumed that even a long-term member has a good understanding of an organisation, its goals, policies and procedures or the roles of key office bearers even if they know the people in these roles. "Proper orientation for volunteers enables them to perform their role as required and ensures they understand their responsibilities and their rights within the organisation" (Volunteering Victoria, 2018, no page).

Nel et al. (2016) describe induction as the link between recruitment and retention. In employment settings the "objective of the induction process is to ensure the new employee's transition to the organisation is positive" (Nel et al., 2016, p. 300). The benefits of induction include: less stress for the new employee, reduced cognitive dissonance between expectations and reality, quick progress to productivity, reduced turnover and withdrawal behaviour, quicker adoption of group norms and an organisation's values and culture, and the development of positive attitudes all of which are likely to apply to new volunteers. Researching VSO board member performance, Doherty and Hoye (2011, p. 120) noted that "performance may be expected to be positively influenced by efforts to reduce individuals' ambiguity with regard to what they are supposed to do and how their work fits in with the organization's overall goals".

Volunteers new to an organisation and those continuing, either in the same or a different role, usually need general and role specific knowledge and skills training to perform their tasks effectively. The choice of training method will usually depend upon factors such as cost, timing, specificity, flexibility, delivery mode, prior knowledge and the availability of volunteers. With the increasing sophistication of learning management systems and greater access to the internet, volunteer training and development programmes can be self-paced, customised and delivered at times that suit the schedules of volunteers irrespective of their physical location. Government sport agencies, sport NSOs, major sport event organisers and professional associations have long recognised the benefits of well-trained volunteers. They have become adept at developing and promoting volunteer training and development programmes for coaches, officials, administrators and sports trainers.

Having volunteers inducted and trained for the job they are expected to do does not necessarily guarantee job performance. Pearce (1993, p. 178) noted that "it is widely assumed that volunteers are less productive than employees ... [but] ... we do not really know in what ways". Volunteer job performance is likely to be affected by the personal attributes of volunteers and by organisational issues. Factors such as volunteers' abilities, motivation, commitment and competing demands (e.g., work and family) coupled with organisational factors such as management style and working conditions affect volunteer job performance and satisfaction.

Performance management in mainstream settings is "a process that consolidates goal setting, performance appraisal and employee development into a unified system with the aim of ensuring that the employee's performance is aligned with the company's strategic aims" (Nel et al., 2016, p. 315). In a voluntary organisation setting performance management is applied by "setting performance expectations, monitoring progress, measuring outcomes, appraising consequences, correcting actions and rewarding accomplishments" (Cross & Hobbs, 2012, p. 288). The process described by Cross and Hobbs is similar to performance appraisal which according to Nel et al. (2016, p. 315) is the "depiction of the strengths and weaknesses of employees in a non-continuous manner, typically just once a year". This approach is compliance focussed, bureaucratic and sometimes perceived as a waste of time particularly by the person being appraised.

Managing volunteer performance can be challenging for VSOs because "volunteers are not as dependent on their organizations as are employees, and their independence ... leads to less volunteer subordination to the system of organizational behavior" Pearce (1993, p. 128). Like many voluntary organisations, VSOs tend to operate on the basis of informal, interpersonal and values-based control mechanisms rather than bureaucratic or managerial control. VSOs can manage volunteer performance through informal social or normative controls and/or more explicit bureaucratic controls but, as Pearce argued, "no organization can be effective with neither one" (p. 179).

Performance management is often tied to reward systems amongst employees. However, the benefits of volunteer work are not clear and "rewards that seem to be most important ... [to volunteers] ... are not under the control of the organization" (Pearce, 1993, p. 181). Therefore, performance management is likely to be ineffective if it is simply adapted to VSOs from mainstream paid employment performance management systems. This is not to suggest that performance management is unimportant to volunteers or VSOs. Clearly, volunteers who feel as though their performance is supported and recognised by others are more likely to continue to contribute time and effort than those who feel unappreciated. Cnaan and Cascio (1999) found evidence that variation in volunteer performance could be explained in part by volunteer management practices. They concluded that screening practices and the use of symbolic rewards influenced commitment and tenure.

Retaining volunteers

VMPs advocate the application of appropriate management practices to retain sport volunteers. Clearly, there is a direct relationship between volunteer retention and recruitment. Higher rates of volunteer retention mean that VSOs can focus less on the challenging tasks of recruiting new volunteers or expecting increased levels of productivity from current volunteers. As indicated earlier, induction is the link between recruitment and retention. Sport England (2018a, no page) argued that providing volunteers with "a great experience won't only help keep volunteers at your club, but they'll also become your best ambassadors for recruiting volunteers in the future". Over and above an induction or welcome process, Sport England recommend a role statement with clear responsibilities, connecting regularly with volunteers through social media, meetings or social events as well as recognising and rewarding volunteers. Making the volunteer experience meaningful will improve the benefits for volunteers as well as the outcomes for sport clubs, and volunteering should be structured in ways that make it fun as well as making a difference.

There is some evidence that the adoption of volunteer management practices influences volunteer retention. Hager and Brudney (2004) found that volunteer management practices centred on making the volunteer experience worthwhile positively influence volunteer retention in what have been described in this chapter as programme management organisations. Specifically, offering training and development opportunities to volunteers, screening to identify suitable volunteers and matching them to appropriate tasks are associated with higher volunteer retention rates (Hager & Brudney, 2004). These findings are consistent with those of a Canadian study which identified ongoing appreciation and respect, meaningful volunteer experiences, and communicating and being responsive to volunteers as important factors in their retention (Phillips, Little, & Goodine, 2002). Schlesinger and Nagel (2018) investigated individual and contextual factors that influence volunteer retention (measured as intention to continue or quit volunteering) in voluntary sports clubs. Using multilevel models they found that at the individual level having children belonging to the club, strong club identification, collective solidarity and job satisfaction predicted stable voluntary activity. In addition, contextual factors including rural (as opposed to urban) sports clubs and clubs that value conviviality were more likely to have stable volunteer engagement. Interestingly, and in contrast to earlier research, Schlesinger and Nagel (2018) found that measures to promote volunteering such as having clearly defined volunteering responsibilities had no significant effect on voluntary commitment.

The HRM management approach advocated by VMPs is cyclical in nature and the loop is closed at the point where volunteers decide whether to continue volunteering. A volunteer may decide to either continue in their present position or, if there is a vacancy, continue but take up a new or additional position within the same organisation. Continuing volunteers in new positions may require additional training, support and mentoring as they transition and extend their involvement by moving to other roles. However, continuing volunteers might normally be expected to have a good understanding of the organisation, its purpose, reporting relationships, culture and traditions. When a volunteer decides to discontinue their involvement, the organisation initiates what is described in VMPs as a succession plan and begins a recruitment process to fill the vacant position with a new volunteer. As discussed earlier, membership management organisations tend to have high levels of volunteer loyalty and lengthy involvement. As a consequence, they generally have low rates of turnover but can find it difficult to fill some core volunteer positions. In contrast, programme management organisations are adept at dealing with volunteer turnover. Both organisational types may benefit from having a succession plan but for different reasons. For example, membership management organisations might use a succession plan to encourage turnover in key positions, avoiding the problems associated with martyred leadership (Pearce, 1993) such as burdening core volunteers with additional responsibilities. Programme management organisations might be better positioned to maintain high standards of service quality and continuity if they can minimise significant fluctuations by using past experience to predict volunteer turnover rates. A succession plan does not necessarily reduce turnover, but it can put a VSO in a stronger position to better cope with the impact of volunteer attrition.

Conclusion

This chapter has examined the challenging issue of managing sport volunteers. It has critically discussed the application of traditional HRM processes advocated by volunteer management programs to VSOs. Volunteer management was considered within the context of the contrasting approaches of programme management and membership management. There are benefits with a more planned approach to volunteer management to VSOs, their members, the volunteers themselves and sport development more broadly. However, HRM models are generally based on the assumption that the interests of management are the most legitimate. This assumption does not sit well with VSOs because "volunteers experience significant uncertainty stemming from the fact that they frequently find themselves holding contradictory formal positions in relation to the organization" (Pearce, 1993, p. 151). Not infrequently, sport volunteers are simultaneously owners of VSOs (as club members), as well as being workers expected to follow directives from other volunteers, and also clients who are service recipients of the VSOs of which they are members. Each of these "distinct formal organizational roles comes with its own set of behavioral expectations" (Pearce, 1993, p. 151). Even the widespread adoption of HRM as advocated by VMPs is unlikely to disentangle the complexity of volunteers' roles in VSOs or lead to significant improvement in volunteer management practices.

References

Atchley, R. C. (1989). A continuity theory of aging. *The Gerontologist, 29*, 183–190.

Atchley, R. C. (1999). *Continuity and adaptation in aging: Creating positive experiences*. Baltimore, MD: Johns Hopkins University Press.

Australian Sports Commission. (2014). *Volunteers market segmentation*. Canberra: Australian Government.

Australian Sports Commission. (2018) *Volunteers in sport*. Canberra: Author. Retrieved from www.clearinghouseforsport.gov.au/knowledge_base/sport_participation/community_participation/volunteers_in_sport (Accessed 24 July 2018).

Canadian Centre for Ethics in Sport. (2018). *Programs: Club excellence*. Ontario: Author. Retrieved from https://cces.ca/about-club-excellence (Accessed 3 September 2018).

Cnaan, R. A., & Cascio, T. A. (1999). Performance and commitment: Issues in management of volunteers in human service organizations. *Journal of Social Service Research, 24*(3–4), 1–37.

Collings, D. G., & Wood, G. (2009). *Human resource management: A critical approach*. London: Routledge.

Cross, J. A., & Hobbs, S. (2012). Volunteer performance management: The impact wheel. In T. D. Connors (Ed.), *The volunteer management handbook: Leadership strategies for success*. Hoboken, NJ: Wiley.

Cuskelly, G. (2004). Volunteer retention in community sport organizations. *European Sport Management Quarterly, 4*, 59–76.

Doherty, A., & Hoye, R. (2011). Role ambiguity and volunteer board member performance in nonprofit sport organizations. *Nonprofit Management and Leadership, 22*(1), 107–128.

Frisby, W., & Kikulis, L. (1996). Human resource management in sport. In B. L. Parkhouse (Ed.), *The management of sport: Its foundation and application* (2nd ed.). St Louis, MO: Mosby.

Hager, M. A., & Brudney, J. L. (2004). *Volunteer management practices and retention of volunteers*. Washington, DC: The Urban Institute.

Hallmann, K. (2015). Modelling the decision to volunteer in organised sports. *Sport Management Review, 18*, 448–463.

International Labour Organization (ILO). (2011). *Manual on the measurement of volunteer work*. Geneva: International Labour Office.

Investing in Volunteers. (2018). *About Iiv*. London: Author. Retrieved from https://iiv.investinginvolunteers.org.uk/about (Accessed 7 September 2018).

LIRC. (2003). *Sports volunteering in England 2002*. London: Sport England.

Meijs, L. C. P. M., & Hoogstad, E. (2001). New ways of managing volunteers: Combining membership management and programme management. *Voluntary Action, 3*(3), 41–61.

Meijs, L. C. P. M., & Karr, L. B. (2004). Managing volunteers in different settings: Membership and programme management. In R. A. Stebbins, & M. Graham (Eds.), *Volunteering as leisure/leisure as volunteering: An international assessment* (pp. 177–194). Oxfordshire: CABI.

Nel, P., Werner, A., Fazey, M., Pillay, S., Wordsworth, R., Du, P. A., ... Suseno, Y. (2016). *Human resource management in Australia*. Retrieved from https://ebookcentral-proquest-com.libraryproxy.griffith.edu.au.

Nichols, G. (2005). Issues arising from the Sport England survey of volunteers in sport 2002/3. In G. Nichols, & M. Collins (Eds.), *Volunteers in sports clubs* (pp. 1–14). Eastbourne, England: Leisure Studies Association.

Østerlund, K. (2013). Managing voluntary sport organizations to facilitate volunteer recruitment. *European Sport Management Quarterly, 13*(2), 143–165.

Pearce, J. L. (1993). *Volunteers: The organizational behavior of unpaid workers.* London: Routledge.

Phillips, S., Little, B., & Goodine, L. (2002). *Recruiting, retaining, and rewarding volunteers: What volunteers have to say.* Ontario: Canadian Centre for Philanthropy.

Rochester, C. (2006). *Making sense of volunteering.* London: Volunteering England.

Schlesinger, T., Egli, B., & Nagel, S. (2013). 'Continue or terminate?' Determinants of long-term volunteering in sports clubs. *European Sport Management Quarterly, 13*(1), 32–53.

Schlesinger, T., & Nagel, S. (2018). Individual and contextual determinants of stable volunteering in sport clubs. *International Review for the Sociology of Sport, 53*(1), 101–121.

Seippel, O. (2004). The world according to voluntary sport organizations: Voluntarism, economy and facilities. *International Review for the Sociology of Sport, 39*(2), 223–232.

South Australian Government. (2018). *V-Star.* Adelaide: Author. Retrieved from www.vstar.sa.gov.au (Accessed 7 September 2018).

Sport England. (2016). *Volunteering in an active nation: Strategy 2017–2021.* London: Author.

Sport England. (2018a). *Club people: Volunteers.* London: Author. Retrieved from www.sportenglandclubmatters.com/club-people/volunteers/ (Accessed 7 September 2018).

Sport England. (2018b). *Clubmark.* England: Author. Retrieved from https://www. sportenglandclubmatters.com/club-mark/ (Accessed 3 September 2018).

Sport New Zealand. (2006). *Finding and keeping volunteers.* Wellington, New Zealand: Author. Retrieved from https://sportnz.org.nz/assets/Uploads/attachments/ managing-sport/officials-and-volunteers/Finding-and-Keeping-Volunteers.pdf (Accessed 17 September 2018).

Sport New Zealand. (2018). *Sport compass.* New Zealand: Author. Retrieved from https://sportnz.org.nz/managing-sport/search-for-a-resource/tools-and-resources/ sport-compass (Accessed 3 September 2018).

Stebbins, R. (2004). Introduction. In R. Stebbins, & M. Graham (Eds.), *Volunteering as leisure/leisure as volunteering: An international assessment* (pp. 13–30). Wallington: CABI Publishing.

Taylor, T., Doherty, A., & McGraw, P. (2007). *Managing people in sport organizations: A strategic human resource management perspective.* Oxfordshire: Elsevier.

Vezina, M., & Crompton, S. (2012). *Volunteering in Canada.* Ottawa: Statistics Canada.

Volunteering Australia. (2015). *The national standards for volunteer involvement.* Canberra: Author.

Volunteering Victoria. (2018). *Designing a volunteer role.* Melbourne: Author. Retrieved from http://volunteeringvictoria.org.au/resources-and-tools/ (Accessed 17 September 2018).

Chapter 7

Volunteer administrators

Volunteer administrators are often the largest category of sport volunteers around the globe, conducting much of the day to day management of VSOs as well as key board roles and planning/organising functions in regional, state/provincial and national level sport organisations. The strategic planning and logistical organising of sport systems and programmes often falls to the work of many dedicated volunteer administrators. As an example of the size and scope of their effort, 7% of Canadians reported volunteering as an administrator for an amateur sport organisation, compared to coaching (5%) and officiating (2%; Canadian Heritage, 2013). Although men are more likely to report involvement in this capacity than women, this gap has shrunk since 1992. In 2010, 8% of Canadian men indicated that they volunteer in amateur sport administration versus 6% of Canadian women (Canadian Heritage, 2013). This is notable in Canada where sport and recreation make up the largest sub-group of the voluntary sector, which is the second largest in the world (Hall et al., 2005). Further, the most recent data in Canada reveals that sport and recreation organisations account for 19% of all volunteer hours with individuals volunteering approximately 120 hours per year (Vézina & Crompton, 2012).

Given the scale of volunteer effort, the development and management of volunteer administrators is crucial for sustaining sport systems at all levels, particularly in light of increasingly complex operating environments. This chapter will review the nature and scope of volunteer sport administration, key roles of volunteer administrators, some of the complex trends influencing administrators and provide a summary of the core principles required to effectively develop and manage these volunteers.

Nature and scope of volunteer sport administration

Volunteer sport administrators are essential to the effective delivery of sport (Nichols, 2012). Sports programmes and events require careful planning, budgeting and organisation that often occurs out of the spotlight. Some categories of sport volunteers (e.g., officials and coaches) are viewed as front-line volunteers given their high visibility and face-to-face interaction with sport participants and the public. In contrast, volunteer administrators often perform their roles "behind the scenes" through board meetings, conference calls and administrative work. Nevertheless, volunteer administrators are crucial to planning, organising and delivering quality sport opportunities. For the most part, volunteer sport administrators work in a variety of roles that include, among other things, planning, budgeting and managing finances, managing human resources including paid staff and other volunteers, evaluating programmes and events, and liaising with external stakeholders (e.g., government, sponsors, governing bodies). Volunteer administrators facilitate the development of opportunities for sport participation that are usually delivered by other types of sport volunteers, although many of the latter fulfil multiple roles (Wicker, 2017).

Volunteer administrators are sometimes described as "core" volunteers and comprise a large proportion of third-sector sport and non-sport volunteers (Ringuet-Riot, Cuskelly, Auld, & Zakus, 2014). Core volunteers are classified as "core" to reflect the involvement and commitment levels as opposed to roles that are typically operational in nature and involve less time and commitment (Breuer, Wicker, & von Hanau, 2012; Ringuet-Riot et al., 2014). Volunteer administrators usually make a greater commitment in time and duties as compared to other categories of sport volunteers (Breuer et al., 2012). Further, core volunteers are often more critical to the successful operation of VSOs because they encounter more of the problems that need to be overcome in the organisation, have greater exposure to the tasks that the organisation performs and are more central to the workflow of the organisation (Ringuet-Riot et al., 2014). Administrative roles tend to operate on year-long commitments, where other volunteer roles may be seasonal in nature and only last for a few months (e.g., coaching, officiating).

Although some sport organisations are managed by a management committee, most sport organisations from community sport through to national sport governing bodies are governed by boards of directors. Much of the work of volunteer sport administrators occurs within this context. Boards of directors, known more colloquially as "boards", are charged with the responsibility to govern an organisation on behalf of its members. The work of these committees is central to the organisation, as boards are responsible for maintaining, preserving, further developing and expending resources to ensure that the organisation's activities benefit its current and future members (Hoye & Doherty, 2011). Sport organisations that are incorporated with their government as a legal entity and even community sport board members have legally enforceable roles and responsibilities. For example, the board has a fiduciary responsibility: it must act honestly, in good faith and in the best interests of the organisation. The board has a duty of care to be informed about the state of the affairs of the organisation. Members of the board or management committee must not let personal interests conflict with those of the organisation, and must work with its interests in mind. In doing this, a board is normally responsible for the following duties among others (adapted from the Sports Governance Principles published by the Australian Sports Commission, 2012):

- establishing the overall vision and direction of the organisation;
- developing strategic and operational plans and budgets to ensure the aims of the organisation are fulfilled;
- coordinating the planning of programmes and activities;
- monitoring operations and evaluating results;
- approving the budget and securing and monitoring effective management of the organisation's financial resources;
- carrying out the recommendations of members as expressed at the annual general meeting;
- providing members with detailed information regarding the management of the organisation;
- monitoring the performance of organisation officials, subcommittees and paid executive employees;
- ensuring organisational compliance with relevant federal, provincial or local legislation and by-laws and the organisation's own policies;
- determining volunteer training needs and organising training opportunities;
- ensuring the organisation has standards of ethical behaviour and promotes a culture of social responsibility; and
- providing written and oral records and job descriptions to a newly elected committee.

In addition to sitting on boards, volunteer administrators often sit on committees. Committees are bodies of one or more individuals, elected or appointed by the board or the members, to conduct work on a certain area of business or technical aspect of sporting competition (i.e., athlete eligibility, competition rules, coach accreditation). Boards often use standing committees, meaning that they exist and operate on an ongoing basis, or special committees, which are only formed for the special purpose to which they have been assigned and cease to exist upon the completion of that work. Task forces and work groups are also similarly structured groups which are considered as committees. Committees report back to the board on the work they've executed or conduct research and provide recommendations for the board to consider. In voluntary sport organisations, committees may be established for functions of the following nature:

- technical;
- financial;
- programmes or competitions committee;
- fundraising;
- nominations;
- risk management; and
- strategic planning.

Many volunteer sport administrators are motivated to be involved at the higher levels of their particular sport. This includes, for example, volunteers representing their local club as elected or appointed delegates on either the regional or state/provincial board or representing state/provincial organisations at the NSO level. The delegate system is also evident at the international federation level with many positions comprising elected or appointed representatives from NSOs. The nature of involvement at higher levels in the sport system may vary according to the role to which one is elected or appointed. In some sports, volunteer administrators may be elected as delegates whose role it is to represent the organisation or stakeholder group that elected them (e.g., state/provincial representative on an NSO). Such involvement requires the delegate to adopt a position in decision making that best protects the interests of the organisation from which they derive their mandate. Alternatively, some volunteer administrators may be elected or appointed to a specific administrative position (e.g., treasurer, media liaison, national team selector) necessary to manage the next level of the sport system. In this case their responsibility lies with the higher level in which they perform this role.

However, the boundaries between these different roles and their responsibilities are sometimes blurred, resulting in problems and inefficiencies at the next level of decision making. There have been calls to replace the representation/delegate system with skill-based appointments to management committees or boards, particularly at the NSO and state/provincial levels of many sports, but the traditional system is still common (Ingram & O'Boyle, 2018).

Volunteer sport administrator roles

Boards are comprised of committee members, called directors. According to the Australian Sports Commission, a board must have at least three members, but the structure and needs of the organisation will determine the exact size of the board beyond those three positions (ASC, 2015). Although it used to be more common to have a large board of ten to fifteen directors, it has now become more common to have a smaller board of five to nine directors.

While all committee positions are important to the successful management of VSOs, it is generally acknowledged that a smaller number of positions have higher levels of responsibility and play key roles in effectively managing sport organisations. The chairperson and/or president, secretary and treasurer often fall under this category. These positions also sometimes make up what's known as the "executive". The executive acts on behalf of the board during the intervals between board meetings.

Recently, research has emphasised the importance of having a clear understanding of one's role in a voluntary setting, given that role ambiguity has been found to be associated with decreased effort, lower satisfaction, lower job performance and increased job stress (Doherty & Hoye, 2011; Sakires, Doherty, & Misener, 2009). Given that volunteer administrators operate in environments that can be uncertain, with pressure from multiple stakeholders, the impact of role ambiguity may be particularly critical in shaping a volunteer's attitude and performance. In turn, this may affect the nature of the board environment and its functioning. It is therefore important to ensure role clarity given that it is directly associated with "board members' perceptions of the meaningfulness and quality of their contributions to the board" (Doherty & Hoye, 2011, p. 119). The following sections outline several of the key roles typically represented within sport boards.

The chairperson/president

While some non-profit organisations utilise both positions it is usually the case that a sport organisation's president also has the role of chairing board meetings. The chairperson is the principal organisational leader, has overall responsibility for the organisation's administration and controls management committee meetings. Generally, the chairperson's duties are to:

- facilitate discussion among, and provide leadership to, the board;
- have a good working knowledge of the by-laws, rules and financial position of the organisation;
- manage all meetings under their purview;
- manage the organisation's annual general meeting;
- liaise on behalf of a sport organisation at other levels of sport including local, regional and national levels;
- act as a facilitator for organisational activities; and
- ensure that planning and budgeting are carried out in accordance with the wishes of the members.

Secretary

Many of the day to day administration tasks are carried out by the secretary who is essentially the chief administration officer of a sport organisation. The secretary is the person responsible for recording the business of the organisation and maintenance of records, aside from the treasurer's books and any duties assigned to other people. The secretary is often the coordinating link between members, the executive committee and external stakeholders. The secretary largely controls the rate, amount and manner in which information is communicated to different internal stakeholders. Typically, a secretary's duties are to:

- record all the proceedings of the organisation – usually called the minutes;
- maintain files of all committee reports;
- maintain registration records (except where those duties are assigned to a registrar);
- handle the correspondence of the organisation;
- set the agenda for meetings in consultation with the chairperson/president; and
- circulate relevant communications, such as calls for meetings, or other relevant meeting documentation.

Treasurer

This position has responsibility for managing the financial affairs of VSOs and, given the more complex environment in which VSOs operate, it is an increasingly difficult role. The volume and nature of the treasurer's work will vary in relation to the size of the organisation, the degree of complexity of its activities and whether the VSO owns facilities or employs staff. Larger sport organisations often have a finance subcommittee to assist the treasurer. The treasurer's duties are to:

- prepare the budget and help plan the financial future;
- collect registration and other payments and disburse funds for bill payments;
- maintain accurate financial records;
- report the financial position of the organisation to the board and membership, annually and as otherwise required;
- liaise with the financial auditor and prepare tax statements as required; and
- assist other committee members with financial issues.

Other directors

While the roles listed above are the central administrative positions within most non-profit organisations, many sport organisations, particularly at the community level, also have a number of other operational areas or roles represented on their boards or management committees. These may include:

- a registrar;
- a volunteer coordinator;
- a coaching coordinator;
- membership;
- publicity/promotions and media liaison;
- a social events coordinator;
- a fundraising coordinator;
- a club captain;
- team managers; and
- a community outreach coordinator.

Trends influencing volunteer administrators

As indicated above, the majority of the work of volunteer sport administrators tends to occur in a specific context – the VSO board. It is also
within boards that many of the consequences of professionalisation are
manifested. As sport has become more professionalised and commercialised, enhanced levels of specialised knowledge and different types of skills
are required to manage sport in this more complex environment (Nichols,
Taylor, Barrett, & Jeanes, 2014). Professionalised environments and more
complicated structures contribute to added pressure on remaining volunteers to take on more roles and responsibilities, and demand more time
commitment from volunteers (Breuer et al., 2012). Given these developments, many VSOs seek the assistance and involvement of paid staff when
possible, which may further translate into a greater degree of professionalisation. Consequently, VSOs are evolving from primarily volunteer-
managed organisations to a combination of staff and volunteer managed
clubs. However, professionalisation is more than just the employment of
paid staff. The trend towards professionalisation has encouraged VSOs to
look outside of their sport's community to recruit professionals who bring
key knowledge and competencies to the board table and to other administrative roles. Evidence suggests that VSOs have come to rely extensively
on the knowledge and skills of paid staff to help run and strategically
manage sport organisations (Auld & Godbey, 1998), and to recruit, train
and retain volunteer administrators who must also possess those knowledge and skills. Further evidence of professionalisation lies in the business-like management practices that have been adopted to increase
effectiveness and which are becoming normalised within the voluntary
sector. As clubs interact with many stakeholders and interorganisational
partners (e.g., suppliers, sponsors, local government), they may be
expected to interact with these partners in more formalised and business-
like ways, rather than relying on informal connections and handshake-
based contracts (Misener & Doherty, 2014).

Professionalisation has perhaps been the single most important factor impacting on VSOs in the last two decades, with far reaching implications as the process continues to evolve. While increased effectiveness and efficiency may seem like desirable outcomes of professionalisation, sport leaders must also be cognisant of possible trade-offs and unintended consequences that can occur when sport organisations head in this direction (Nagel, Schlesinger, Bayle, & Giauque, 2015). In particular, shifts in values and processes such as representation and democracy may result from professionalisation and must be carefully examined in order to prevent a loss of culture and disengaged volunteers (Houlihan & Green, 2009).

Organizational-level certification programmes have emerged as a method of standardising operations and professionalising the management of sport activities. These programmes enable organisations to demonstrate compliance with particular standards in order to achieve an accreditation category or be associated with a certified brand. As a result, many of the responsibilities of volunteer administrators are also becoming more systematic and standardised. These programmes are intended to help volunteers to effectively manage their clubs in a wide range of topics. However, not all administrators have the capacity and interest to pursue these programmes and must carefully assess the benefits to determine if this is a worthwhile pursuit at that time. Given the range of different types of sport clubs and corresponding degrees of formality and professionalisation (Nichols, Padmore, Taylor, & Barrett, 2012), organisational certification may represent an additional task requiring different forms of investment and support depending on the organisation's current capacity.

Sport England's Club Matters programme combines several previous programmes – Club Leaders, Help for Clubs and Clubmark – by providing online support, workshops, a club improvement plan and the Clubmark programme to provide practical guidance to improve and develop the VSO's volunteers, and the VSO as a whole (Sport England, n.d.). The programme offers resources on a variety of topics that relate to the themes of club finances, management, people and marketing. The Clubmark programme is a universally acknowledged cross-sport accreditation scheme for VSOs in England. VSOs must demonstrate their proficiency in four key club development areas: an activity/playing programme, a duty of care and welfare, knowing the club and community, and club management. Many NSOs in England have their own sport specific accreditation that utilises the Clubmark criteria (Sport England, n.d.).

Similarly, in Canada, both sport-specific and multi-sport certification schemes are rapidly evolving, and clubs are being encouraged and even required to participate in order to standardise their operations and enhance their organisational capacity. In turn, clubs may use certification as a way to strengthen their legitimacy in the eyes of key stakeholders, although this outcome is not guaranteed and may vary based on the strength of the certification scheme's brand (Misener, Schlesinger, Doherty, Rogalsky, & Johnson 2016). The Australian Sports Commission (2015) has also published mandatory sport governance principles, which have been implemented in a number of sports. The mandatory sport governance principles have several criteria for each of the following: structure for sport; board composition and operation; and sport transparency, reporting and integrity (ASC, 2015).

This trend towards certification has important implications for volunteers since attaining and maintaining status in the programme represents a new demand for administrators and requires substantial time and effort, specialised knowledge as well as policy and partnership management capabilities. While the intent of certification is to strengthen organisational functioning and capacity, it may also create an additional burden on volunteers and jeopardise the nature of voluntary civic engagement (cf. Nichols et al., 2014). While certification may be viewed as an improvement in the strategic capability of an organisation, implications for volunteer board engagement must also be considered given the balance required to navigate the added demands for strategic action with existing policy and operational responsibilities (Shilbury & Ferkins, 2011).

Sport organisations are faced with ever-changing compliance regimes that require them to adapt their modes of practice and programmes. Many of these regimes require system or process changes to the governance, rules and regulations of sport organisations. For example, in Canada, the national and provincial governing bodies in both soccer and ice hockey have recently implemented new regulations governing youth sport as a foundation for long-term athlete development, changing the form of play and rules at the community sport level. These changes involve major philosophical shifts and programmatic alterations that significantly influence club capacity, resource allocation, parent communication and volunteer time (Legg, Snelgrove, & Wood, 2016; Riehl, Snelgrove, & Edwards, in press).

Beyond these programmatic examples, sport organisations around the world are also facing increasingly complex compliance regimes related to issues such as member protection, child safety, discrimination and racism. Indeed, the philosophy that "everyone involved in sport and activity, whether they are a volunteer, participant, spectator or an elite athlete, should never have to worry about abuse or harassment" (Sport England, n.d., no page) is the premise behind the notion of safeguarding in sport. By developing, monitoring and reinforcing safeguarding, a safe space in which to play sport and be active can be fostered (Sport England, n.d.). Many government agencies, sport governing bodies, multi-sport organisations and single sport organisations now support the capacity of sport to safeguard children. For example, the Child Protection in Sport Unit in

England works with sport organisations to offer support, resources and training guided by a framework of ten standards, originally published in 2002 (Sport England, 2018). Similarly, the Australia Childhood Foundation and Australian Sports Foundation have partnered to develop a research-based framework for child safe sport (Tucci & Mitchell, 2015). While further research is needed related to the appropriate structures and policies for preventing and responding to child protection issues, it is clear that "doing nothing" is no longer an option as community attitudes about the nature of sport have changed and the values of safety, accessibility and inclusion must be reflected in the organisation and leadership of sport.

The increasing complexity of sport compliance regimes does not only apply to children and youth. Rather, citizens of all ages around the globe are demanding safe, principle-driven sport which requires innovation within the processes, systems and culture which guide sport leaders' actions (e.g., True Sport Foundation, 2016; Vicsport, 2014). In addition to formal compliance regimes, other organisations such as the True Sport Foundation in Canada have a growing presence within the sport sector as leaders advocating for change in the sport system in order to promote participation among diverse and marginalised groups including teen girls, at-risk youth, seniors, newcomers, individuals with a disability, LGBTQ+ communities, indigenous people, low-income families, and rural and remote communities. The True Sport Foundation (2016) reminds us that "sport is never neutral – it has the potential to provide a positive effect just as much as a negative outcome" (p. 14). As such, both compliance and advocacy are responsibilities of volunteer administrators who have the power to challenge the status quo and reshape the future of sport.

Where traditional pressures such as time demands, not enough people to do the work and conflict with family commitments are still highly relevant for today's volunteer administrators, these individuals must also take part in new training and compliance programmes and lead the way for other volunteers (e.g., volunteer coaches, timekeepers, officials). The additional responsibilities associated with new regimes and advocacy work, in addition to other compliance programmes related to issues such as integrity in sport, employment equity, tax legislation and concussion management, are indicative of a wider scope of responsibilities than previously conceived and require leaders to be open-minded, inclusive, forward-thinking and adaptable as the nature of volunteer commitment continues to evolve.

Developing volunteer administrators

The development and management of volunteer administrators is important for sustaining sport systems dependent on volunteers to govern and manage organisations from the local, state/provincial to national and international levels. Over the last 20 years, there has been a shift to being more aware of the personal qualities and relationships necessary to manage sport. Indeed, the True Sport Foundation in Canada (2016) notes that Canadians are demanding values-based sport participation opportunities and those who plan and implement sport programmes must be leaders in this domain. Bell-Laroche, MacLean, Thibault, and Wolfe (2014) explored the concept of managing sport organisations through management by values (MBV). "MBV involves the development of management systems that integrate values into the policies, procedures, and programs of an organization" (Bell-Laroche et al., 2014, p. 69). MBV represents an alternative model of management for sport organisation boards, where the personal values of sport administrators are acknowledged, the collective values of the organisation are articulated and recognised, and where the organisational culture is developed to support and reflect the shared values in every aspect of the organisation's management. Bell-Laroche and colleagues (2014) reported that empirical work in different organisational contexts uncovered increased performance when values were collectively shared by employees. When values are espoused by an organisation, it has an increased ability to attract people whose values are congruent with it (Bell-Laroche et al., 2014). It is therefore imperative to train administrators to understand, demonstrate and implement value-based principles in order to truly change the culture of sport and eliminate issues that have long plagued the sector, such as homophobia and bullying (True Sport Foundation, 2016).

Because VSOs are generally led by volunteers, the practice of properly orienting and training new volunteers is often overlooked, especially when administrative volunteers have such a high level of responsibility. Providing new volunteers with all the material and information they need to do the job well, connecting them to someone in the VSO as a "buddy" in case they have any questions, and checking in with volunteers are key to ensuring they have a positive experience and better work performance (Breuer et al., 2012; Griffiths & Armour, 2012). Other actions may include maintaining accurate records in a volunteer training manual in order to minimise the loss of knowledge and productivity often resulting from the transition between volunteers, an issue that is often a cause for concern for VSOs.

Continued development of volunteers and staff through training is an important strategy for ensuring that the human resources needs of the organisation are continually met. Frawley, Favaloro, and Schulenkorf (2018) examined experience-based leadership development in professional sport organisations within the Australian sport marketplace. Exposing individuals with leadership potential to experience-based opportunities for development was important to the development of leadership (Frawley et al., 2018). Connecting them to others for support, feedback and discussion will help volunteer administrators grow and develop from their experiences. These networking opportunities will lead to further leadership development and offer opportunities to put their newly earned abilities to work for the sport organisation (Frawley et al., 2018). Investing in volunteers and supporting them to pursue training to develop the skills required for the roles they possess is an effective way to increase satisfaction and retain volunteers.

One of the key issues related to the effectiveness of volunteer committees is the turnover of members. The very nature of committee work means that inefficiencies can arise when there is a continual loss of organisational memory. It seems that poor procedures and inefficiencies in committee operations impact on the willingness of members to maintain their involvement and, like other areas of sport volunteering, the administrative function is under threat from problems with recruitment and retention. In this regard, appropriate succession planning is essential to ensuring that remaining volunteer administrators are not overburdened.

Sport organisations which plan for the future are better able to develop those with leadership potential to help prepare for periods of leadership transition (Frawley et al., 2018). Understanding the required skills and abilities of an organisation, maintaining an accurate appraisal of the organisation's strengths and challenges, regularly updating job descriptions and keeping up-to-date records are all methods that help to ease succession. Furthermore, initially recruiting people into smaller roles, and having open discussions about their interests to move into larger roles and transitioning roles internally, can assist in more easily and successfully having succession when people intentionally or unintentionally vacate their roles (Ringuet-Riot et al., 2014). These efforts can help to build volunteer pathways and enable volunteers to draw on their past experiences as a foundation for more significant commitment in the future (Hallmann & Dickson, 2017).

The trend towards professionalisation and increasing institutional pressures at all levels of sport have shifted expectations of volunteer administrators and the nature of their experience. In response, as discussed briefly in Chapter 4, psychological contracts have recently been explored as a possible tool for promoting volunteer engagement and satisfaction as clubs seek to manage the diverse needs of their volunteers (Taylor, Darcy, Hoye, & Cuskelly, 2006). Grounded in social exchange theory, a psychological contact is "a cognitive state that is subjective and interpretative and refers to the development and maintenance of the relationship between the individual and the organisation" (Taylor et al., 2006, p. 126). The psychological contract involves independent dimensions of exchange which can be characterised as transactional (i.e., economic currency) or relational (i.e., socio-emotional currency), where the psychological contract with volunteers is more often relational in nature (Taylor et al., 2006). While there has been some research on the psychological contract of volunteer coaches (e.g., Harman & Doherty, 2014), Taylor et al.'s (2006) study of sport club volunteers in Australia found that

> club administrators and volunteers place different emphases on the transactional, assurance of good faith and fair dealing, and intrinsic job characteristic components of the psychological contract. Notably, club administrators had substantial expectations of volunteers in relation to adherence to professional, legal and regulatory standards. Volunteers were primarily concerned with doing rewarding work in a pleasant social environment that was able to fit within their often tight time restrictions.
>
> (p. 123)

Given the ever-changing nature of volunteer administration, and increasing demands for compliance and systematic approaches via certification, there may be a disconnect between what is required of a volunteer and what role they had expected to perform. Thus, developing psychological contracts may contribute not only to greater role clarity, but offer a means of assessing whether an organisation is meeting a volunteer's expectations. Kappelides, Cuskelly, and Hoye (2018) note that a clear understanding of psychological contracts during the volunteer recruitment phase may help establish realistic outcomes and lead to greater retention. This may also have important implications for how volunteers are rewarded and recognised, and enable organisations to highlight the significant impact of a volunteer's role and counter the largely accepted view that voluntary work is unappreciated (Breuer et al., 2012).

Conclusion

A "large proportion of sports participation takes place in clubs run by the members themselves" (Nichols, 2012, p. 155). Thus, the importance of volunteer administrators in the sport sector cannot be overstated. However, sport organisations in many countries have experienced a significant decrease in volunteers over the last decade (Breuer et al., 2012). Research shows that volunteering is diminishing in both size and scope. Ringuet-Riot et al. (2014) report that, in Australia, those currently volunteering are contributing less time to their duties. Similarly, data from Germany reports that less people overall are contributing their time to volunteering (Breuer et al., 2012). In Canada, the number of volunteers has been on an upward trend, yet the number of hours of volunteer work has generally plateaued (Vézina & Crompton, 2012). In light of the current trends, volunteer administrators remain the lifeblood of many sport organisations and we must consider all factors which influence their participation and experience.

Many of the trends facing voluntary sport organisations mirror those within the wider voluntary sector as they are not immune to general trends in civil society. For example, the voluntary sector must navigate the changing nature of citizenship where the rise of individualistic forms of participation comes at the expense of collective forms of action (e.g., Pattie, Seyd, & Whiteley, 2004). As a result, we see a trend towards "the weakening of the institutions which support collective action and which encompass representative interests" (Pattie et al., 2004, p. 275). Relatedly, the voluntary sector has been confronted with increased pressure to do "more with less" resulting from of lack of human and financial resources and shifts in government spending environments (Cheng & Yang, 2018). These sector-wide trends remind us that innovative strategies are needed to advance the sector and continue to offer the important services that the public expects from non-profit organisations. Similarly, Nichols (2012) reminds us to think about how voluntary organisations would respond if core volunteers become too difficult to replace. While some voluntary sport organisations are able to supplement their loss of volunteer administrators and other core administrators with more casual volunteers, partnerships and paid roles, the resulting increased costs may be downloaded onto the participants and end users (Breuer et al., 2012).

Further, the increasingly formalised environment in which volunteers must work and encroaching private market values such as commercial revenue generation, the influence of funding bodies and donors, and contract competition (Eikenberry & Drapal Kluver, 2004) may challenge the impact of non-profit organisations and their role in promoting citizenship through volunteering. Although there have been significant changes to sport management practices and procedures brought about by professionalisation, the responsibility for effective service delivery still rests largely with volunteer administrators. Volunteer sport administrators make substantial contributions, often behind the scenes, to the provision of services to members and the public and ensure the continuing viability of voluntary sport organisations. However, their roles, probably more so than other types of volunteers, have been altered by the professionalisation of sport systems internationally over the past two decades. Professionalisation and, relatedly, standards such as certification represent a double-edged sword. VSOs must seek to benefit from professionalisation while being acutely aware that it may impact on committee functioning and board effectiveness, contribute to declining volunteer levels as well as alter the very nature of their experience. Sport organisations must continue to find new and effective methods to engage and retain administrative volunteers – if they do not, they will be forced to answer questions such as who will sustain our sport systems when volunteer administrators no longer want to pursue this important role and become too difficult to replace (Nichols, 2012).

References

Auld, C. J., & Godbey, G. (1998). Influence in Canadian national sport organizations: Perceptions of professionals and volunteers. *Journal of Sport Management*, 12(1), 20–38.

Australian Sports Commission. (2012). Sports governance principles. Retrieved from www.sportaus.gov.au/__data/assets/pdf_file/0011/686036/CORP_33978_Sports_Governance_Principles.pdf (Accessed 21 February 2018).

Australian Sports Commission. (2015). Mandatory sports governance principles. Retrieved from www.sportaus.gov.au/__data/assets/pdf_file/0003/686046/Mandatory_Sports_Governance_Principles_FINAL.pdf (Accessed 26 October 2018).

Bell-Laroche, D., MacLean, J., Thibault, L., & Wolfe, R. (2014). Leader of perceptions management by values within Canadian national sport organizations. *Journal of Sport Management*, 28, 68–80.

Breuer, C., Wicker, P., & von Hanau, T. (2012). Consequences of the decrease in volunteers among German sports clubs: Is there a substitute for voluntary work? *International Journal of Sport Policy and Politics*, 4(2), 173–186.

Canadian Heritage. (2013). Sport participation 2010. Retrieved from http://publications.gc.ca/collections/collection_2013/pc-ch/CH24-1-2012-eng.pdf

Cheng, Y., & Yang, L. (2018). Providing public services without relying heavily on government funding: How do nonprofits respond to government budget cuts? *The American Review of Public Administration*. doi:10.1177/0275074018806085

Doherty, A., & Hoye, R. (2011). Role ambiguity and volunteer board member performance in nonprofit sport organizations. *Nonprofit Management and Leadership*, 22(1), 107–128.

Eikenberry, A., & Drapal Kluver, J. (2004). The marketization of the nonprofit sector: Civil society at risk? *Public Administration Review*, 64(2), 132–140.

Frawley, S., Favaloro, D., & Schulenkorf, N. (2018). Experience-based leadership development and professional sport organizations. *Journal of Sport Management*, 32, 123–134.

Griffiths, M., & Armour, K. (2012). Mentoring as a formalized learning strategy with community sports volunteers. *Mentoring & Tutoring: Partnership in Learning*, 20(1), 151–173.

Hall, M. H., de Wit, M. L., Lasby, D., McIver, D., Evers, T., … Johnson, C. (2005, June). *Cornerstones of community: Highlights of the national survey of nonprofit and voluntary organizations*. (Catalogue No. 61-533-XPE, Rev. ed.). Ottawa, ON: Statistics Canada.

Hallmann, K., & Dickson, G. (2017). Non-profit sport club members: What makes them volunteer? *Voluntary Sector Review*, 8(2), 87–204. doi:10.1332/204080517X14975367943041

Harman, A., & Doherty, A. (2014). The psychological contract of volunteer youth sport coaches. *Journal of Sport Management*, 28, 687–699.

Houlihan, B., & Green, M. (2009). Modernization and sport: The reform of Sport England and UK sport. *Public Administration*, 87(3), 678–698.

Hoye, R., & Doherty, A. (2011). Nonprofit sport board performance: A review and directions for future research. *Journal of Sport Management*, 25(3), 272–285.

Ingram, K., & O'Boyle, I. (2018). Sport governance in Australia: Questions of board structure and performance. *World Leisure Journal*, 60(2), 156–172.

Kappelides, P., Cuskelly, G., & Hoye, R. (2018). The influence of volunteer recruitment practices and expectations on the development of volunteers' psychological contracts. *Voluntas*. doi:10.1007/s11266-018-9986-x

Legg, J., Snelgrove, R., & Wood, L. (2016). Modifying tradition: Examining organizational change in youth sport. *Journal of Sport Management*, 30(4), 369–381.

Misener, K., & Doherty, A. (2014). In support of sport: Examining the relationship between community sport organizations and sponsors. *Sport Management Review*, 17(4), 493–506. doi:10.1016/j.smr.2013.12.002

Misener, K., Schlesinger, T., Doherty, A., Johnson, K., & Rogalsky, K. (2016). Legitimacy for capacity? An investigation of the role of certification in community sport organizations. Paper presented at the 31st annual conference of the North American Society for Sport Management (NASSM), Orlando, Florida.

Nagel, S., Schlesinger, T., Bayle, E., & Giauque, D. (2015). Professionalization of sport federations: A multi-level framework for analysing forms, causes and consequences. *European Sport Management Quarterly*, 15(4), 407–433.

Nichols, G. (2012). Sports volunteering. *International Journal of Sport Policy and Politics*, 4(2), 155–157.

Nichols, G., Padmore, J., Taylor, P., & Barrett, D. (2012). The relationship between types of sports club and English government policy to grow participation. *International Journal of Sport Policy and Politics*, 4(2), 187–200.

Nichols, G., Taylor, P., Barrett, D., & Jeanes, R. (2014). Youth sport volunteers in England: A paradox between reducing the state and promoting a big society. *Sport Management Review*, 17(3), 337–346.

Pattie, C., Seyd, P., & Whiteley, P. (2004). *Citizenship in Britain: Values, participation and democracy*. Cambridge: Cambridge University Press.

Riehl, S., Snelgrove, R., & Edwards, J. (in press). Mechanisms of institutional maintenance in minor hockey. *Journal of Sport Management*. doi:10.1123/jsm.2018-0041

Ringuet-Riot, C., Cuskelly, G., Auld, C., & Zakus, D. H. (2014). Volunteer roles, involvement and commitment in voluntary sport organizations: Evidence of core and peripheral volunteers. *Sport in Society*, 17(1), 116–133.

Sakires, J., Doherty, A., & Misener, K. (2009). Role ambiguity in voluntary sport organizations. *Journal of Sport Management*, 23(5), 615–643.

Shilbury, D., & Ferkins, L. (2011). Professionalization, sport governance, and strategic capability. *Managing Leisure*, 16(2), 108–127.

Sport England. (n.d.). *Club matters*. Retrieved from www.sportenglandclubmatters.com/on (Accessed 28 October 2018).

Sport England. (2018). Standards for safeguarding and protecting children in sport. Retrieved from https://thecpsu.org.uk/media/445556/web_cpsustandards.pdf (Accessed 18 December 2018).

Taylor, T., Darcy, S., Hoye, R., & Cuskelly, G. (2006). Using psychological contract theory to explore issues in effective volunteer management. *European Sport Management Quarterly*, 2, 123–147.

True Sport Foundation. (2016). Sport and belonging, 2016 Vital Signs Report. Retrieved from http://communityfoundations.ca/wp-content/uploads/2016/04/Vital_Signs_Sport_and_Belonging.pdf

Tucci, J., & Mitchell, J. (2015). Safeguarding children in sport: A national blueprint to build the capacity of sport to protect children and young people from abuse, harm and exploitation. Australian Childhood Foundation. www.childabuseroyal commission.gov.au/sites

Vézina, M., & Crompton, S. (2012). Volunteering in Canada. *Canadian Social Trends, Statistics Canada Catalogue no. 11-008*. Ottawa: Statistics Canada.

Vicsport. (2014). *Everybody's business: State and regional sport organisations and safeguarding children in Victorian sport*. South Melbourne: Vicsport.

Wicker, P. (2017). Volunteerism and volunteer management in sport. *Sport Management Review, 20*(4), 325–337.

Chapter 8

Volunteer officials

From suburban parks and sports facilities to international competitions, sports officials have a prominent role in almost every sporting contest. Sports officials are an essential part of organised competitive sport to the extent that they are responsible for applying the rules of the game or judging the performance of athletes. The capabilities of sports officials can directly impact on the quality of the sport experience for players, coaches and spectators alike, many of whom feel the need to challenge the decisions of officials, at times in an abusive manner. In some sports the knowledge and skills of officials and how they interpret and apply the rules of a match or contest can affect participant safety and wellbeing. Because community level sport accounts for a large proportion of overall sports participation most officiating is undertaken either voluntarily or in low paid positions in VSOs. A widely held view across sport is that officials are increasingly difficult to attract, develop and retain and to some extent the availability of officials may affect the capacity of VSOs to deliver sporting competitions and events. The purpose of this chapter is to explore the importance and significance of sports officiating, the roles of sports officials, problems and issues in sports officiating, and the development and management of sports officials.

Scope of sports officiating

A sports official is any person who controls the actual play of a competition (e.g., umpire, referee or judge) by the application of the rules and laws of the sport to make judgements on the rule infringements, performance, time or score to ensure the proper conduct of a sporting fixture in a safe environment (Government of Western Australia, 2018). Dell, Gervis, and Rhind (2016) assert the "role of a referee [official] is multi-faceted ... [and includes] ... implementing the rules and regulations of the game; dealing with events that occur during the match; managing coaches and players and dealing with conflict" (p. 109) and further claim that because sport officials make a high number of decisions during a game these jointly contribute to officiating being a complex and pressured role.

"Sports official" is a collective term and depending upon the context includes umpire, referee, judge, lines person, scorer, timekeeper and in some cases adjudicator, marshal and scrutineer. Sports officials apply the laws and rules of sport in many competitive environments from community, school and local sport through to elite and professional sports such as national leagues and championships, international sport events and world championship and Olympic competitions. They officiate at team and individual sports whether played on courts, arenas, fields or tracks, in pools or a in a variety of natural settings. MacMahon and Plessner (2008) describe three categories of sport officials: those who interact, those who react and those who judge. Officials who *interact* are integral to and often move within the contest arena or field of play itself (e.g., football, basketball, hockey or combat sports). Officials who *react* tend to have little interaction with players or athletes but are required to observe and make decisions about particular aspects of a game (e.g., assistant football referee or a tennis or volleyball line judge). Decisions are often binary (e.g., the ball is either in or out). The third category is officials who *judge* a particular performance aesthetically or for the quality of particular elements on a routine and assign a score (e.g., gymnastics, equestrian, diving, surfing or ice skating). Although officials in this category have to deal with a much greater level of information than officials in the *react* category, they tend to have more time to make decisions than officials in the *interact* category. While technology such as decision review by video systems is increasingly common in elite and professional sporting contests, sports officials in VSOs rarely have access to such technology.

Cognitive skills are important across all categories of sports officiating and are exemplified in a study of rugby league referees. Morris and O'Connor (2017) found that the top six ranked skills of elite level referees were all cognitive skills and included decision-making accuracy, reading the game, communication, game understanding, game management and knowledge of the rules. Based on self-efficacy theory (Bandura, 1997), Myers, Feltz, Guillén, and Dithurbide (2012) developed and validated a referee self-efficacy scale which identified four dimensions of officiating: game knowledge, decision making, pressure and communication (see Figure 8.1). Game knowledge is the confidence that a referee has in their knowledge of their sport. Decision making is the confidence that a referee has in their ability to make decisions during a competition. Pressure is the confidence that a referee has in their ability to be uninfluenced by pressure. And finally, communication is the confidence that a referee has in their ability to communicate effectively.

Different categories or types of officials require different skills and varying levels of physical fitness. However, all officials need to develop a range of general skills and knowledge specific to a particular sport or officiating role. General skills include communication, perception,

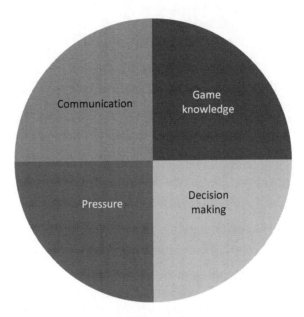

Figure 8.1 Four dimensions of sports officiating (inspired by Myers et al., 2012)

cognitive and decision-making skills. Sport specific skills and knowledge include understanding the rules of the game or contest and the roles and responsibilities of officials in a particular sport or discipline within a sport. The training and development of sports officials is an important aspect of delivering quality sport experiences for players, coaches and spectators and is discussed later.

Sport New Zealand (2018, no page) contends that officials "undertake an important role ... [through] ... leadership and guidance to participants, ensuring that the competition is conducted in a safe and fair manner" and list integrity, honesty, trustworthiness and respect as qualities required in the role of official. Further, officials are responsible for how they present themselves, their attitudes and actions, including how they behave before, during and after a competition (Sport New Zealand, 2018). While there are expectations that apply to officials there are a number of benefits of being a sports official. The Government of Western Australia (2018) lists enjoyment and satisfaction, career path and development to elite level, personal development, the potential for financial rewards, social inter-action and opportunities for family to be involved, fitness and health, and travel opportunities amongst the benefits or rewards of being a sports official.

Involvement and trends

Sports officiating is amongst the most practised non-playing roles in sport. The Ausplay 2018 survey (Sport Australia, 2018a) reported that 1.08 million Australians aged 15 years and over participated in a non-playing role as a sports official in the 12 months prior to the survey (see Table 8.1). This figure represented 5.3% of the relevant population and was only exceeded by people in coaching, instructing, training or teaching roles (8.0%). Other non-playing roles including administrator or committee member (2.9%), team manager or coordinator (1.8%) and medical support (0.3%) involved far fewer members of the population than officiating. Canada Heritage (2013) reported that 2.1% of the population aged 15 years and over participated as a referee, official or umpire in amateur sport. This participation rate was less than half the rate observed for Australia. The rate of coach participation was 4.8% and administrator/helper was 7.2%. Sport England (2018) reported that almost one-quarter (24.6%) of 6.6 million adult volunteers in sport (representing 15% of the population of England) volunteered as a referee, official or umpire. This rate was lower than both coaching or instructing (38.8%) and administration or committee roles (35.1%). Although not directly comparable due to year of reporting and different data collection methods, there is some level of consistency in participation rates across several nations.

Rates of participation in sports officiating vary by age group and gender with younger age groups over-represented and females under-represented (see Table 8.1). In Australia, 15 to 17 year olds participated

Table 8.1 Gender and age of Australians (aged 15 years or more) who participate in sport as an official (adapted from Sport Australia, 2018a)

	Sport officials (000s)	Participation rate (% of population)
Total	1,077.4	5.3
Gender		
Male	655.0	6.5
Female	422.5	4.1
Age group		
15–17	116.1	14.2
18–24	134.0	5.8
25–34	139.5	3.7
35–44	238.7	7.1
45–54	231.5	7.1
55–64	122.9	4.2
65 and over	94.6	2.4

at a much higher rate (14.2%) than any other age group including the 18 to 24-year-old age group (5.8%) suggesting that there is possibly a very high attrition rate amongst younger aged sports officials (Sport Australia, 2018a). Canadian and British participation rates by age group (tables not shown) were somewhat consistent with the highest rate of participation as a sports official reported at 5.6% for the 15 to 19-year-old age group in Canada (Canada Heritage, 2013) and 38.1% for 16 to 24 year olds in England (Sport England, 2018). Canada Heritage (2013) reported an increased level of involvement for women officiating in amateur sport. In 1992 males outnumbered female sports officials by five to one and by 2010 this ratio had closed to three males to one female. Gender differences between male and female participation rates, while not as stark as in Canada, are evident in the Australian population (see Table 8.1). Of a total of almost 1.08 million sports officials less than 40% (422,500) are female.

Drawing on earlier data from a report on involvement in organised sport by the Australian Bureau of Statistics (2005), Sport Australia (2018b, no page) revealed the majority (78.5%) of "all officials were unpaid volunteers who worked part-time, although 60% received some in-kind compensation for their time and effort". Payment for officiating is not inconsistent with Cnaan, Handy, and Wadsworth's (1996) conceptual model of volunteering which categorises remuneration for volunteering on a continuum from no payment to stipend/low pay. Of the 78,600 Australian sport officials who reported some level of paid involvement, 71,800 (91%) were paid in goods or services only, or earned less than AUD5,000 from officiating in the year prior to the survey. Nominal payments such as stipends or low pay have become increasingly important as sport organisations face the challenge of recruiting and retaining officials in sufficient numbers to deliver organised sport in the community. Sports officials, irrespective of their age, experience or the level of competition at which they officiate, are expected to perform at a high standard. Spectators, coaches and players make few concessions to young or inexperienced officials which places their decisions under high levels of scrutiny. These factors, in addition to requiring officials to be trained to high standards at all levels of competition, suggest there is an increasing need to pay individuals to officiate.

Problems in the retention of sports officials

According to Cuskelly and Hoye (2013), "having an adequate number of sufficiently trained and experienced sports officials is an important issue for sport organisations particularly when the average career length of many officials is relatively short" (p. 451). Data from the

Australian Bureau of Statistics (2010) revealed that about one in two officials (51.9%) were involved for less than five years and only about one in four officials (27.2%) have ten years or more experience. As well as relatively short careers, the total number of officials may also be declining. Analysing the results of successive Australian Bureau of Statistics surveys between 1993 and 2004, Sport Australia (2018b) reported a 21% decline in the number of sports officials and noted a further decline of 6.6% from 2004 to 2010. Sport Australia (2018b, no page) suggested that "similar trends have been seen in statistics from the United States and Canada" and further commented that the frequency of participation as an official (e.g., number of games offici-ated over a season) and the number of years of service as an official have also declined. They speculated that there may be a number of reasons for this trend including "an increasingly 'time poor' society, particularly among parents who contribute to their children's sporting involvement by becoming a volunteer official" (Sport Australia, 2018b, no page). According to Sport Australia (2018b) and a report by Cus-kelly and Hoye (2004), there are many reasons volunteers, particularly early career officials, leave their position including:

- finding that they are not suited to the role of officiating;
- psychological stress caused by frequent verbal abuse and threats of physical violence from players, coaches and spectators;
- pressure to perform with a high level of proficiency irrespective of level of experience and training;
- burnout caused by physical and mental stress stemming from being expected to officiate too frequently to cover for a shortage of officials;
- unrealistic expectations of rapid advancement to elite levels of officiat-ing or perceived lack of opportunities to advance one's "career" as an official;
- lack of ongoing support, training and recognition by sport clubs and associations;
- low pay or lack of sufficient stipends or reimbursement for personal expenses;
- too much time away from family, friends and social activities;
- full time work or study taking priority over officiating; and
- fear of liability arising from injuries sustained by players or athletes and other legal issues.

A body of research has focussed on stress, burnout, coping and intention to quit amongst sports officials. The germination for much of this research was a study by Taylor and Daniel (1987) who investigated sources of stress amongst Canadian soccer (football) officials. Subsequent studies have demonstrated that stress is a predictor of burnout and intention to terminate among officials in a number of sports (Anshell & Weinberg, 1996; Dorsch & Paskevich, 2007; Rainey, 1995; Rainey & Duggan, 1998; Rainey & Hardy, 1999; Schmidt & Stein, 1991; Taylor, Daniel, Leith, & Burke, 1990). A number of sources of stress have been identified amongst officials across a number of sports. These include: performance concerns (or fear of failure or making a bad call); confrontation or abuse and fear of physical harm; interpersonal and role conflict; and time pressure (Rainey & Hardy, 1999; Voight, 2009). Performance concerns include having a "bad" game, making a bad decision and maintaining concentration. Fear of physical harm is associated with abuse or assault by a coach or player, whether actual or threatened. Interpersonal and role conflict includes little recognition for officials dealing with abusive players, personality clashes with players or coaches and dealing with hostile or over-excited coaches. Time pressure is concerned more with extraneous factors not directly associated with the job of officiating and includes conflicts between officiating, work and family or the social demands of others who would prefer that the official spent more time with them.

Anshell, Kang, and Jubenville (2013) developed a scale to measure sources of acute stress for sports officials. They found the most severe causes of stress were making an incorrect call, being out of position, having a problem with their (officiating) partner and receiving verbal abuse from coaches. Interestingly, receiving verbal abuse from players was amongst the least severe sources of acute stress. Whether through experience as a player, coach or spectator, when an individual decides to become a sports official they do so with the expectation of being subjected to verbal abuse. Kellet and Shilbury (2007) found no evidence that the attrition of sports officials is related to abuse and argued that officials consider abuse a part of their role. However, earlier studies have found evidence that burnout amongst officials is predicted by several sources of stress, particularly performance concerns (Rainey, 1995; Taylor et al., 1990), interpersonal conflict and time pressure (Rainey & Hardy, 1999; Taylor et al., 1990) and that burnout, in turn, is a mediator between stress and intention to quit (Rainey & Hardy, 1999). Notwithstanding the cognitive and emotional processes that cause individual sports officials to make a decision to quit, retention of officials is a significant concern for many stakeholders across the sport system and particularly in VSOs where younger and inexperienced individuals are most likely to be found officiating.

Support and pathways for officials

The retention of sports officials is necessary to support government policy objectives which aim to increase participation in organised sport. Increases in sports participation put upward pressure on the capacity of officials to be available for more competitions and events. Increased sports officiating capacity is achievable through three strategies: attraction, productivity and retention, or some combination of these. Attraction refers to recruiting more individuals to become involved in sports officiating. Productivity refers to finding efficiencies amongst current sports officials and can be improved in several ways: by increasing the workloads of current officials, allocating more games per official per season or appointing fewer officials per game (e.g., three judges at a diving competition rather than five). Retention focusses on increasing the average career length of officials by reducing rates of attrition. Retaining officials is a good strategy because it "not only reduces recruitment and training costs, it increases the depth of officiating talent available to sport" (Cuskelly & Hoye, 2013, p. 461) and does not increase the pressure on current officials through increased workloads or demands for higher productivity. Attracting new officials is necessary to replenish and expand the officiating workforce. However, high recruitment rates can "exacerbate the abuse problem faced by younger or less experienced officials" (Cuskelly & Hoye, 2013, p. 453).

While officials may consider abuse and conflict a normal expectation of their role, they were more likely to be retained if they felt they were supported by their organisation, codes of conduct were applied when abuse occurred and that tribunals displayed minimal tolerance of abuse by imposing sanctions on players and others (Cuskelly & Hoye, 2004). Whether through retirement, changing work or family demands, stress or burnout, a certain level of attrition will occur irrespective of how much attention is focussed on the retention of sports officials. In effect, a recruitment strategy is also necessary to maintain or expand sports officiating capacity. As discussed in Chapter 6, many volunteers have a prior association with sport, often as a player, and the decision to adopt a different role, such as officiating, is essentially a transition process. The initial recruitment of sports officials represents a transition into a new role or a new VSO or both. Examples of the transition into officiating are those that occur when a former athlete, player, coach or administrator or the parent of a junior player becomes a volunteer official for the first time.

Sports officials often have a desire to advance their "career" and develop their capabilities as an official particularly if they find the role enjoyable. Examples of progression along officiating development pathways are the transitions that occur as officials move from volunteer to paid status or those that occur as officials are promoted from local or regional to state/provincial, national and ultimately to international level competition. Many NSOs have clearly defined pathways for officials who are motivated by advancing their "career" either as a voluntary or paid sports official. An example of a sports official "career" development pathway is the Netball Australia National Umpire Development Framework (see Table 8.2). This pathway outlines the theory and practical assessments and prerequisites and levels of qualification

Table 8.2 Example of an officiating development pathway (adapted from Netball Australia National Umpire Development Framework, 2013)

Pathways	Prerequisites	Theory exam	Practical test	Qualifications
Participating in rules discussion workshops. Attending rules in action course(s). Mentoring. Practice umpiring at appropriate level. Attend umpire development programmes. Self-reflection. Individual development. Screening for AA. Introductory level general officiating principles (on-line). Advanced level officiating general principles.	Level 1 course (integrated with introductory level officiating general principles)	Section 1 70–79%	Local game (4 x 10, 12 or 15 minute quarter game)	C Badge
		Section 1 80–89%	Local game (4 x 15 minute quarters)	B Badge
	Rules in Action (two parts) plus Level 2 course (includes advanced level officiating general principles)	Section 1 90–100%	State League game (4 x 15 minute quarters)	A Badge
		Section II 90–100%	Two quarters of two State League games. One game at highest level of competition in the country.	AA Badge
		International umpire theory exam	Highest level of competition in the country with international experience	International Umpire Award (IUA)

for a netball umpire to advance from officiating local club games as a volunteer (C badge), through to National (AA badge) and international competitions. As sports officials gain more experience and advance their qualifications they create entry level vacancies that need to be filled. Most often this occurs through recruiting new officials and it is therefore incumbent on sport organisations to incorporate strategies for the recruitment, development and retention of officials across all levels of sport.

Training and development of officials

Building officiating capacity in sport is more than simply a numbers game. Standards of officiating impact on the quality of the sport experience for players, coaches and spectators alike and poor quality officiating can compromise participant safety and be a source of conflict. Increasing participation and quality standards requires not only greater numbers of officials but also higher standards of officiating. Governments and associations of sports officials such as the National Association of Officials (NASO) in the United States have a role to play in the development of sports officiating through policy development, training resources and other initiatives. NASO is a membership association of sports officials which is independent of any particular sport. Its mission is to be a leading source of information, programmes and services for sports officiating (NASO, 2018) which it aims to achieve through enhancing the image of officiating, creating alliances, improving performance through education and training materials and advocating for the recruitment and retention of sports officials.

Government agencies often develop policy and strategic frameworks as well as generalised training in order to address issues such as the number and quality standards of sports officiating. Governments also have a role to play in improving the overall status of officiating and respect for sport officials. For example, Sport Australia (2018c) has developed a series of online learning modules on general principles of community officiating. The modules are designed as foundation knowledge upon which NSOs can build their sport specific accreditation requirements for officials. The general principles course covers: (1) a snapshot of a good official; (2) preparing to officiate; and (3) the official in action. The training course includes content that matches the capabilities, skills and attitudes typically observed in successful officials. The first module explores motivations, fair play, legal responsibilities, ethics, safety and risk management, and impartiality and professionalism. The second module focusses on preparation including sport rules and laws, physical and mental preparation, goal setting and improvement as an official. The third and final module aims at developing communication skills and confidence in dealing with participants, coaches, spectators and other officials, and strategies for dealing with abuse and resolving conflicts. An advanced level general principles of officiating course is also offered online and also designed to be incorporated within training and development programmes offered by NSOs.

NSOs or the referees associations that provide officiating services have a significant role in recruitment, development and retention of officials within their particular sport from the community to regional and national levels. NSOs typically develop and govern matters including the rules or laws of the sport and their interpretation, accreditation programmes for officials, competency standards and roles of officials, codes of practice, participant safety, performance monitoring, assessment and grading, talent identification and development, and career pathways for officials. NSO strategic plans often include objectives and key performance indicators for officiating in terms of recruitment, retention and development. For example, the Football Association (FA) (2018, no page) in England has developed a comprehensive National Referee Strategy (NRS) which "sets out the organisational blueprint of the key principles, frameworks and structures for referee recruitment, retention and development".

NSOs generally work towards at least two broad goals; increasing the number of officials and increasing officiating standards. The FA strategy has eight strands covering not only recruitment, retention and development but also the officiating structure, governance, curriculum, participation, core values and raising the profile of refereeing. The FA referee development pathway which, not unlike many sport development frameworks, has a pyramid structure with a broad base of trainee, junior and county referees through to a narrow apex of national list referees. The NRS categorises officials into two broad groups which they label "the majority" and "the ambitious". The majority group are what is best described as community level officials. They "provide a consistent service to football at all levels of the game ... and have little or no desire for promotion" (Football Association, 2018, p. 4). In contrast, the ambitious are those referees with the motivation to progress to higher levels of the game.

Refereeing with the FA sits under the FA Referee's Committee. The NRS outlines, in what it describes as the DNA of English Refereeing, the underpinning and shared values, which are defined as respect, empathy, fitness, evaluation, reliability, education and excellence. The structure of refereeing is the second strand and has separate pathways for men, women, futsal, small-sided and disability football with no direct comparability or transferability from one pathway to another. However, referees can be classified on more than one pathway. The national referee curriculum is the third strand of the NRS and sets out the design and implementation of referee training at all levels of football with greater consistency and differentiated content for the majority and the ambitious categories of referees. The strategy encourages players to transition into refereeing and aims to meet targets for female referees as well as disability and minority group representation and identifies clubs as having a role in producing referees. The participation and coverage strand of the NRS is focussed on maintaining high referee numbers as well as raising the knowledge and skill levels of current referees. The development and opportunities strand outlines a pyramidal core structure which aims to develop the potential of referees in both on-field technical performance and off-field behaviours and attitudes. The governance and administration strand of the NRS is quite brief and is focussed on the issue of integrity. The final strand outlines strategies to raise the profile of refereeing including creating a positive perception of refereeing, emphasising career opportunities available within refereeing and the development of life skills through refereeing.

Due to resource constraints many NSOs are not in the position to develop comprehensive recruitment, development and retention programmes for sports officials that are as extensive as the FA NRS. However, the problems faced by sport officials are unlikely to improve unless NSOs respond to the need for more and better trained and supported officials, particularly at the VSO level. However, there are practical resource constraints to be overcome in many situations. The goal of NSOs to recruit more females as sport officials, for example, is laudable but may not be achievable at the VSO level of sport because many local facilities have not been designed with separate female-friendly change room amenities.

Officiating codes of ethics

The decisions made by sports officials can directly affect the result or outcome of most sporting contests. It is therefore the duty of sports officials to impartially judge competitions with accuracy, consistency, objectivity and high integrity. Government agencies with responsibility for sport policy and many NSOs have developed codes of conduct or ethics for various categories of sports participants including players or athletes, coaches, administrators, spectators and officials. Codes of conduct or behaviour in sport are designed to encourage fair play and assist in the provision of sport which is inclusive, safe and free of integrity issues. For example, concussion has emerged as an important safety issue, particularly in those sports which have high rates of physical contact and risks of serious head injuries. Sports officials clearly have a role to play in stopping a game or contest where there is a reasonable belief that a serious injury may have occurred.

Play by the Rules is a collaboration between Sport Australia, the Australian Human Rights Commission and other government and not-for-profit partner agencies and runs national campaigns and provides resources, information and online training for anyone involved in sport, including officials, at no cost. Play by the Rules (2018, no page) state that "coaches and officials ... play a crucial role in helping keep sport safe, fair and inclusive". From the perspective of sports officials, codes of ethics provide an important mechanism for promoting the values of fair play, safety and integrity. Many sports such as Canada Soccer have developed comprehensive codes of ethics that include players, coaches, spectators and officials. The code of ethics for match (sport) officials is displayed in Table 8.3. Canada Soccer (2018, p. 2) states that the purpose of the code of conduct and ethics is to make

> individuals aware that there is an expectation, at all times, of appropriate behaviour consistent with Canada Soccer's core values. Canada Soccer supports equal opportunity, prohibits discriminatory practices, and is committed to providing an environment in which all individuals are treated with respect.
>
> (p. 2)

With increasing levels of gambling, even at the community level of the sports system, betting and match fixing has emerged as an important integrity issue and many NSOs have developed policies or guidelines. For example, within a code of conduct framework, the Football Federation

Table 8.3 Canada Soccer Code of Ethics for Match Officials (adapted from Canada Soccer, 2018)

Match Officials must:

i. Conduct themselves with dignity both on and off the field of play, and by example seek to inspire the principles of fair play in others;
ii. Adhere to all standards and directives established by Canada Soccer, International Football Association Board and FIFA;
iii. Be neat in appearance and maintain a high level of physical and mental fitness;
iv. Study and enforce the current Laws of the Game and any event-specific rules and regulations;
v. Perform his/her designated duties, including attending organized clinics and lectures, etc. and shall assist their colleagues in upgrading and improving their standards of officiating, instructing and assessing;
vi. Adhere to the Canada Soccer's Anti-Doping Policy;
vii. Honour any appointments accepted, unless unable to do so by virtue of illness or personal emergency;
viii. Not publicly criticize other referees or Canada Soccer;
ix. Not make any statement to the media (newspaper, television, radio, etc.) related to a game in which the referee has officiated, or to the performance of the players or other officials;
x. Not accept any appointment to officiate in any competitive game in which an immediate member of his/her family by marriage or common law is a registered player or coach. An immediate member of the family is a parent, a spouse, a son or daughter, a brother or sister;
xi. Not accept any appointment to officiate in unsanctioned events;
xii. Be fair, equitable, considerate, independent, honest, and impartial in all dealings with others;
xiii. When writing reports, set out the true facts and not attempt to justify any decisions; and
xiv. Report any approach to fix the result of a match.

Australia (FFA) (2013) released sports betting and match fixing guidelines which provide specific advice for match officials.

Alleged breaches of the code of conduct or ethics by sports officials are usually handled by NSOs or their member associations which may take disciplinary action in accordance with the principles of natural justice. Most codes provide for disciplinary measures which range from verbal or written apologies to deregistration or the withdrawal of the official's accreditation for a set period of time. Serious or repeated violations may result in life bans for officials and, depending on the circumstances, possible criminal investigation for being involved in substantial integrity issues such as match fixing.

Governance

The governance of sports officiating usually sits within a broad framework such as A Code for Sports Governance in the United Kingdom (UK Sport,

2018). Though targeted at the Boards of NSOs, the UK code sets out five principles: structure, people, communication, standards and conduct, and policies and processes. Together these principles guide sport organisations towards appropriate governance structures, high standards of integrity, compliance with laws and regulations, transparency and accountability, and decision-making processes. An important consideration regarding sports officials is how they are governed in the context of their NSO. For example, in the sport of rugby at the state (provincial) level in Queensland, Australia, the peak rugby match officials' body is the Queensland Rugby Referees Association (QRRA). The QRRA is separately constituted to the Queensland Rugby Union (QRU), the controlling body of rugby in the State of Queensland. While the QRAA states it works closely with the QRU, the two governing bodies are independent and separate entities. The QRAA has sole responsibility for the appointment of referees to a range of matches across senior, junior, school and social rugby competitions. Basketball Australia has a governance structure in which referees from local association to state level are incorporated within the sport in terms of training, accreditation and appointments to games.

Across the sport system there are essentially two officiating governance structures, termed the independent model and the integrated model. The independent model has some or all of the following features:

- a governance structure that ensures complete separation between the body responsible for sports officiating at local, state/provincial and NSO levels;
- the officiating governing body assumes responsibility for all aspects of officiating including recruitment, training and accreditation, appointment to competitions, assessment, talent identification and development; and
- a service-provider approach whereby the officiating body enters into a contractual type of arrangement to officiate at competitions officially sanctioned by VSOs or NSOs.

In contrast, the integrated model has some or all of the following features:

- a governance structure in which sports officials are members of the NSO or VSO with similar rights and responsibilities as other members such as players, coaches and administrators;
- the NSO or VSO assumes responsibility for all aspects of officiating; and
- officials work with and under the direction of the NSO or VSO.

The integrated model enables sports officiating to be more closely aligned with the strategies, policies and operations of NSOs and VSOs for the mutual benefit of both parties. Communication problems which tend to exist between separate bodies can be minimised. Matters such as the management of recruitment and retention, training, accreditation, development, support and recognition of officials are often dealt with more effectively when they are part of the regular deliberations of committee and board members within an NSO or a VSO rather than the subject of ongoing negotiations between two separate entities. The integrated sports officiating model may also alleviate other officiating problems and issues which include support for officials, particularly when they are verbally or physically abused, over-rostering of officials to compensate for under-recruitment, lack of performance feedback and access to career pathways. Some of these issues were raised earlier in relation to stress and burnout amongst officials. A disadvantage of the integrated model is a lack of independence between officials and other stakeholders within a sport. Depending upon the quality of the governance and administration of a sport, a lack of separation between sports officials and other volunteer groups (e.g., coaches and administrators) could invite potential conflicts of interest in the selection, appointment and promotion of officials.

Conclusion

This chapter has focussed on the recruitment, development and retention of sports officials as well as the standards of sports officiating. The application and interpretation of the rules or laws of the game is a necessary but often under-appreciated task in many sports. The role of sports officials is becoming more complex and NSOs and government agencies responsible for sport develop policies and guidelines for issues such as inclusive practices, concussion and sports betting. The standard of the quality of sports officiating can have a direct impact on the quality, enjoyment and safety of the sport experience for competitors, coaches and other officials, and spectators alike. Increasingly, government and sport NSOs are taking a strategic interest in the recruitment and retention of officials, the standards of officiating and the public's perception of sports officials. Stress and burnout are amongst a number of reasons for high rates of attrition amongst officials, particularly those who are young or inexperienced. Pay and other rewards are being used as incentives to recruit and retain officials. It is also apparent that significant structural reform is necessary in some sports to ensure a more integrated governance structure in which NSOs and VSOs assume greater responsibility for officiating and that officials enjoy the rights and responsibilities enjoyed by other members such as coaches and players. Government policies, strategies and programmes seem to be well advanced in addressing the problems and issues associated with sports officiating. However, the under-representation of females does not appear to be a high priority issue for all government agencies and NSOs.

References

Anshell, M. H., Kang, M., & Jubenville, C. (2013). Sources of acute sport stress scale for sports officials: Rasch calibration. *Psychology of Sport and Exercise, 14*, 362–370.

Anshell, M. H., & Weinberg, R. S. (1996). Coping with acute stress among American and Australian basketball referees. *Journal of Sport Behaviour, 19*, 180–203.

Australian Bureau of Statistics. (2005). *Involvement in organised sport and physical activity 2004, cat. no. 6285.0.* Canberra: Commonwealth of Australia.

Australian Bureau of Statistics. (2010). *Involvement in organised sport and physical activity, cat. no. 6285.0.* Canberra: Commonwealth of Australia.

Bandura, A. (1997). *Self-efficacy: The exercise of control.* New York: Freeman.

Canada Soccer. (2018). *Code of conduct and ethics.* Retrieved from www.canada soccer.com/files/CSA_Code_of_Conduct_and_Ethics_FINAL_22.09.17.pdf (Accessed 16 December 2018).

Canadian Heritage. (2013) *Sport participation 2010* (Catalogue No. CH24-1/2012E-PDF). Author.

Cnaan, R. A., Handy, F., & Wadsworth, M. (1996). Defining who is a volunteer: Conceptual and empirical considerations. *Nonprofit and Voluntary Sector Quarterly, 25*(3), 364–383.

Cuskelly, G., & Hoye, R. (2004). *Problems and issues in the recruitment and retention of sports officials.* Canberra: Australian Sports Commission.

Cuskelly, G., & Hoye, R. (2013). Sports officials' intention to continue. *Sport Management Review, 16*, 451–464.

Dell, C., Gervis, M., & Rhind, D. J. A. (2016). Factors influencing soccer referee's intentions to quit the game. *Soccer and Society, 17*(1), 109–119.

Dorsch, K. D., & Paskevich, D. M. (2007). Stressful experiences among six certification levels of ice hockey officials. *Psychology of Sport and Exercise, 8*, 585–593.

Football Association. (2018). *National referee strategy.* Retrieved from www.thefa.com/get-involved/referee/the-fa-national-referee-strategy-and-dna (Accessed 17 December 2018).

Football Federation Australia. (2013). *FFA sports betting and match fixing guidelines.* Retrieved from www.ffa.com.au/sites/ffa/files/2017-09/FFA%20Sports%20Betting%20and%20Match%20Fixing%20Guidelines.pdf (Accessed 20 December 2018).

Government of Western Australia. (2018). Retrieved from www.dsr.wa.gov.au/support-and-advice/people-development/officiating (Accessed 4 December 2018).

Kellet, P., & Shilbury, D. (2007). Umpire participation. Is abuse really the issue? *Sport Management Review, 10*, 209–229.

MacMahon, C., & Plessner, H. (2008). The sport official in research and practice. In D. Farrow, J. Baker, & C. MacMahon (Eds.), *Developing sport expertise: Researchers and coaches put theory into practice* (pp. 172–192). Abingdon, Oxford: Routledge.

Morris, G., & O'Connor, D. (2017). Key attributes of expert NRL referees. *Journal of Sports Sciences, 35*(9), 852–857.

Myers, N. D., Feltz, D. L., Guillén, F., & Dithurbide, L. (2012). Development of, and initial validity evidence for the referee self-efficacy scale: A multistudy report. *Journal of Sport & Exercise Psychology, 34,* 737–765.

National Association of Sports Officials. (2018). *Mission statement.* Retrieved from www.naso.org/about-naso/mission-statement/ (Accessed 19 December 2018).

Netball Australia. (2013). *National umpire development framework.* Retrieved from https://netball.com.au/wp-content/uploads/2013/09/National-Umpire-Development-Framework-Revised-2013.pdf (Accessed 16 December 2018).

Play by the Rules. (2018). *Coaching and officiating.* Retrieved from www.playbytherules.net.au (Accessed 19 December 2018).

Rainey, D. W. (1995). Stress, burnout, and intention to terminate among umpires. *Journal of Sport Behavior, 18,* 312–323.

Rainey, D. W., & Duggan, P. (1998). Assaults on basketball referees: A state-wide survey. *Journal of Sport Behavior, 21,* 113–120.

Rainey, D. W., & Hardy, L. (1999). Sources of stress, burnout and intention to terminate among rugby union referees. *Journal of Sports Sciences, 17,* 797–806.

Schmidt, C., & Stein, G. L. (1991). Sport commitment: A model integrating enjoyment, dropout and burnout. *Journal of Sport and Exercise Psychology, 13,* 254–265.

Sport Australia. (2018a). *AusPlay national results.* Retrieved from www.clearinghouseforsport.gov.au/research/smi/ausplay/results/national (Accessed 7 December 2018).

Sport Australia. (2018b). *Community sports officiating.* Retrieved from www.clearinghouseforsport.gov.au/knowledge_base/sport_participation/community_engagement/community_sport_officiating (Accessed 4 December 2018).

Sport Australia. (2018c). *Community sports officiating general principles.* Retrieved from https://learning.ausport.gov.au (Accessed 19 December 2018).

Sport England. (2018). *Active lives adult survey.* Retrieved from www.sportengland.org/media/13052/active-lives-adult-survey-nov-16-17-report.pdf (Accessed 7 December 2018).

Sport New Zealand. (2018). Retrieved from https://sportnz.org.nz/managing-sport/search-for-a-resource/guides/roles-of-officials (Accessed 4 December 2018).

Taylor, A. H., & Daniel, J. V. (1987). Sources of stress in soccer officiating: An empirical study. In T. Reilly, A. Lees, K. Davids, & W. J. Murphy (Eds.), *Science and football: Proceedings of the first world congress of science and football* (pp. 538–544). London: E and FN Spon.

Taylor, A. H., Daniel, J. V., Leith, L., & Burke, R. J. (1990). Perceived stress, psychological burnout and paths to turnover intentions among sport officials. *Journal of Applied Sport Psychology, 2,* 84–97.

UK Sport. (2018). *A code for sports governance.* Retrieved from www.uksport.gov.uk/resources/governance-code (Accessed 19 December 2018).

Voight, M. (2009). Sources of stress and coping strategies of US soccer officials. *Stress and Health, 25,* 91–101.

Chapter 9

Volunteer coaches

Coaches are an important and indeed "distinct" category (Harman & Doherty, 2014) of sport volunteers. The nature and scale of the contribution made by coaches is undeniable as they can inspire people to be physically active and also make valuable, social and economic contributions to society (Sport England, 2016). Cuskelly, Hoye, and Auld (2006, p. 123) argued that "coaches are often the most tangible manifestation of organizational quality and effectiveness in the sport context and are a crucial component of the sport experience for most participants". Harman and Doherty (2014) further suggested that youth sport volunteer coaches are front-line volunteers with the key responsibility for delivering the primary functions and services of sport clubs and organisations. Most volunteer coaches tend to engage with youth/children in community level programmes. In the UK, 50% of children (compared to around 7% of adults) participate regularly in guided sport activities (Lyle, 2011).

In addition to their direct impacts on sport participants, coaches can also positively influence a wide range of other related behaviours of those they coach (Thompson, 2017; UK Coaching, 2017). Data from the UK provide strong evidence that a range of broader benefits from coaching can be delivered to individuals and communities. While it might be somewhat axiomatic, UK research results indicate that people who were coached tend to lead healthier lifestyles and exhibit "more resilient sport and physical activity habits" than those who were not coached (Thompson, 2017, p. 4). More specifically, according to Thompson, based on an analysis of coaching data from the 2006–2016 Active People Surveys, those who were coached were more likely than those who were not coached to:

1. be more physically active;
2. be active for longer periods; and
3. engage in a greater number of physical activities.

Thompson (2017, p. 22) further argued that the Active People Survey data also revealed that coaching not only helps to get people engaged but also improves retention in sport and physical activity. Coached participants were more "likely to overcome the barriers associated with taking part in sport and activity and ... to continue" (Thompson, 2017, p. 22). The report concludes that the data "presents a strong case for investment in coaching to increase participation and retention in sport and physical activity" (Thompson, 2017, p. 22).

However, despite their acknowledged central role, Wicker (2017) reported that research on volunteer coaches has attracted somewhat less attention than that for other voluntary roles. Dawson and Phillips (2013) posit that research on coach professional development is "embryonic" and Trussell (2016) later argued that, despite community sport comprising the largest sector of sport volunteers, grassroots sports volunteering remains relatively under-researched. However, Wicker (2017) also indicated that volunteer coach research appears to be gathering momentum with new areas of focus, including that of parent coaches, though volunteer coaches deserve more research attention in the future.

There is little doubt therefore that volunteer coaches are crucial to the sport sector and understanding the factors that influence their recruitment and retention is essential to ensuring the long term sustainability of sport, especially for youth programmes at the community/grass-roots level. This chapter reviews the key issues influencing the development of volunteer coaches and provides a summary of the core principles required to effectively develop and manage this important cohort of volunteers. Examples of national coaching schemes from different countries are provided. Given the structure and nature of sport delivery systems in most jurisdictions, the chapter concentrates on volunteer coaches who are most likely to coach junior sport at the community/recreational level.

Volunteer coaching data

As indicated above, volunteer coaches are often the most prominent or overt component of the sport delivery system and research from a variety of jurisdictions reaffirms the scale and importance of their contribution. Data from the Canadian Survey of Giving, Volunteering and Participating indicated that, in 2013, 17% of all volunteers were involved in coaching, refereeing or officiating, accounting for around 7% of all volunteer hours (Statistics Canada, 2015). Males and females exhibit different patterns of volunteering as coaches. Men were more than twice as likely to coach (24% compared to 11% of women).

In Australia a series of reports released by the Australian Bureau of Statistics (ABS) over a number of years also reinforce the scale of the contribution made by coaches. It should be noted that, while the data reported here are similar in many respects, they do reflect different time periods, methodologies and approaches to sampling (e.g., in some cases including paid as well as volunteer coaches). Richards (2018), through the Clearinghouse for Sport Australia, developed a collated report on community coaches in Australia, partly based on the series of ABS data releases. This section is largely based on that summary.

According to Richards, the 2010 ABS survey "Involvement in Organised Sport and Physical Activity" indicated that there were about 643,300 people engaged as coaches, instructors or teachers of sport. Of these, 370,300 (57.5%) were men and 273,000 (42.5%) were women. More than 60% of coaches were involved at the junior sport level and more than half (56%) of coaches had a relevant qualification. Richards also reported that other surveys conducted by the ABS in 2001, 2004 and 2007 revealed a downward trend over this period in the number of non-playing sport participants, including coaches. For example, the 2007 survey revealed that 659,000 individuals (4.0% of the Australian population aged 15 years and over) were involved as a coach, instructor or teacher. Of these, 78% participate as volunteers. More males (386,000 or 58.6%) than females (273,000 or 41.4%) worked as a coach, instructor or teacher. Other ABS data showed that over half (54%) of total sport volunteers in 2006 were involved in coaching, refereeing or judging. In other related work, Shilbury and Kellett (2010) reported that each week, in Australia, coaches engage with more than 7 million sport participants. Furthermore, the results of a survey of 1,374 coaches in Australia indicated that 59% of respondents reported they were volunteers (Dawson, Wehner, Phillips, Gastin, & Salmon, 2013).

In the UK, two different reports, both released in 2017, also point to significant levels of involvement in volunteer coaching. As is the case with the Australian data, however, there are some variations in time frames, methodologies and sampling, so any trend analysis or comparisons across jurisdictions are indicative only. According to UK Coaching (2017), in 2016, 3.6 million adults coached sport or physical activity, a workforce bigger (by head count) than the entire UK National Health Service. Of these, 1.67 million were volunteer coaches, representing more than 213 million hours dedicated to coaching sport and physical activity per year. Of those who were involved as volunteer coaches, 69% were male and 31% female. Half of all volunteer coaches were in the 16 to 34 age group, followed by 37% who were aged 35 to 54.

The second report indicated that, at some point in their lifetime, almost 14 million adults (about 25% of the UK population) have coached sport or physical activity (Thompson & McIlroy, 2017). Furthermore, in the previous 12 months over 3 million (6% of the UK population) were categorised as active coaches, having coached sport or physical activity during that period. More than half of active coaches started before the age of 25 and most started while still participating in sport and physical activity. Thompson and McIlroy also noted that:

- coaches are most commonly active in sports clubs, community settings and schools;
- the majority coach less than three hours a week;
- 57% coach in a voluntary capacity, providing around 5.2 million coaching hours per week, and 18% coach in both a paid and volunteer capacity, providing around 4.5 million hours per week; and
- volunteer coaching hours account for 47% of all coaching activity.

In the USA, data indicate that overall, in 2015, 5.5% of all volunteer hours were devoted to coaching, refereeing or supervising sports teams. As in the other jurisdictions, men (9.3% of all male volunteers hours) were more likely than women (2.7%) to be involved in this category of volunteering (US Department of Labor, 2016).

The data reported here from a number of different countries clearly indicate, despite some variations in survey design and sampling, a broadly comparable pattern of high levels of engagement in volunteer coaching. The data also demonstrate that males are more likely than females to volunteer as a coach and, as indicated in Chapter 1, sport appears to be serving as a key nursery for volunteers and early volunteer "training", given the relatively young profile of volunteer coaches. The data underscore the central importance of volunteer coaches to the sport sector, especially at the community and junior sport levels.

Volunteer coaching trends

Coaches, like almost every other category of sport volunteer, are subject to the same global and organisational trends impacting on all volunteers. However, it could be argued that for coaches the impacts of these trends may be even more significant given the necessity, inherent in the coaching context, for face-to-face engagement, coupled with the relatively inflexible nature of coaching interactions with participants (e.g., spatially and temporally fixed training sessions and competitions). It is also the case that during the sport season coaches are typically required to commit to both mid-week and weekend sessions that often involve considerable amounts of time. As noted by Harman and Doherty (2014), coaches tend to contribute more hours than other volunteers.

Thompson (2017) reported that one of the key trends impacting on coaches are the changes to sport participation and consequently the number of people seeking to be coached. For example between 2006 and 2016 in the UK, despite a 1% increase in overall sports participation from 46% of adults aged over 16 in 2005/2006 to 47% in 2015/2016, participation in organised sport declined by 9% during the same period. Similar trends had also been reported earlier in Australia. Hajkowicz, Cook, Wilhelmseder, and Boughen (2013, p. 6) noted that, in Australia, due to "busy and time fragmented lifestyles" and a more health-conscious society, participation in individualised physical activity was increasing whereas "participation rates for many organised and team sports … have held constant or declined".

Perhaps of most relevance to volunteer coaches, however, is that data from a number of sources reveal a mixed picture about participation in junior sport. Although Meân (2015, p. 340) argued that "participation in organized youth sport is growing globally and sport and childhood are becoming increasingly bound", there are some data sources indicating otherwise. For example in Australia Trost (2012) reported that, while the majority of young people in Australia participate in organised sport and participation had remained relatively stable over the previous 15 years (at just over 60%), almost one-third of young people do not participate in organised sport. Trost also reported that sports participation declines with age (especially for girls), is higher in boys than girls and tends to peak between the ages of 9 and 11 years. Trost did note however that inconsistencies in measurement, sampling and survey design made it difficult to accurately comment on participation trends.

Richards and May (2018) in a summary report on sports participation in Australia indicated that an analysis of data from the 2013–2014 ABS Multi-Purpose Household Survey Participation in Sport and Physical Recreation revealed that the percentage of those persons aged 15 years and over who reported that they had participated in sport and physical recreation at least once during the 12 month declined from 65% in 2011/2012 to 60% in 2013/2014. The ABS (2013) reported that approximately 60% of all children aged 5 to 14 years had participated in at least one organised sport activity outside of school hours in the previous 12 months. However, more recent data from Sport Australia (2018) show declines in junior sport engagement. Those aged 14 and under who participated in sport at least once per week fell from 61.8% in 2016/2017 to 58.0% in 2017/2018. On the other hand, the US Centre for Disease Control and Prevention (2010) reported slight increases in the physical activity levels of Grade 9–12 students between 2000 and 2010.

While the data are mixed it does appear that youth sport programmes, even if participation rates fluctuate or have declined slightly in some jurisdictions, are still of such scope and scale to require significant levels of volunteer labour, especially coaches. However, as indicated above, of all sport related volunteering roles, coaching is likely to have amongst the highest time requirements and the least options for flexible involvement for potential volunteers. Therefore, the increasing demand for micro- and virtual volunteering opportunities is likely to disproportionally impact on the availability and commitment of volunteer coaches.

Most sports clubs and programmes still appear to experience both coach recruitment and retention challenges and sports club officials typically express strong anecdotal opinions on this topic. Data from a variety of jurisdictions reinforce this view and indicate that coaching as a specific form of volunteering is declining. For example, Statistics Canada (2015) reported that while coaching, refereeing or officiating accounted for 20% of volunteers in 2007, this dropped to 18% in 2010 and then again to 17% in 2013. Similarly in Australia, data from a number of sources reveal that the prevalence of coaches is declining. For example, there was a 7.2% drop in the number of accredited coaches in 2002–2003 and this was followed in 2003–2004 with a 9.6% reduction (Australian Sports Commission, 2003, 2004). A later report from the ABS (2011) indicated that while employment as a coach, instructor or teacher in sport had increased from 2000 onwards, this category of engagement in the sport industry started to decline from 2007. There was a 2.3% decrease in 2010 compared to that recorded in 2007.

Thompson (2017) also reported that there had been a decrease in the number of volunteer coaches in the UK. The 2015/2016 UK figure of 1.67 million volunteer coaches, while still significant, represented a 2% (40,000) reduction in the number of volunteer coaches since 2010/2011. Also of note, the average hours per month committed by volunteer coaches dropped from around 11.1 hours to 9.8 hours, meaning that in 2015/2016, there were more than 32 million fewer coaching hours available to sports participants in the UK than in 2005/2006.

As with other sport volunteer categories, coach recruitment, commitment and retention continue to be problematic issues for sport delivery systems in most countries. Despite government policies seeking continued development in sport, a lack of coaches is likely to impede any planned growth. The UK figures reported above are both alarming and concerning given the well-publicised sport legacy that was expected from the 2012 London Olympic Games. A number of reports (Gibson, 2013a, 2013b; Helm, 2013) noted the cuts to both schools sport programmes and public sport and leisure services and facilities in a number of municipalities across the UK. One result has been "enthused children unable to find facilities and coaches" (Gibson, 2013a, no page).

Volunteer coach issues

Consistent with the impacts of broader societal trends on volunteering described in Chapter 1, planning for and the development and support of volunteer coaches also face a number of emerging challenges and needs to adapt to more contemporary contexts. Kaer (2019, p. 50) argues that, in most industrialised countries, sports coaching and youth sports have experienced significant change in recent years and, further, that "competitive youth sport has become an industry influenced by money, ambitious parents, and coaches".

Due to growing concerns about the role, nature and efficacy of coaching on the sport system, Sport England in 2016 released a coaching plan for England for the period 2017–2021 in which it was argued that "there is a need to reconsider the way that coaches are recruited, developed and deployed so that they can reach a wider audience and support more people to reach their goals" (p. 4). The Coaching Plan argues that the environment in which coaching occurs is changing and indicates that coaching is increasingly:

- less about technique and more about the experience;
- more about engaging with people and changing their behaviour; and
- focussed more on behaviours, values and attitudes that reflect the "soft" coaching skills.

The volunteer coaching environment is becoming more complex and volunteer coaches are facing increasing workloads and expectations from community sport stakeholders, especially the clubs for whom they work and often the parents of those children they coach. Cheval, Chalabaev, Quested, Courvoisier, and Sarrazin (2017) suggested that coaches, because of the nature and level of engagement with participants, are assumed to play a critical role in shaping the quality of the sport experience. Volunteer coaches are typically involved with younger age groups and this also then introduces a particular pressure for volunteer coaches: the (often close) scrutiny of parents. This can be especially problematic if the coach is young and inexperienced (Rundle-Thiele & Auld, 2009) and may be even more complex if the coach is also a parent of a child involved in the team. Trussell (2016) suggested that the contributions of parent volunteers are crucial as youth sport volunteers, especially coaches, are more likely to become involved because their children are participating. For example, Busser and Carruthers (2010) found that the majority of coaches (90%) had a child on the team. However, while the research has identified a number of challenges faced by coaches who are parents of children that they coach, for both males and females, the research also indicates that the junior sport coaching context provides a valuable opportunity for parental engagement and positive role modelling (Graham, Dixon, & Hazen-Swann, 2016; Leberman & LaVoi, 2011).

The complexity of the coaching environment is also accentuated due to growing awareness about legal liability and issues related to child safety. Nurse (2018) reported that over the last 20 years, increasing numbers of sport organisations in the US have initiated background checks for coaches, well defined policies and procedures related to adult/child contact, as well compulsory child sexual abuse (CSA) prevention training for staff. This is now a common feature of coach education in many jurisdictions given the unfortunate history of sexual abuse cases in sport and because the nature of sport coaching means that coaches are in a position to recognise signs of child sexual abuse (that could be occurring both within and outside of the sport context). Nurse further reports that training improves coaches' knowledge and boosts their confidence in identifying CSA and engagement in protective actions.

Potrac, Nelson, and O'Gorman (2016, p. 911) expressed the growing complexity of the volunteer coaching context well:

> much of the available coaching literature examining these topics in the context of football has been situated in professional and semi-professional football settings. In comparison with the work undertaken in these environments, little attention has been given to the experiences of volunteer coaches involved in grass-roots football. This situation is somewhat surprising for two reasons. The first relates to the high number of volunteer coaches who are relied upon to provide high-quality sporting experiences to both children and adults, while the second is concerned with neoliberal and rationalistic trends in sporting organisations that expect volunteers to adopt increasingly professional practices, manage larger workloads and subject themselves to detailed scrutiny and evaluation. Indeed, it is rather unfortunate that we continue to know relatively little about how grass-roots football coaches understand these realities in practice and, relatedly, the ways in which their experiences might impact their decisions to continue their respective participation as coaches.

It is argued here that these views apply equally to many (if not all) other junior sport and volunteer coaching settings in most jurisdictions. These issues should also be considered against a backdrop of the increased awareness of the outcomes (both good and bad) resulting from the coached experience. Meân (2015, p. 342) posited that "coaches, parents (or parent-coaches), and officials influence children's understandings of sport and fair play in ways that have a long-lasting impact on identities and life skills". Meân argued further that a failure "to capitalize on teachable moments in youth sport is often compounded in recreational sports by an over-reliance on untrained, volunteer parents in coaching and officiating roles". The implications of the changing nature of the volunteer coaching context relate mostly to education and retention. These are discussed in more detail below.

Coach education

Harman and Doherty (2014, p. 687) noted that given the significant role played by volunteer coaches it is "not surprising, then, that the development of youth sport coaches is the focus of sport strategy in many countries" and later added that "coaches' direct impact on youth programming, participants' experiences, and the achievement of social policies through sport participation has led several countries to develop strategies targeted at recruiting, retaining, and ensuring an effective club environment for volunteer coaches" (Harman & Doherty, 2017, p. 96).

This has now been the case for many years. For example in Australia the National Coaching Accreditation Scheme (NCAS) was initiated in 1979 as a model for coach education and has continued to evolve (now redeveloped as the Community Coaching General Principles course). Dawson and Phillips (2013, p. 482) reported that the Australian Sports Commission, in response to the 2009 report, "The future of sport in Australia" (otherwise known as the Crawford report) commissioned by the Federal Government, identified the strengthening of coach pathways as essential for long-term sport development in Australia and developed two related strategies:

1. Recognizing the importance of quality coaching across the entire sporting spectrum and introducing new funding, training, support and mentoring initiatives to assist coaches; and,
2. Providing additional coaching and officiating training opportunities for up to 45,000 community coaches and officials and subsidized costs associated with training for 5000 new community coaches and officials.

In the UK, Houlihan and White (2002) indicated that national governing bodies for sport had begun to treat coaching more seriously in the 1970s and that this had been prefaced by the formation in 1966 of the British Association of National Coaches and followed, in 1982, by the establishment of the National Coaching Foundation in order to, among other things, "promote and co-ordinate the burgeoning range of coaching courses ... around the country" (p. 46). Kaer (2019) argued that guidelines, benchmarks and systems of formal coach accreditation continue to be developed and advanced.

Given the strong focus on coach development and education in a wide range of jurisdictions over many years, it may be surprising to some to note that, in a number of countries, there is actually a relatively low rate of qualified coaches. For example in Australia slightly more than half (56%) of coaches had a relevant qualification (Richards, 2018). However, Dawson et al. (2013) reported that 75% of 1,374 coaches surveyed in

Australia were accredited through NCAS. In the UK Thompson and McIl-roy (2017) reported that over half (58%) of coaches do not have a formal coaching qualification and that coaches identified the cost of training/ qualifications as amongst the top barriers facing coaches. Dawson et al. (2013) reported that 81% of respondents in an Australian study did not receive any financial support for undertaking further professional development activities and that this was one of the biggest grievances of the coaches in the survey.

Dawson and Phillips (2013) suggested that coaches at all levels in the sport sector are expected to deliver high quality services, exhibit ethical behaviour and produce outcomes that may vary from a fun and safe experience for children to international gold medals. However, despite the significance of their influence and impact, people can volunteer as sport coaches with limited skills and without accreditation or training. More generally, Meân (2015) argued that

> in recreational youth sports many volunteer parent-coaches and officials lack the training, experience, insight and knowledge that should be required to coach the vulnerable population of youth athletes. Equally, there is little monitoring of volunteer performance in these positions. This is highly significant given the power and status of coaches, their influence on young people, and the potential benefits and advantages of being trained by a good coach.
>
> (pp. 342–343)

Busser and Carruthers (2010) indicated that most youth sport coaches are volunteers with little formal training with a resultant gap between the ideal competencies of volunteer youth sport coaches and their actual skills.

Nelson, Cushion, and Potrac (2013, p. 204) argued that, although coach education has long been perceived as a key means to raise the standard of coaching practice, the literature suggests that coach education has only had a "limited impact on the learning and development of coaching practitioners". They further suggested that, rather than a traditional "top down" approach to coach education, future initiatives should engage with "coach learners" to enhance coach education programme delivery and outcomes. Their research findings indicated that in the future:

- pedagogical approaches should actively involve course learners;
- a range of learning resources and mentoring opportunities should be provided; and
- consideration be given to the appropriateness of course venues and costs associated with continuing professional development.

Dawson et al. (2013) reported that coaches engaged in a range of formal and informal learning activities, including formal coach education courses, reading books, on-line coach forums and workshops/conferences. Informal learning activities such as reading books and websites were reported to be the most popular (41%) way coaches learn. However, coaches wanted more opportunities for training and greater resources to facilitate their continuing development. In terms of key areas for future skill development, Dawson et al. (2013) reported that coaches felt they lacked skills in people management, particularly regarding dispute resolution and player counselling/mentoring and dealing with parents, principally concerning unrealistic expectations about their children.

Therefore, coach education has also had to evolve – especially that aimed at the community and youth coaching levels – with a growing recognition that technical skills, although important, are insufficient to meet changing expectations about the nature of the coached experience. Lyle (2008, p. 231) argued that the increased attention "to the nature of the experience for the participant raises the issue of the 'quality' of the coaching episode or programme. Useful criteria here may be enjoyment, activity levels, sociability, success, achieving competence and so on". He suggests that "the social agenda of many sports development initiatives requires a coaching approach that reinforces practices leading to retention, enjoyment" and there was "little doubt that this coaching requires a particular set of coaching skills" (Lyle, 2008, p. 231).

Consequently, in acknowledgement of the increasing complexity and expectations placed on coaches and shifting views about the nature of the coaching role, the focus in coach policies, programmes and strategies in most jurisdictions has developed from somewhat limited and utilitarian concerns about mere coach numbers and technical expertise, to a more evolved concentration on the style, culture and quality of coaching – especially in junior sport. This change is reflected in both research and strategies to improve coach education programmes. For example Toohey et al. (2014) reported that coaches should have, in addition to technical knowledge, well developed "soft" and "people" skills (e.g., interpersonal skills and relationship building, professionalism and problem solving) and should be passionate, approachable, encouraging, motivating, adaptable and honest.

Richards (2018, no page) reported that in Australia in 2017,

> after consultation with the sector and in recognition that since the establishment of the schemes, adult learning theory and practice has shifted, new technologies are available, participant expectations of the sport experience have changed and parental involvement in sport is different,

the ASC discontinued the NCAS. Sport Australia (n.d.) subsequently developed the Community Coaching General Principles (CCGP) course aimed at assisting coaches, particularly those working with children, to learn the basic skills of coaching. The CCGP consists of four modules, covering a range of general topics including: the role and responsibilities expected of a coach, planning, safety, working with parents, communication, group management and inclusive coaching practices. The course (which is free) takes approximately four hours to complete, can be completed online and assessment is incorporated into each module. Completion of the CCGP alone does not provide a coaching accreditation. Each National Sporting Organisation (NSO) determines the specific requirements needed to gain an accreditation in that sport.

Coaches who have moved beyond the beginner level can choose to complete the Intermediate Coaching General Principles. This course comprises 13 modules that are optional for sports to include and deliver within their coaching programmes. It should be noted that the modules go well beyond the "technical only" and now include areas such as inclusiveness:

1. essence of coaching;
2. programme management;
3. planning;
4. sports safety;
5. coaching processes;
6. inclusive coaching;
7. skill acquisition;
8. introduction to physiology;
9. basic anatomy and biomechanics;
10. development and maturation;
11. sports nutrition;
12. sport psychology; and
13. anti-doping in sport.

The Coaching Association of Canada (2019, no page) reports that the National Coaching Certification Program (NCCP), launched in 1974, is also a world leading coach education programme and is "currently the largest adult continuing education program in Canada". The NCCP has been designed and is delivered in partnership with all levels of government and national/provincial/territorial sport organisations. The first level is "Community Sport" and is targeted at those individuals who may already coach at the community level or are considering becoming a coach. This may include parents whose child is involved in sport, or a volunteer who works with participants of all ages that are new to a sport. This is followed by two further levels: "Competition" and "Instruction".

In addition, the Coaching Association of Canada has also established the Responsible Coaching Movement (RCM), which provides a wide range of advice, guidelines and resources to parents, sport organisations and coaches. The key aim of the RCM is to keep sport healthy and safe for children and those with whom they interact. The programme is based on three steps to responsible coaching: Rule of Two, Background Screening, and Ethics Training. The programme is coordinated by the Coaching Association of Canada in collaboration with the Canadian Centre for Ethics in Sport and resulted from extensive consultation with the Canadian sport community.

Volunteer coach retention

As indicated above, a lack of coaches is a major constraint on the growth of sport and the evidence clearly shows across a number of jurisdictions that volunteer coach numbers are declining. Globally, most public sector policies, plans and strategies reaffirm the central role of sports coaches and their importance to the continuing growth and development of sport. It seems axiomatic therefore that a lack of coaches will constrain the development of sport.

Rundle-Thiele and Auld (2009, p. 3) argued that, despite considerable research focussed on the recruitment and retention of coaches, "a comprehensive understanding of these phenomena is still elusive". They noted a considerable amount of research that had identified a wide range of factors affecting the decision to discontinue coaching. These included: burnout; concerns about self-efficacy; lack of enjoyment and challenge; lack of time; work–life balance; administrative problems; and lack of opportunities for professional development. Rundle-Thiele and Auld adopted a different perspective and asserted that the bulk of the research on coach retention was based on identifying the "push" factors that lead to coaches leaving and then developing strategies to ameliorate the impact of these factors. Rather, they examined what was termed "pull" factors in the context of volunteer coaches in junior Australian Rules Football and described them as being "inherent in the nature of the coaching experience and organisational setting (e.g., player enjoyment and the social milieu) that may tend to keep coaches engaged with their sport, their club, and the activity of coaching" (p. 4).

Rundle-Thiele and Auld reported that intrinsic factors associated with the coaching experience may include: the enjoyment derived from seeing athletes improve, learn and perform; learning new skills and reaching their goals; fun; the challenges associated with blending individuals into a team; as well as the need to give something back to the sport. Coaches who gain intrinsic satisfaction are more likely to stay, whereas those motivated by extrinsic factors such as winning were likely to leave if these results were not achieved. Given that winning is a zero-sum game, 50% of coaches are unlikely to experience a "winning" season and, therefore, in clubs that place strong pressures on coaches to win, it seems that a certain proportion of volunteer coach turnover may be structurally locked into most sport competitions.

In their research, Rundle-Thiele and Auld found that sustained involvement in junior coaching occurs when:

1. team dynamics are positive;
2. coaches are intrinsically motivated to continue coaching;
3. clubs have clear and open communication; and
4. coaches feel they are supported.

The important role of the team manager was also a dominant theme in the findings, especially if they were able to sometimes buffer the coach from distracting and potentially stressful interactions with parents. The ability of a club and league to manage parent behaviour, especially when it impacts directly on the coach, is an important factor likely to influence coach retention.

In a similar vein, Toohey et al. (2014) found that club culture was an important factor on the overall experience of sport participants and volunteers. The results of their study on sport talent identification in Australia indicated that a combination of both club structures and processes (e.g., managing the parent relationship), as well as the more subtle influence of informal club cultures (e.g., coach and administrator soft skills and attitudes to winning) are important factors in successful clubs, therefore making them attractive to both participants and volunteers. Toohey et al. (2014) recommended that local sport clubs should focus on the management of parents especially the parent–coach relationship, as well as maintaining a sense of enjoyment and creating a positive and welcoming club culture that reflects team camaraderie (rather than just winning). They also recommended that national and state sporting associations should revise coach education initiatives to recognise the role of soft skills and better support coaches (e.g., by the use of mentors and adjunct staff). Wicker (2017) later indicated that those sport clubs which, among a range of other attributes and actions, place a high value on conviviality, report relatively fewer problems in recruiting and retaining volunteers. Harman and Doherty (2017) found that three key retention issues for coaches included the fulfilment of expectations related to recognition, coach support and club administration. Harman and Doherty (2017) acknowledged however that some sport clubs may find it difficult to meet the expectations of volunteer coaches due to capacity issues.

Conclusion

The recruitment and retention of volunteer coaches continues to be a challenge for the sport sector. The very nature of the required behaviour inherent in the coaching experience makes this category of volunteering particularly susceptible to the broader societal trends that are driving more people to seek virtual and micro-volunteering opportunities. These types of volunteer engagements are generally not available in the coaching context. However, the research does point to a number of areas of sport club and organisational management and culture that may not only make sports clubs and associations attractive to potential volunteers but also better able to assist with retaining volunteers.

Specifically in the coaching context it appears that the management style and culture of sports clubs and organisations are keys to retaining volunteer coaches. Clubs should focus on: an approach to club and team dynamics that are positive and not overly focussed on winning; regular and accurate communication; and ensuring coaches feel they are recognised and supported. A very particular issue related to support is assisting coaches (especially young and inexperienced coaches) to deal with the "parent dynamic" – an issue that features prominently in the research. As suggested by Harman and Doherty (2017, p. 95) a "volunteer-centred approach may be particularly critical in organisations that rely on the goodwill of individuals to dedicate their time, energy and expertise to the operation, governance, and delivery of valued services in the community".

References

Australian Bureau of Statistics. (2011). *Voluntary work, Australia, 2010* (Catalogue Number 4441.0). Retrieved from www.abs.gov.au/ausstats/abs@.nsf/mf/4441.0

Australian Bureau of Statistics. (2013). *Perspectives on sport* (Catalogue Number 4156.0.55.001). Retrieved from www.abs.gov.au/ausstats/abs@.nsf/Products/4156.0.55.001~June+2013~Main+Features~Square+eyes+and+couch+potatoes:+Children's+participation+in+physical+activity+and+screen-based+activities.

Australian Sports Commission. (2003). *Annual report 2002–2003*. Canberra: Australian Sports Commission.

Australian Sports Commission. (2004). *Annual report 2003–2004*. Canberra: Australian Sports Commission.

Busser, J. A., & Carruthers, C. P. (2010). Youth sport volunteer coach motivation. *Managing Leisure*, 15(1–2), 128–139. Retrieved from http://eds.a.ebscohost.com/eds/pdfviewer/pdfviewer?vid=1&sid=0da0c6a6-0ca6-4698-a388-f053561eb3b0%40sdc-v-sessmgr05.

Cheval, B., Chalabaev, A., Quested, E., Courvoisier, D. S., & Sarrazin, P. (2017). How perceived autonomy support and controlling coach behaviors are related to well-and ill-being in elite soccer players: A within-person changes and between-person differences analysis. *Psychology of Sport and Exercise, 28,* 68–77. Retrieved from www.sciencedirect.com/science/article/pii/S1469029216302217.

Coaching Association of Canada. (2019). *The National Coaching Certification Program.* Retrieved from https://coach.ca/coach-training-in-canada-s15408.

Cuskelly, G., Hoye, R., & Auld, C. (2006). *Working with volunteers in sport: Theory and practice.* London: Routledge.

Dawson, A., & Phillips, P. (2013). Coach career development: Who is responsible? *Sport Management Review, 16*(4), 477–487. Retrieved from www.sciencedirect.com/science/article/pii/S1441352313000119

Dawson, A., Wehner, K., Phillips, P., Gastin, P., & Salmon, J. (2013). *Profiling the Australian coaching workforce.* Melbourne: Deakin University, Centre for Exercise and Sport Science. Retrieved from http://dro.deakin.edu.au/eserv/DU:30062342/dawson-profilingtheaustralian-2013.pdf

Gibson, O. (2013a, March 25). Sports and leisure cuts out Olympic legacy at risk. *The Guardian.* Retrieved from www.theguardian.com/society/2013/mar/25/sports-and-leisure-cuts-olympic-legacy

Gibson, O. (2013b, December 27). London 2012: Fears over sporting legacy dull the shine from a golden year. *The Guardian.* Retrieved from www.theguardian.co.uk/uk/2012/dec/27/london-2012-fears-sporting-legacy

Graham, J. A., Dixon, M. A., & Hazen-Swann, N. (2016). Coaching dads: Understanding managerial implications of fathering through sport. *Journal of Sport Management, 30*(1), 40–51. Retrieved from http://eds.a.ebscohost.com/eds/pdfviewer/pdfviewer?vid=1&sid=52dbfeb1-510f-4d0b-82f5-c104138c7073%40sessionmgr4006

Hajkowicz, S. A., Cook, H., Wilhelmseder, L., & Boughen, N., 2013. *The future of Australian sport: Megatrends shaping the sports sector over coming decades.* A Consultancy Report for the Australian Sports Commission. Australia: CSIRO. Retrieved from www.clearinghouseforsport.gov.au/__data/assets/pdf_file/0007/564073/The_Future_of_Australian_Sport_-_Full_Report.pdf

Harman, A., & Doherty, A. (2014). The psychological contract of volunteer youth sport coaches. *Journal of Sport Management, 28*(6), 687–699.

Harman, A., & Doherty, A. (2017). Psychological contract fulfilment for volunteer youth sport coaches. *International Journal of Sport Management and Marketing, 17*(1/2), 94–120.

Helm, T. (2013, January 27). Fury over lost London Games legacy as school sports funds dry up. *The Guardian.* Retrieved from www.theguardian.com/uk/2013/jan/26/fury-lost-london-2012-games-legacy

Houlihan, B., & White, A. (2002). *The politics of sports development.* London: Routledge.

Kaer, J. B. (2019). The professionalization of sports coaching: A case study of a graduate soccer coaching education program. *Journal of Hospitality, Leisure, Sport & Tourism Education, 24,* 50–62. Retrieved from www.sciencedirect.com/science/article/pii/S1473837618301175?via%3Dihub

Leberman, S. I., & LaVoi, N. M. (2011). Juggling balls and roles, working mother-coaches in youth sport: Beyond the dualistic worker-mother identity. *Journal of Sport Management, 25*(5), 474–488. Retrieved from http://eds.b.ebscohost.com/

eds/pdfviewer/pdfviewer?vid=2&sid=25e98582-e9a1-42eb-a237-c734cd90667d%40pdc-v-sessmgr06

Lyle, J. (2008). Sports development and sports coaching. In K. Hylton, & P. Bramham (Eds.), *Sports development: Policy, process and practice* (2nd ed., pp. 214–235). Abingdon: Routledge.

Lyle, J. (2011). Sports development, sports coaching and domain specificity. In B. Houlihan, & M. Green (Eds.), *Routledge handbook of sports development* (pp. 487–500). Abingdon: Routledge.

Meân, L. J. (2015). The communicative complexity of youth sport: Maintaining benefits, managing discourses and challenging identities. In P. M. Pedersen (Ed.), *Routledge handbook of sport communication* (pp. 338–349). Abingdon: Routledge.

Nelson, L., Cushion, C., & Potrac, P. (2013). Enhancing the provision of coach education: The recommendations of UK coaching practitioners. *Physical Education and Sport Pedagogy*, 18(2), 204–218. Retrieved from www.tandfonline.com/doi/abs/10.1080/17408989.2011.649725

Nurse, A. M. (2018). Coaches and child sexual abuse prevention training: Impact on knowledge, confidence, and behaviour. *Children and Youth Services Review*, 88, 395–400. Retrieved from www.sciencedirect.com/science/article/pii/S0190740918300070

Potrac, P., Nelson, L., & O'Gorman, J. (2016). Exploring the everyday realities of grass-roots football coaching: Towards a relational perspective. *Soccer & Society*, 17(6) 910–925. doi:10.1080/14660970.2015.1100900.

Richards, R. (2018). *Community sport coaching*. Clearinghouse for Sport Australia. Retrieved from www.clearinghouseforsport.gov.au/knowledge_base/sport_participation/community_engagement/community_sport_coaching

Richards, R., & May, C. (2018). *Sport participation in Australia*. Clearinghouse for Sport Australia. Retrieved from www.clearinghouseforsport.gov.au/knowledge_base/sport_participation/community_participation/sport_participation_in_australia

Rundle-Thiele, S., & Auld, C. (2009). Should I stay or should I go? Retention of junior sport coaches. *Annals of Leisure Research*, 12(1), 1–21.

Shilbury, D., & Kellett, P. (2010). *Sport management in Australia: An organisational overview*. Crows Nest, NSW: Allen and Unwin (ebook).

Sport Australia. (2018). *Ausplay results 2017–2018*. Retrieved from www.clearinghouseforsport.gov.au/research/smi/ausplay/results/national

Sport Australia. (n.d.). Training for coaches. Retrieved from www.sportaus.gov.au/coaches_and_officials/coaches

Sport England. (2016). *Coaching in an active nation: The coaching plan for England 2017–21*. Retrieved from www.sportengland.org/media/11317/coaching-in-an-active-nation_the-coaching-plan-for-england.pdf

Statistics Canada. (2015). *Volunteering in Canada, 2004 to 2013*. Retrieved from www.150.statcan.gc.ca/n1/en/pub/89-652-x/89-652-x2015003-eng.pdf?st=9mCSANWZ

Thompson, B. (2017). *Coaching in the Active People Survey 2006–2016*. Armley, Leeds: The National Coaching Foundation. Retrieved from www.ukcoaching.org/resources/research/coaching-in-the-active-people-survey

Thompson, B., & McIlroy, J. (2017). *Coaching in the UK: Coach survey*. Armley, Leeds. The National Coaching Foundation. Retrieved from www.ukcoaching.

org/UKCoaching/media/coaching-images/Entity%20base/Guides/Coaching-in-the-UK_Coach-Experience_FINAL.pdf

Toohey, K., MacMahon, C., Weissensteiner, J., Thomson, A., Auld, C., Beaton, A., Bourke, M., & Woolcock, G. (2014). *Improving the identification and development of Australia's sporting talent: Overall findings*. A report to the Australian Research Council.

Trost, S. G. (2012). *Review of junior sport framework draft briefing paper: Trends in sport and physical activity participation in Australian children and youth*. Brisbane: UniQUest. Retrieved from www.clearinghouseforsport.gov.au/__data/assets/pdf_file/0008/496862/715_-_Trost_-_Trends_in_Sport.pdf

Trussell, D. E. (2016). Young people's perspectives of parent volunteerism in community youth sport. *Sport Management Review*, 19(3), 332–342. Retrieved from https://ac.els-cdn.com/S1441352315000789/1-s2.0-S1441352315000789-main.pdf?_tid=e9ba23eb-8bda-4929-9b56-38585ea2ba7f&acdnat=1547073866_0edb5f0bfee143db77a6ec1017394fe7

UK Coaching. (2017). *The case for coaching*. The National Coaching Foundation. Retrieved from www.ukcoaching.org/UKCoaching/media/coaching-images/Entity%20base/Guides/The-Case-for-Coaching.pdf

US Centers for Disease Control and Prevention. (2010). *Physical activity and fitness*. Retrieved from www.cdc.gov/nchs/data/hpdata2010/hp2010_final_review_focus_area_22.pdf

US Department of Labor. (2016). *Volunteering in the United States*. Retrieved from www.bls.gov/news.release/volun.toc.htm

Wicker, P. (2017). Volunteerism and volunteer management in sport. *Sport Management Review*, 20(4), 325–337.

Chapter 10

Sport event volunteers

International multi-sport events such as the Olympic, Paralympic and Commonwealth Games rely on significant numbers of volunteers to deliver core event services. Without their efforts, organisations such as the International Olympic Committee (IOC) and the Commonwealth Games Federation (CGF) could not afford to sustain the scale and scope of these global events which, since 2007, have grown faster than international GDP (Collignon & Sultan, 2014). Indeed event organisers at all levels utilise the knowledge and skills of event volunteers to administer competitions, liaise with visiting teams, work with media and security organisations, manage hospitality and catering services, and provide a myriad of other services for athletes, sponsors, spectators and other organisations associated with sport events. Quite simply, most sport events would not be feasible without the input of volunteers.

The purpose of this chapter is to explore the importance and significance of sport event volunteers, and in particular the unique management environment of sports events that involve large numbers of volunteers. The chapter is presented in four parts: first a brief description of major sport events, the organisations that manage them and the scope of sport event volunteering; second, an examination of the roles of event volunteers; third, an exploration of a number of unique aspects of sport event volunteers and the nature of the sport event volunteer experiences; and finally, a discussion of the implications for working with sport event volunteers.

Sport events and volunteers

The size and level of sophistication of sport events can vary enormously. Volunteers play a critical role in the operation and success of many events that differ in terms of scale, scope and complexity, ranging from the community driven through to mega-sporting events (Lockstone-Binney, Holmes, Smith, Baum, & Storer, 2015). Volunteers carry out a variety of roles, some of which may involve major responsibilities, such as planning and organising the event, through to helping on the day with relatively simple support tasks. Sport events can be "held annually or more frequently, conducted on a single day or over a number of days, staged in a single venue or multiple venues, focused on one sport or recreation activity or involve a variety of activities" and can be conducted for participants of differing age groups or ability (ASC, 2000, p. 3). Arthur (2004, p. 322) argued that an all-encompassing definition of a special event "has proved difficult to achieve, largely due to the scope of events in existence". For the purpose of this chapter, sport events are defined as any event held where sporting activity or competition is the focus and may include finals of sporting competitions, multi-sport events such as the Olympic or Commonwealth Games, or single sport state/provincial, national or international level championships. Such a definition excludes events such as parades, fairs and other community activities. Additionally, the focus of the chapter is on the role of volunteers within sport events, thus the discussion concentrates on those events that rely heavily on a significant volunteer labour force.

It is necessary to also make a distinction between sport event organisations and VSOs. Organisations such as the IOC or the CGF exist primarily to facilitate multi-sport events with long intervening periods, whereas VSOs exist to govern and manage the affairs of a discrete membership engaged in regular and typically frequent sporting activities or competitions. While both types of organisations rely on volunteers to sustain their operations and deliver core services, the nature of the volunteer experience and the relationships between organisations and volunteers differ. These differences and the implications for how to manage volunteers within the context of sport events are also key issues addressed in this chapter.

The scale of volunteer involvement in major sport events is significant. Volunteer numbers for the 2012 and 2016 summer Olympic Games exceeded 65,000 and 70,000 respectively, while the 2017 Commonwealth Games at the Gold Coast, Australia and the 2018 Asian Games in Jakarta each utilised more than 15,000 volunteers. Single sport events such as the 2019 Rugby World Cup (10,000 volunteers) and the 2019 ICC Cricket World Cup (4,000 volunteers) will also depend on considerable numbers of volunteers even though many of the competitors and their associated staff are professionals. Ironically, major sport events are not financially sustainable without the use of volunteer labour yet many competitors and event organisers receive substantial remuneration.

Koutrou (2018) explored the contribution of volunteers to major sport events, in particular the value of volunteer work at the 2010 Women's Rugby World Cup (WRWC). The event was an international sport competition with over 300 volunteers involved during the event period. Koutrou (2018, p. 16) found that certain variables, such as "socio-economic background, prior sport engagement and satisfaction with volunteering at the 2010 WRWC determined future volunteering behaviours, promoted further volunteering in the event context, as well as the transfer of volunteer efforts across other sporting contexts, such as clubs".

Events such as Olympic Games or World Cup tournaments in major sporting codes, often referred to as mega- or hallmark events, are frequently supported by governments both directly (e.g., financial assistance) and indirectly (e.g., sport infrastructure, tax incentives) and the respective communities that host the events for the legacies (economic and social benefits) they create. These benefits may be "economic, social, physical, cultural, technical or psychological in nature" (Ritchie, 2001, p. 156). The most obvious legacies are the physical infrastructure created to host such events like new stadia, improved public transport systems or athlete or visitor housing that is often converted to public housing after an event. Economic benefits from increased tourism activity and capacity to host further events are also common reasons cited to support the public funding and support for hosting sport events. Ritchie (2001, p. 156) argued that some of the most valuable benefits of hosting major events may be psychological or social in nature and cited the example of the 1998 Winter Olympics in Calgary, Canada which enjoyed an "enhanced international awareness/image of the city". In addition, "the strengthened social structure related to the strengthening of community volunteerism were regarded as perhaps the most valuable of all the legacies left behind by this highly successful event" (Ritchie, 2001, p. 156). This legacy has provided the city of Calgary with momentum to build "strong social networks that have inspired the desire and confidence to pursue the hosting of more mega-events" (Ritchie, 2001, p. 160).

This overwhelmingly positive view of events is balanced by critics such as Mules (1998, p. 42) who found that, unless allied sectors such as tourism that benefit as a result of major events are encouraged to contribute to the costs of hosting events, "it is difficult to avoid the conclusion that the taxpayer is generally the loser in the hosting of major sporting events". Sandy, Sloane, and Rosentraub (2004, p. 292) argued that "public sector support for major sporting events is a highly contentious issue ... [and that] ... economic theory casts doubt on the likelihood of a substantial windfall for the host city for such events". In addition, research in recent years by Benson, Dickson, Terwiel, and Blackman (2014) has focused on the long-term legacies of large-scale sport events in areas such as maintaining or improving volunteer participation rates in VSOs. Their research focused on the training and legacy of volunteers at the Vancouver 2010 Olympic and Paralympic Winter games and found that, when bidding and planning the delivery of mega events, social and human capital legacy related to volunteers needs to be part of the overall legacies for a mega-event and not an afterthought. This paper suggests that there is a "legacy gap" between the rhetoric and the reality in achieving a volunteering legacy, and that a key aspect of this is the planning, design and execution of training in terms of a best practice model for delivering both the games and development (legacy) opportunities. Benson et al. argue that, consistent with the training and development literature pertaining to effective knowledge acquisition and transfer of training into a new workplace or context, a legacy will only eventuate when the required long-term learning outcomes have been identified, developed into the training plan and delivered in an appropriate manner in partnership with the relevant agencies, such as the community organisations who may benefit from the volunteer legacy (Benson et al., 2014).

Sport event volunteer roles

There is typically a substantial reliance on volunteers to facilitate all types and sizes of sport events and to fulfil various roles that are undertaken for their successful outcome (Cuskelly, Hoye, & Auld, 2006). Rogalsky, Doherty, and Paradis (2016) highlighted that sport event volunteers can be asked to perform one or more roles ranging from pre-event planning and organising to event day registration, marshalling or athlete management. Importantly they also identified that sport event volunteers need to clearly understand their roles and how they are contributing to the overall event. This understanding may allow event volunteers to perform their roles with a higher level of effort and performance, ensuring that tasks are completed. In turn, this may be expected to be associated with greater overall satisfaction and further intentions to volunteer at another sports event.

The impact of the event on the community may extend beyond its fundamental focus on the delivery of the competition itself and provide a strong volunteer legacy (Doherty, 2009; Kristiansen, Skirstad, Parent, & Waddington, 2015; Ralston, Downward, & Lumsdon, 2004). Although research on corporate social responsibility (CSR) in the realm of sport events is relatively new, Kotler and Lee (2005) defined CSR as the discretionary business practices committed to improving the well-being of the community and to believing these practices should be completely voluntary. As such, it is vital for event managers to understand the importance of giving back to their communities and to taking an active lead in contributing to enhanced community outcomes that may be derived from volunteering. For example, Bason and Anagnostopoulos (2015) identified that employees of several UK companies had the opportunity to be involved in the 2012 London Olympic Games. A number of employees volunteered in various aspects of the event, and nearly 20% of these volunteered to assist the Paralympics and Special Olympics. This also suggests, as found by Fairley, Lovegrove, and Brown (2016), that engagement in an event volunteering experience can be an impetus for the development of a volunteer role identity, which can also lead to repeat volunteering (Fairley, Green, O'Brien, & Chalip, 2014; Jiménez, Fuertes, & Abad, 2010).

The issues associated with recruiting, training and managing sport event volunteers are explored later in this chapter. These volunteers may be involved in various areas of event management and operations, including:

- team management and liaison;
- media roles;
- catering and hospitality;
- marketing;
- venue management;
- crowd control;
- finance and budgeting;
- risk management;
- first aid provision;
- event operations;
- registration; and
- volunteer supervision and management.

These diverse roles require a range of skills, experiences, knowledge and in some cases accreditation or specialised training. The degree of complexity of these roles will vary according to the type, duration and size of the event, and the anticipated number of participants and spectators. Some roles require very little preparation while others, such as venue management or team liaison, may require volunteers to be involved over long lead times prior to the event period such as Pioneer Volunteers discussed in Chapter 1.

Most studies of sport event volunteers provide a brief description of the demographic profile of volunteers, with little analysis or critical examination of the implications for volunteer management. In addition, comparisons with non-event volunteer characteristics are rarely reported. Kim, Fredline, and Cuskelly (2018) examined the demographic characteristics and motivational segmentation of sport event volunteers from three events and found that men and women tended to volunteer differently, dependent on the nature of the event. They also found that they, similar to most sport volunteers, are more likely to be highly educated and come from more professional occupations than the general population. However, they concluded that

> tourists who are willing to volunteer with the intention of travelling can be regarded as potential volunteers for sport events. Such volunteers tend to be a diverse group and have different motivations. Sport

event organizers therefore need to pay more attention to motive profiles of different groups to better understand the characteristics of event volunteers with a view to maintain a good relationship with volunteers and develop the effective volunteer management strategies.

(Kim et al., 2018, p. 385)

Issues related to sport event volunteers

Much of the research into volunteer motivation, satisfaction, commitment, performance and retention has been undertaken in the context of sport events and organisations with paid staff in which the programme management approach is the dominant volunteer management paradigm (see Chapter 4). The episodic nature of volunteering for sport events has a number of implications for these elements of volunteering.

Volunteer motivation

Volunteers play an important role in sport events – identifying the motivation for participating in and supporting such events is essential for volunteer management. As discussed at length in Chapter 4 a number of volunteer motives have been identified in the literature (Clary et al., 1998; Khoo & Engelhorn, 2011; Kim, 2018; Pearce, 1983). We revisit some of the key literature focused on sport event volunteer motives in this section. According to Clary et al. (1998) volunteer motivation can be defined as a drive of individuals to seek out volunteer opportunities, to commit themselves to volunteer helping and to sustain their involvement in volunteering over extended periods of time. In one of the first published studies of volunteer motivations within a sport event context, Andrew (1996, p. 24) concluded that "individuals will be attracted by and expect different material and personal incentives when volunteering for a cause". This implies that sport event managers need to be cognisant of the variety of motivations that might exist amongst their volunteer labour force and hence should utilise a diversity of management techniques to sustain these motivations over the duration of an event.

Farrell, Johnston, and Twynam (1998, pp. 288–289) identified the importance of sport event organisers understanding volunteer motivation so they could "respond effectively to management needs in the areas of recruitment, retention, and daily operations". In addition, if organisers managed volunteer experiences appropriately, such investment would pay dividends for the "maintenance of a strong volunteer base in the community for future events" (Farrell et al., 1998, p. 289). The results of their study suggested that the motivation of sport event volunteers differed from sport volunteers in other settings. The motivations of sport event volunteers could be grouped into four categories: purposive, solidary, external traditions and commitments.

Purposive motivation is based on a desire to do something useful and contribute to a society or community, while solidary motivation was based on the need for social interaction, group identification and networking. These two categories matched those originally proposed by Caldwell and Andereck (1994) as incentives for volunteering. The additional factors identified in the study of external traditions (an emphasis on extrinsic motivations) and commitments (expectations from others for volunteering) were the lowest ranking in terms of importance to event volunteers. In other words, the nature of sport events and the volunteer experiences they provide attracted individuals for different reasons than for the longer term volunteer roles typical of VSOs. Slaughter (2002) supported these findings but argued that the motivations of sport event volunteers may change over time. Sport event volunteers involved on a long-term basis tend to volunteer their time in order to give something back to the community rather than a need for social interaction or networking which may have been part of the initial motivation to be involved in a sport event.

Bang and Chelladurai (2003) established the volunteer motivation scale for international sporting events (VMS-ISE) in the sample of the 2002 FIFA World Cup. This six-factor scale consisted of an expression of values (related to altruistic values for other people), patriotism (feeling of belonging, pride, community spirit), interpersonal contacts (friendship and social network), career orientation (opportunities for new career and learning career-relevant skills), personal growth (feeling of self-worth and self-esteem) and extrinsic rewards (related to free admission, uniform and food). Bang and Ross (2009) proposed seven factors with the inclusion of one more, named love of sport (loving the sport and liking any event of the sport), and changed a factor name from patriotism to community involvement. They investigated whether volunteers were willing to support the country and the sport event to make it a success. In this sense, the VMS-ISE explained the attractiveness of sport as one of volunteers' strong motives.

The adaption of VMS-ISE has provided a better understanding of various subgroup differences in volunteer motivation at sport events. Giannoulakis, Wang, and Gray (2007) examined the Olympic volunteer motivation scale (OVMS) including three categories: Olympic related (a desire of volunteers to be associated with the Olympic movement or meet with Olympic athletes), egoistic (a need for social interaction and networking) and purposive (a willingness of volunteers to benefit with their actions). Although the OVMS factors consisted of fewer items, Olympic-related motivation was found to be a main factor and important to volunteers in this area. Understanding the use of this scale will allow VSOs and volunteer managers working with large sport events to identify the motives and necessary support for individuals to volunteer.

The uniqueness of the event and affinity with the sport are important reasons volunteers continue an association with a sport event over a long period of time. Retaining volunteers from year to year is a challenge for organisers at many major sport events. Large annual sport events often put elaborate strategies in place to encourage and reward repeat volunteering. Like other marketing contexts, it is more efficient to retain volunteers than it is to recruit new ones. Retaining event volunteers from year to year has the added benefit of retaining the skills and knowledge that volunteers obtain through their event experience. However, not all events occur at the same destination each year. Fairley et al. (2014) found initial volunteer motivations were based on identifiable personal rewards but these changed as volunteers remained involved in successive events. In other words, sport event volunteer motives are somewhat dependent on the length of time they have been associated with a particular event and how they choose to continue volunteering. For example, results from Fairley, Kellett, and Green's (2007) research on the Olympic games suggested the utility of providing opportunities for volunteers to network and exchange stories and ideas about their experiences, both during and after an event. The provision of such opportunities could encourage ongoing camaraderie and friendships among volunteers that they found led to ongoing involvement in subsequent Olympic Games.

Ralston et al. (2004, p. 13) investigated the expectations of volunteers in the lead up to the 2002 Manchester Commonwealth Games, an event which utilised "the largest volunteer workforce in the UK in recent decades", more than 10,500 volunteers. Ralston et al. (2004, p. 15) reported that sport event volunteering "tends to be sporadic and episodic and is highly dependent on the availability of tangible and intangible incentives and awards to attract and motivate volunteers". Other factors that influence volunteer motivations and identified by Ralston et al. (2004) included:

- a feeling of connectedness with something special;
- an empathy with the spirit or philosophy of the event;
- general commitment as local and national citizens;
- support for an event that leads to the development and image of a local community, region or nation; and
- volunteers' expectations of the experience itself.

Ralston et al. (2004) found that volunteers at the 2002 Games were motivated by three factors: altruism, involvement and the uniqueness of the event. Such factors have a direct impact on how volunteers should be recruited and trained, and in shaping their expectations of the particular roles they may play in an event. A study of the motivations of polyclinic volunteers (medical and allied health professionals) at the 2002 Salt Lake City Winter Olympic Games yielded similar results to Ralston et al. (2004) (Reeser, Berg, Rhea, & Willick, 2005). The highest ranking motivating factors were a sense of altruism, wanting to be involved in working with a variety of people and elite athletes, and to feel part of a unique event. Reeser et al. (2005) concluded that polyclinic volunteers were motivated by a complex process they described as enlightened self-interest, where volunteer motives were not solely altruistic but based on a sense of reciprocity, with identifiable benefits accruing not just to the event organisers and participants but to the volunteers themselves.

In summary, based on studies conducted on the motives of sport event volunteers, several conclusions can be made: first, the variety of motives held by them suggest they should not be treated as a homogeneous group; second, they tend to be motivated for reasons that differ from volunteers regularly involved in VSOs; and third, these motivations may well change over time for volunteers involved repeatedly in the same event.

Volunteer satisfaction

Job satisfaction is an overall measure of the degree to which the employee is satisfied and happy with the job (Millette & Gagné, 2008). In comparison with satisfied employees, volunteers with high levels of satisfaction also have an increased probability of volunteering with an organisation (Farrell et al., 1998; Green & Chalip, 2004). As identified by Doherty (2009) event volunteers are more likely to engage in future volunteering behaviour based on the extent to which they are satisfied with past experiences. This was also found in Clary et al. (1998) who wrote that "overall satisfaction indicates emotional state and fulfillment gained from serving within the volunteering activity" (p. 1524). There are a number of factors that contribute to a satisfying volunteer experience, such as interpersonal relationships with staff and volunteers, and appreciation by the athletes towards the volunteer's role (Reeser et al., 2005). The above-mentioned factors provide important insights for managers to design specific and unique tasks to each individual volunteer and help fulfil their motivations and expectations (Millette & Gagné, 2008). This provides an opportunity to match expectations of the volunteer and the organisation (Kim, Zhang, & Connaughton, 2010). There have been a variety of academic studies exploring sport event volunteer satisfaction (Bang & Ross, 2009; Green & Chalip, 2004; Hwang, 2010; Reeser et al., 2005) which found that intrinsic motivation plays an important role in overall volunteer satisfaction for event volunteers, which appears to be closely related to motivation. Specifically, factors such as personal networking, being a part of the celebratory atmosphere, job-related competence, welfare issues and job characteristics have been identified as important components of sport event volunteer satisfaction (Elstad, 2003; Farrell et al., 1998). For example, Green and Chalip (2004) found a sense of community for volunteers at the 2000 Sydney Olympic Games was the stronger predictor of satisfaction, followed by learning and excitement.

Importantly, Jiang, Potwarka, and Xiao (2017, p. 724) found that

> if participants attained valued benefits from volunteering in the form of accomplishment/belonging; perceived their volunteering in terms of helping others or "giving back" to the community; and perceived event organizers in favourable terms; they were more likely to experience satisfaction with the volunteer experience and intend to volunteer for future events.

In other words, the way sport event volunteers are managed has a direct bearing on their level of satisfaction. Similarly, Reeser, Berg, Rhea and Willick (2005) concluded that feedback on performance and recognition of volunteer efforts by event managers has a significant effect on the level of satisfaction of volunteers.

Volunteer commitment, performance and retention

While the reported studies of volunteer motives, expectations and satisfaction go some way to explaining the nature of the volunteer experience within the context of sport events, they do not explain the behaviour of sport event volunteers. The study of commitment has also received significant attention in the volunteer context, mainly focussing on the relationship between volunteer motives and commitment (MacLean & Hamm, 2007). The research suggests that commitment impacts on retention: the more committed volunteers are, the more likely they are to remain with the organisation (Cuskelly & Boag, 2001; MacLean & Hamm, 2007). Organisational influences on commitment have been well established within a voluntary setting where it is evident that positive supervisor support and effective leadership (Bennett & Barkensjo, 2005) result in increased commitment of volunteers. The literature has also suggested that commitment has positive effects on volunteer roles (Dawley, Stephens, & Stephens 2005) and also enhances performance (Stephens, Dawley, & Stephens, 2004).

As discussed in Chapter 4, Cuskelly, Auld, Harrington, and Coleman (2004) also investigated the behavioural dependability of sport event volunteers in a number of sport event contexts. Behavioural dependability was defined as the extent to which the performance and attendance of sport event volunteers meets or exceeds the expectations of event organisers. As we have pointed out earlier in this book, the authors argued that the duration of an event and subsequent expectations placed upon volunteers by event organisers as well as support from the family and friends of event volunteers were important determinants of their behavioural dependability. Event managers should not ignore the likelihood that sport event volunteers will maintain their intrinsic motivation through "enjoyment of the activity of volunteering, interacting socially with other volunteers and event participants, and contributing to the larger social good", elements that are largely outside the control of sport event organisers (Cuskelly et al., 2004, p. 87).

Working with sport event volunteers

Differences between sport event and VSO volunteers' motivation, satisfaction and commitment have several implications for sport event volunteer performance and retention. These factors require them to be managed in slightly different ways than volunteers in ongoing roles with VSOs. As discussed in Chapter 6 traditional HRM processes are based on the assumption that the motives, needs and interests of volunteers can be matched with the strategic and operational requirements of VSOs. The same logic can be applied to the context of sport events, except there are differences in the timeframes over which the HRM processes can be applied. For instance, Hanlon and Cuskelly (2002) identified that staffing for major annual sport events can be referred to as "pulsating", as sport events require a larger workforce for a short period of time prior to, during and directly following the event. Generally, a smaller workforce of both paid and volunteer staff may be needed for the rest of the year. Carlsson-Wall, Kraus, and Karlsson (2017) explained how this rapid increase and decline in staffing requires systematic recruitment, selection and orientation programmes (different from the ones required for traditional/ongoing volunteers) to attract volunteers and simple yet effective evaluations and rewards systems to retain them.

In order to better understand volunteer motivation, satisfaction and commitment it is essential to differentiate among the types of volunteers involved with sport events. A useful way to do this is to examine how long they volunteer. Common terms used to describe length of service of a volunteer are "long term", "short term" and "episodic volunteering" (Connors, 2011). Long-term or traditional volunteers offer regularly occurring service to an organisation for an extended period of time without a specified end date. Short-term volunteers do the same but for a limited amount of time. As highlighted in Chapter 1, this type of volunteer is identified as an occasional episodic volunteer or a volunteer who provides a service regularly for short periods of time (Hustinx & Lammertyn, 2003). Episodic volunteers provide infrequently occurring service to an organization, typically for a single day or multiday event. Because they participate in volunteering during a short period, their supervision tends be different from that associated with traditional/long-term volunteers (Macduff, Netting and O'Connor, 2009).

A further assumption of the HRM approach to managing volunteers is that the commitment, satisfaction and ultimately the performance and retention of sport event volunteers are logical outcomes of appropriately deployed HRM practices. The differences in volunteer motives and the antecedents of satisfaction and commitment require HRM processes such as recruitment, selection, orientation, training, development, performance management, recognition and reward of volunteers to be adapted for the particular strategic and operational contexts of sport events.

As discussed earlier, Farrell et al. (1998) argued that the manner in which sport event volunteers are managed has a direct bearing on their level of satisfaction. Specifically, event managers need to focus on providing volunteers with "positive experiences during the event, particularly in the areas of operations and facilities" (Farrell et al., 1998, p. 298). These areas are generally under the control of event managers so it is important they pay attention to those aspects of the volunteer experience that will directly impact on volunteer satisfaction and the likelihood of volunteers returning for subsequent events.

The success of most sport events relies on recruiting adequate numbers of appropriately motivated and skilled volunteers. Pegg (2002, p. 266) argued that "the success of future voluntary action will depend upon organizations enhancing volunteer participation" and that this can be achieved by "attracting and recruiting new volunteers, supporting and training them and importantly, by channelling the many different values, motivations and contributions of volunteers such that they are personally satisfied with their participation". Pegg (2002) investigated how to match sport event volunteer motivations with elements of the volunteer experience by using the six elements of the Volunteer Job Satisfaction Scale: contingent rewards, the nature of supervision, operating conditions, co-workers, the nature of the work itself and communication. From a traditional HRM perspective, sport event managers may be able to use the scale to identify volunteers' preferences in order to assist matching individuals' needs and expectations with the most appropriate volunteer roles. For example, the scale could be administered to volunteers and the results used to reassign volunteers to particular roles that offer them more attractive rewards, better role design or improved opportunities to work with other volunteers or in other work settings.

An important part of the HRM process is the induction of volunteers into the roles and responsibilities of specific volunteer positions at a sport event. The induction process is particularly important in the context of sport events, which share the characteristics of pulsating organisations, where volunteer numbers increase substantially in the lead up to an event, peak and then decrease rapidly (Hanlon & Cuskelly, 2002). Induction in most organisations with a stable workforce tends to occur on an individual basis, whereas "induction is more likely to be performed on a group basis at pulsating major sport event organizations, due to the influx of personnel over a limited time" (Hanlon & Cuskelly, 2002, p. 232). In order to manage the group induction process, Hanlon and Cuskelly (2002) recommended the use of comprehensive induction manuals, group induction sessions involving presentations and training elements, and a range of specific checklists, venue tours and documentation to facilitate volunteers' understanding of sport event operations and the specific roles of newly appointed volunteers.

It is commonly acknowledged that high levels of personnel turnover are associated with poor organisational performance, ineffectiveness and instability in the workforce. High turnover rates also impose additional recruitment and training costs on organisations. Retention of sport event volunteers in the lead up to major sport events, during events and in between the staging of a series of events present sport event organisations with some significant challenges. Garner and Garner (2011) argued that non-profit organisations must ensure that volunteers feel supported and have the opportunity to express their opinions so as to maximise their retention of volunteers. Volunteer departures in the lead up stage to an event can threaten the viability of an event as the preparatory work in event planning, staff and volunteer training, and development of operational systems is largely dependent on a stable workforce. Volunteer departures and low levels of behavioural dependability during the staging of an event are even more problematic for event operations. For seasonal sport events that depend on core volunteers returning each year, higher volunteer retention rates minimise the time and financial costs required to recruit and train a new volunteer labour pool each year.

Aisbett and Hoye (2015) found that the applicability of traditional HRM practices apply but with minor alterations. They found that sport event volunteers most valued the informal support from their immediate supervisor but appreciated the formal support from the organisation. As such, sport event organisations should focus on developing their volunteer supervisors to have the skills, knowledge, attitude and experience to better manage and support their volunteers as well as ensuring that the HRM systems incorporate both elements of formal and informal management systems. The transitory nature of major sport events with distinct operating stages also requires event organisers and managers to utilise a variety of retention strategies at each of the pre-, during and post-event stages. Hanlon and Jago (2004) recommended a number of volunteer retention strategies for sport event organisers for each of these stages. In the pre-event, organisers should emphasise the status of the event, ensure the timing of the event suits the majority of volunteers (although this may be impractical), implement recognition schemes, and develop a sense of ownership amongst volunteers by involving them in event planning and other decisions. During the event, particularly events of more than several days duration, investing time in debriefing volunteers on issues associated with their roles and the efficacy of the support provided to them was recommended. In the immediate post-event period social functions designed to thank volunteers and recognise them for the efforts are considered effective. Post-event functions also present an opportunity to conduct debriefing sessions to gather feedback from volunteers regarding event operations and support provided to volunteers. In addition, organisers of seasonal sport events should attempt to maintain regular contact with their volunteer workforce through such things as sending birthday cards, event newsletters, surveying their requirements for subsequent events or promoting other volunteer opportunities.

Treuren and Monga (2002) argued that the majority of volunteers involved in special events (including sport events) run on a regular or annual basis are repeat volunteers. In addition, they assert that these volunteers are sourced from organisations related to the event organisation, through the social networks of previous volunteers, or from prior participants. This suggests that "a combination of targeted recruitment and planned training" may substantially increase the effectiveness and efficiency of volunteer recruitment efforts for sport events (Treuren & Monga, 2002). In addition, sport event organisers should recognise that if the majority of their volunteers are repeat volunteers or that their involvement is part of a long term "career" in volunteering at sport events, then the typical sport event volunteer will be familiar with many of the volunteer management practices previously utilised. This suggests that organisers of sport events that are held on a regular or annual basis need to be innovative in how they manage volunteers to avoid dissatisfaction with volunteer management and support practices.

Conclusion

Volunteers are central to the success of international multi-sport events such as the Olympic, Paralympic and Commonwealth Games as well as sport events at the local, state/provincial and national level. Sport event organisers rely on the knowledge and skills of event volunteers to administer competitions, liaise with visiting teams, work with media and security organisations, manage hospitality and catering services, and provide services for athletes, sponsors, spectators and other event stakeholders. The scale of volunteer involvement in sport events is significant, enabling major events to create the potential for a range of economic, social, physical, cultural, technological and psychological legacies. The unique environment of sport events, in particular their episodic nature and the increasing commodification of major events, has a number of implications for volunteer motivation, satisfaction, commitment, performance and retention. Consequently, these differences in volunteer motives and the antecedents of satisfaction and commitment require volunteer management practices to be adapted for the context of sport events.

References

Aisbett, L., & Hoye, R. (2015). Human resource management practices to support sport event volunteers. *Asia Pacific Journal of Human Resources*, 53(3), 351–369.

Andrew, J. (1996). Motivations and expectations of volunteers involved in a large scale sports event: A pilot study. *Australian Leisure*, 7(1), 21–25.

Arthur, D. (2004). Sport event and facility management. In J. Beech, & S. Chadwick (Eds.), *The business of sport management*. Essex: Prentice Hall.

Australian Sports Commission (ASC). (2000). *Volunteer management program: Managing event volunteers*. Canberra: Australian Sports Commission.

Bang, H., & Chelladurai, P. (2003, May). Motivation and satisfaction in volunteering for 2002 World Cup in Korea. In Conference of the North American Society for Sport Management. Ithaca, New York.

Bang, H., & Ross, S. D. (2009). Volunteer motivation and satisfaction. *Journal of Venue and Event Management*, 1(1), 61–77.

Bason, T., & Anagnostopoulos, C. (2015). Corporate social responsibility through sport: A longitudinal study of the FTSE100 companies. *Sport, Business and Management: An International Journal*, 5(3), 218–241.

Bennett, R., & Barkensjo, A. (2005). Internal marketing, negative experiences, and volunteers' commitment to providing high-quality services in a UK helping and caring charitable organization. *Voluntas: International Journal of Voluntary and Nonprofit Organizations*, 16(3), 251–274.

Benson, A. M., Dickson, T. J., Terwiel, F. A., & Blackman, D. A. (2014). Training of Vancouver 2010 volunteers: A legacy opportunity? *Contemporary Social Science*, 9(2), 210–226.

Caldwell, L. L., & Andereck, K. L. (1994). Motives for initiating and continuing membership in a recreation-related voluntary association. *Leisure Sciences*, 16(1), 33–44.

Carlsson-Wall, M., Kraus, K., & Karlsson, L. (2017). Management control in pulsating organisations: A multiple case study of popular culture events. *Management Accounting Research*, 35, 20–34.

Clary, E. G., Snyder, M., Ridge, R. D., Copeland, J., Stukas, A. A., Haugen, J., & Miene, P. (1998). Understanding and assessing the motivations of volunteers: A functional approach. *Journal of Personality and Social Psychology*, 74(6), 1516.

Collignon, H., & Sultan, N. (2014). Winning in the business of sports. *AT Kearney*, 1.

Connors, T. D. (Ed.). (2011). *The volunteer management handbook: Leadership strategies for success* (Vol. 235). New York: John Wiley & Sons.

Cuskelly, G., Auld, C., Harrington, M., & Coleman, D. (2004). Predicting the behavioral dependability of sport event volunteers. *Event Management*, 9(1–2), 73–89.

Cuskelly, G., & Boag, A. (2001). Organisational commitment as a predictor of committee member turnover among volunteer sport administrators: Results of a time-lagged study. *Sport Management Review*, 4(1), 65–86.

Cuskelly, G., Hoye, R., & Auld, C. (2006). *Working with volunteers in sport: Theory and practice*. Abingdon: Routledge.

Dawley, D. D., Stephens, R. D., & Stephens, D. B. (2005). Dimensionality of organizational commitment in volunteer workers: Chamber of commerce board members and role fulfillment. *Journal of Vocational Behavior*, 67(3), 511–525.

Doherty, A. (2009). The volunteer legacy of a major sport event. *Journal of Policy Research in Tourism, Leisure and Events*, 1(3), 185–207.

Elstad, B. (2003). Continuance commitment and reasons to quit: A study of volunteers at a jazz festival. *Event Management*, 8, 99–108.

Fairley, S., Green, B. C., O'Brien, D., & Chalip, L. (2014). Pioneer volunteers: The role identity of continuous volunteers at sport events. *Journal of Sport & Tourism*, 19(3–4), 233–255.

Fairley, S., Kellett, P., & Green, B. C. (2007). Volunteering abroad: Motives for travel to volunteer at the Athens Olympic Games. *Journal of Sport Management*, 21(1), 41–57.

Fairley, S., Lovegrove, H., & Brown, M. (2016). Leveraging events to ensure enduring benefits: The legacy strategy of the 2015 AFC Asian Cup. *Sport Management Review*, 19(4), 466–474.

Farrell, J. M., Johnston, M. E., & Twynam, G. D. (1998). Volunteer motivation, satisfaction and management at an elite sporting competition. *Journal of Sport Management*, 12, 288–300.

Garner, J. T., & Garner, L. T. (2011). Volunteering an opinion: Organizational voice and volunteer retention in nonprofit organizations. *Nonprofit and Voluntary Sector Quarterly*, 40(5), 813–828.

Giannoulakis, C., Wang, C. H., & Gray, D. (2007). Measuring volunteer motivation in mega-sporting events. *Event Management*, 11(4), 191–200.

Green, B. C., & Chalip, L. (2004). Paths to volunteer commitment: Lessons from the Sydney Olympic Games. In R. A. Stebbins, & M. Graham (Eds.), *Volunteering as leisure/Leisure as volunteering: An international assessment*. Cambridge, MA: CABI.

Hanlon, C., & Cuskelly, G. (2002). Pulsating major sport event organizations: A framework for inducting managerial personnel. *Event Management*, 7, 231–243.

Hanlon, C., & Jago, L. (2004). The challenge of retaining personnel in major sport event organizations. *Event Management*, 9, 39–49.

Hustinx, L., & Lammertyn, F. (2003). Collective and reflexive styles of volunteering: A sociological modernization perspective. *Voluntas: International Journal of Voluntary and Nonprofit Organizations*, 14(2), 167–187.

Hwang, J. (2010). Does sport really matter to volunteers? Implications from an empirical comparison between sport volunteers and nonsport volunteers. Electronic Theses, Treatises and Dissertations. Paper 3376. http://diginole.lib.fsu.edu/etd/3376

Jiang, K., Potwarka, L. R., & Xiao, H. (2017). Predicting intention to volunteer for mega-sport events in China: The case of Universiade event volunteers. *Event Management*, 21(6), 713–728.

Jiménez, M. L. V., Fuertes, F. C., & Abad, M. J. S. (2010). Differences and similarities among volunteers who drop out during the first year and volunteers who continue after eight years. *The Spanish Journal of Psychology*, 13(1), 343–352.

Khoo, S., & Engelhorn, R. (2011). Volunteer motivations at a national special Olympics event. *Adapted Physical Activity Quarterly*, 28(1), 27–39.

Kim, E. (2018). A systematic review of motivation of sport event volunteers. *World Leisure Journal*, 60(4), 306–329.

Kim, E., Fredline, L., & Cuskelly, G. (2018). Heterogeneity of sport event volunteer motivations: A segmentation approach. *Tourism Management, 68*, 375–386.

Kim, M., Zhang, J. J., & Connaughton, D. P. (2010). Comparison of volunteer motivations in different youth sport organizations. *European Sport Management Quarterly, 10*(3), 343–365.

Kotler, P., & Lee, N. (2005). Best of breed: When it comes to gaining a market edge while supporting a social cause, 'corporate social marketing' leads the pack. *Social Marketing Quarterly, 11*(3–4), 91–103.

Koutrou, N. (2018). The impact of the 2010 Women's Rugby World Cup on sustained volunteering in the Rugby community. *Sustainability, 10*(4), 1030.

Kristiansen, E., Skirstad, B., Parent, M. M., & Waddington, I. (2015). 'We can do it': Community, resistance, social solidarity, and long-term volunteering at a sport event. *Sport Management Review, 18*(2), 256–267.

Lockstone-Binney, L., Holmes, K., Smith, K., Baum, T., & Storer, C. (2015). Are all my volunteers here to help out? Clustering event volunteers by their motivations. *Event Management, 19*(4), 461–477.

Macduff, N., Netting, F. E., & O'Connor, M. K. (2009). Multiple ways of coordinating volunteers with differing styles of service. *Journal of Community Practice, 17*(4), 400–423.

MacLean, J., & Hamm, S. (2007). Motivation, commitment, and intentions of volunteers at a large Canadian sporting event. *Leisure/Loisir, 31*(2), 523–556.

Millette, V., & Gagné, M. (2008). Designing volunteers' tasks to maximize motivation, satisfaction and performance: The impact of job characteristics on volunteer engagement. *Motivation and Emotion, 32*(1), 11–22.

Mules, T. (1998). Taxpayer subsidies for major sporting events. *Sport Management Review, 1*, 25–43.

Pearce, J. L. (1983). Job attitude and motivation differences between volunteers and employees from comparable organizations. *Journal of Applied Psychology, 68*(4), 646.

Pegg, S. (2002, July 15–16). Satisfaction of volunteers involved in community events: Implications for the event manager. In University of Technology, Sydney, Australian Centre for Event Management, Events and Place Making Conference Proceedings, pp. 253–274. Sydney: University of Technology, Sydney.

Ralston, R., Downward, P., & Lumsdon, L. (2004). The expectations of volunteers prior to the XVII Commonwealth Games, 2002: A qualitative study. *Event Management, 9*, 13–26.

Reeser, J. C., Berg, R. L., Rhea, D., & Willick, S. (2005). Motivation and satisfaction among polyclinic volunteers at the 2002 Winter Olympic and Paralympic Games. *British Journal of Sports Medicine, 39*(4), e20.

Ritchie, J. R. B. (2001). Turning 16 days into 16 years through Olympic legacies. *Event Management, 6*, 155–165.

Rogalsky, K., Doherty, A., & Paradis, K. F. (2016). Understanding the sport event volunteer experience: An investigation of role ambiguity and its correlates. *Journal of Sport Management, 30*(4), 453–469.

Sandy, R., Sloane, P. J., & Rosentraub, M. S. (2004). *The economics of sport: An international perspective.* New York: Palgrave.

Slaughter, L. (2002, July 15–16). Motivations of long term volunteers at events. In University of Technology, Sydney Australian Centre for Event Management Events and Place Making Conference Proceedings, pp. 232–252. Sydney: University of Technology, Sydney.

Stephens, R. D., Dawley, D. D., & Stephens, D. B. (2004). Commitment on the board: A model of volunteer directors' levels of organizational commitment and self-reported performance. *Journal of Managerial Issues*, *16*(4), 483–504.

Treuren, G., & Monga, M. (2002, July 15–16). Are special event volunteers different from non-SEO volunteers? Demographic characteristics of volunteers in four South Australian special event organizations. In University of Technology, Sydney, Australian Centre for Event Management, Events and Place Making Conference Proceedings, pp. 275–304. Sydney: University of Technology, Sydney.

Chapter 11

A sport volunteering research agenda

The earlier chapters of this book have highlighted the central role played by volunteers in sustaining community based sport systems and for the delivery of major sport events. The earlier chapters have also emphasised that governments are increasingly reliant on volunteers to support the delivery of government funded sport programmes and to achieve broader policy objectives such as social integration and inclusion, increased sport participation and greater health among citizens. We have explored the concepts of the scale and nature of sport volunteering, the impact that sport volunteers have on society and the manner in which government policies and actions affect the sport volunteer experience. In addition, we have reviewed the core concepts associated with the psychology of sport volunteering, identified the potential that eliciting engagement of volunteers from more diverse population groups has for sport and examined contemporary sport volunteer management practices. We have also devoted a considerable part of this book to reviewing four major volunteer contexts unique to sport volunteering: administration, coaching, officiating and sport events. In each of these chapters we have utilised the existing literature and the seminal pieces of published research to articulate what we know about each of these important aspects of sport volunteering. The writing of this book has also allowed us to identify what is now known about sport volunteering and to ponder what, indeed, we should strive to understand more in relation to this complex phenomenon. This final chapter, therefore, is our attempt to elucidate a research agenda for sport volunteering.

It is clear that many volunteers across all sectors are seeking shorter volunteer experiences with reduced commitments, as well as enhanced control over the nature and scope of their voluntary experience. This trend presents significant challenges for those who manage sport volunteers to not only recruit and retain people to fulfil their voluntary workforce requirements, but also to be keenly aware that in a more contemporary world, they are increasingly attracting individuals with different volunteering values and principles (i.e., motivated less by altruistic and social motivations) than regular core, continuous or stalwart volunteers. This development has the potential to diminish the efficacy of traditional approaches to volunteer programmes and is testing sport organisations to develop new management practices better suited to the current generation of volunteers. We simply do not know enough about the changing nature of volunteer attitudes and expectations and how sport organisations of varying types should go about designing, implementing and evaluating the utility of innovative approaches to volunteer management.

As we stated in the opening chapter, sport organisations have to be able to straddle both the more traditional requirements of sport volunteers, as well as the emerging wants, needs and behaviours of an emerging cohort of younger, more diverse volunteers. The implications of an alternative future delivery model that may involve more "paid volunteer" roles, an increase in virtual volunteers and a shifting focus to the use of face-to-face volunteers only in frontline service and programme delivery roles present many resourcing and cultural challenges for sport organisations. Further research is required to explore how sport organisations might adopt more flexible delivery models to not only provide services to a more demanding user, member or customer base but in the context of having to recruit, develop and retain a more sophisticated and diverse volunteer workforce. The utility of continually evolving technologies is likely to also play a major role for sport organisations in adapting to the responses of potential volunteers to what has been popularly labelled the Fourth Industrial Revolution.

We have argued that volunteers play a vital role in the sport sector in supporting the delivery of sport, providing independent governance, contributing to community capacity building and supporting sport for development programmes and the delivery of government policy agendas associated with sport. The questions of whether this model should continue and if sport should move to a user-pay approach with fewer volunteers does suggest we need to know more about the feasibility and implications of such a change, especially in regard to the potential marginalisation of sport volunteers. As noted earlier in this book, Breuer, Wicker, and von Hanau (2012), in their study of German sports clubs, examined whether there is a viable substitute for voluntary work. While, at an instrumental or transactional level, the work of sport volunteers can be replaced with paid staff, they found that such a move had the potential to diminish the contribution of community sport to social capital development. The question of how VSOs might reduce the voluntary burden through the use of more professional, paid staff without diminishing the social value or contribution of their organisations to social capital is an important one, especially in the context that much of the social value of sport organisations is generated through the interactions of their members and their volunteers.

Government policy also clearly impacts on the volunteer experience in sport, both in terms of encouraging volunteer involvement in sport and increasing the compliance burden for sport volunteers and VSOs alike. The intersection of government policy with the world of the sport volunteer offers many opportunities for research. We need to know more about how different political ideologies influence: the development of sport policy that impacts on volunteers; the utility of different policy instruments for improving the experience, safety or behaviour of sport volunteers; the effectiveness and influence that VSOs and their constituent interest groups have on the development of sport policy. We know very little about how effective various policy initiatives that have increased the regulatory and compliance burden of volunteers and their VSOs (i.e., child safety, food safety, risk management, member privacy and protection, enhanced governance requirements) have on improving the overall sport experience of participants in terms of safety, satisfaction or performance. This appears to be a fundamental question not yet addressed in a comprehensive manner. Government sport policy will continue to be an important driver for how volunteering takes place in the sport sector including imposing a number of constraints and challenges on the operations of VSOs and the volunteers on whom they rely. Future research should continue to explore the impacts of government policy on VSOs in general and on the experience of sport volunteers specifically.

Our review of the psychology of sport volunteering focused on volunteer motives, satisfaction, commitment, future intentions and performance. We demonstrated that these concepts are clearly interrelated with important implications for the management of volunteers in sport events and more traditional modes of volunteering. Despite the volume of research already published on these key topics, we argue that there still remains much to be discovered about sport volunteers' motivation and commitment, and how volunteer management practices should be designed and implemented to maximise volunteer performance, satisfaction and retention. Future research efforts should, however, move beyond descriptive studies of volunteer motives or satisfaction and address the lack of a consistent and coherent theoretical foundation, including the lack of agreement on the dimensionality of sport volunteer motivation. A key problem for the field is the diverse range of bespoke measurement scales developed by researchers and thus a valuable piece of future research would be the development of a comprehensive volunteer motivation scale applicable to a range of sport volunteer contexts. As we point out, the ability to reliably explain or predict the commitment or future intentions of sport volunteers must improve.

We cited the work of Cuskelly (2017, p. 458) who argued that sport volunteer management research lacks its own research paradigms, methods and traditions which has resulted in the field of sport volunteer research having "little coherence or agreement about the most important research priorities or directions necessary to advance the body of knowledge independent of the mainstream management literature". In relation to understanding the experiences of sport volunteers and to address the perennial issue of volunteer retention, the field clearly needs a coherent and coordinated international research agenda, an agreed definition and measurement tool for volunteer retention, and a more robust set of measurement tools for variables associated with the psychology of the sport volunteering experience. Consistent measurement, in addition to using more contemporary qualitative methods such as narrative analysis, creative analytic practice and photovoice, would support the ability of researchers to move beyond cross-sectional, descriptive studies of attitudes or engagement of sport volunteers to a much more comprehensive and useful understanding of the complexity of the sport volunteer experience. We would argue that these types of research outcomes would then underpin efforts to develop more contemporary volunteer management approaches that address individual volunteer needs but also support sport organisations in maintaining appropriate human resources for the delivery of sport programmes, participation opportunities and events.

An important contribution of this book is an examination of the possibilities and challenges of social inclusion through volunteering by opening access to more diverse communities into mainstream sport volunteering, particularly mature-aged people, those with a disability, and CALD and LGBTQI communities. As we argue throughout this book, volunteers are essential for the sustainability of the sport sector and there is an untapped opportunity for the sector to more actively engage with diverse population groups to both support their own operations and also to support the development of a more socially inclusive sport system. Our review suggests that there is a dearth of research in regards to volunteers from diverse backgrounds. A first step would be for future research efforts to focus on identifying how organisational leaders and key decision makers in sport such as committee members and volunteer managers and coordinators understand the nuances of inclusive volunteering and current levels of inclusivity within their own organisations. Government policy initiatives to support inclusive volunteering are not evidence based; in fact sport policies in general fail to adequately address the lack of diversity and inclusivity amongst the sport volunteer workforce. Future research that explored how governments could support greater diversity amongst sport volunteers and actions to support sport organisations to provide greater access to volunteer opportunities would benefit sport organisations and individuals facing inherent barriers to participation as a sport volunteer.

We have also devoted considerable space in this book to critically reviewing the application of traditional HRM processes advocated by volunteer management programmes to VSOs. While we argued that there are benefits with a more planned approach to volunteer management to VSOs, their members, the volunteers themselves and sport development more broadly, these HRM models are generally based on assumptions and approaches that privilege and legitimise the interests of management over other stakeholders. The somewhat contradictory context of VSO operations, where sport volunteers are simultaneously owners of VSOs (as club members), volunteer workers are expected to follow directives from other volunteers, and clients are service recipients of the VSOs of which they are members, calls for a more nuanced and bespoke management system, particularly in regard to the core issues of volunteer recruitment, retention and performance management.

It seems paradoxical that while governments of all persuasions continue to enact sport policies designed to increase the numbers of people playing organised sport that is largely delivered by volunteer run sport organisations, we are still somewhat in the dark about how best to manage this large volunteer workforce. We need to know far more about the drivers that will keep volunteers in their roles for longer, how to increase the number of hours each volunteer devotes to sport and how to design more attractive voluntary experiences.

Kappelides and Hoye (2014) argued that the sport sector has appeared somewhat reluctant to align itself to the general voluntary or non-profit sector agendas around volunteer recognition schemes or management standards developed by organisations such as Volunteering Australia or Volunteer Canada. Perhaps this is partly due to the highly specialised roles of some sport volunteers such as coaches and officials. If VSOs are in need of a more nuanced management approach to their volunteer workforce that moves beyond the application of standard HRM models, there seems to be a need for future research to assess how sport might adopt volunteer management practices from other sectors.

The core sport volunteer roles – administrators, officials, coaches and event volunteers – each have their own challenges related to recruitment, development and retention, as well as the standards to which volunteers perform these functions. The roles in each of these contexts are becoming increasingly complex as NGBs and government agencies develop guidelines for best practice, require adherence to accreditation standards, demand increased reporting, compliance and accountability, and seek to ensure these volunteer roles are carried out safely, with integrity and in line with both community expectations and regulatory demands. The expectations of these roles must be continually re-evaluated given the complex demands on contemporary parents, who are typically a large portion of sport volunteers in many countries.

The more structured and formalised volunteer roles of officials and coaches, with their respective technical accreditation systems and structured competency development frameworks, are, somewhat ironically, the volunteer roles under the most pressure due to the incidence of stress and burnout and the impact on attrition rates. In that context we need to know more about what intervention practices ameliorate these effects, or indeed address the underlying causes amongst these volunteers. We have flagged the need to investigate the impact of pay and other rewards as incentives to recruit and retain officials and coaches as well as what strategies will address the under-representation of females in sports officiating and coaching roles, especially in senior ranks, and in light of the growth in participation numbers in women's sport.

Concluding thoughts

The future delivery of community based sport is clearly dependent on having access to a sustainable, diverse, skilled and motivated voluntary workforce. The value in maintaining the voluntary nature of sport also lies beyond the instrumental requirements of running clubs or putting athletes and teams onto the playing arena. There is also inherent value in grassroots sport facilitating the interactions between volunteers and other community members, in order to help maintain a sense of community in an increasingly fragmented and privatised world. Globally, community integration is under threat. Future research efforts must address the inherent value of what volunteers provide sport with and the associated management issues involved in facilitating voluntary experiences in sport, as well as the social value sport delivers to society through voluntary action. We hope this book helps to assist those working with sport volunteers to facilitate such outcomes.

References

Breuer, C., Wicker, P., & von Hanau, T. (2012). Consequences of the decrease in volunteers among German sports clubs: Is there a substitute for voluntary work? *International Journal for Sport Policy and Politics*, 4(2), 173–186.

Cuskelly, G. (2017). Volunteer management. In R. Hoye, & M.M. Parent (Eds.), *The Sage Handbook of Sport Management* (pp. 442–462). London: Sage.

Kappelides, P., & Hoye, R. (2014). Volunteering and sport. In M. Oppenheimer, & J. Warburton (Eds.), *Volunteering in Australia* (pp. 168–179). Sydney: The Federation Press.

Index

Page numbers in *italics* refer to figures. Page numbers in **bold** refer to tables.

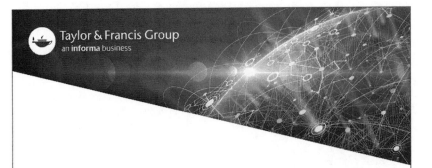